# Innovations in Healthcare Technologies in India

Varinder Garg • Manoj Goyal
Harish Kumar
Editors

# Innovations in Healthcare Technologies in India

## An Initiative of ICMR-CIBioD (Centre for Innovation and Bio-Design)

Springer

*Editors*
Varinder Garg
ICMR-Centre for Innovation and Bio-Design (CIBioD)
Postgraduate Institute of Medical Education and Research (PGIMER)
Chandigarh, Chandigarh, India

Manoj Goyal
Department of Neurology
Postgraduate Institute of Medical Education and Research (PGIMER)
Chandigarh, Chandigarh, India

Harish Kumar
Department of Computer Science and Engineering
University Institute of Engineering and Technology (UIET) Panjab University
Chandigarh, Punjab, India

ISBN 978-981-97-0243-5 ISBN 978-981-97-0244-2 (eBook)
https://doi.org/10.1007/978-981-97-0244-2



This Springer imprint is published by the registered company Springer Nature Singapore Pte Ltd.
The registered company address is: 152 Beach Road, #21-01/04 Gateway East, Singapore 189721, Singapore

*This book is dedicated to my parents (Sh. Surinder Mohan Garg and Smt Raksha Devi), my wife Rama, My daughter Bhavaya, my teachers, friends a colleagues. Their love, care, mentoring and unconditional support is a powerhouse for me.*

सर्वे भवन्तु सुखिनः सर्वे संतु निरामया ।
सर्वे भद्राणि पश्यन्तु मा कश्चित
दुखभागभवेत। ।

*"Sarve bhavantu sukhinah sarve santu niramaya.*
*Sarve bhadrani pashyantu maa kashchit dukhbhaagbhavet."*

*"May all be happy; May all be free from infirmities;*
*May all see good; May none partake suffering."*

*"Let us be a small component to achieve this goal. We are trying our best to contribute our bit to achieve the enormous task."*

# Preface

At Centre for Innovation and BioDesign (CIBioD), our vision is to encourage collaboration among Indian clinicians and technocrats for joint research. Our goal extends beyond identifying obstacles; we aim to foster research that transforms India into a healthcare device manufacturing hub. We are dedicated to devising innovative solutions to overcome challenges and utilize our expertise to make healthcare accessible to all. We aim to unite our efforts to realize our shared vision of universal well-being. This book delves into the realm of health innovation, portraying it as both a practice and a discipline. It underscores the significance of health innovation and research, seeing India's progressive health growth as a pivotal event in modern economic and social history. Unlike conventional perspectives that regard innovation as a spontaneous gift or inspiration, this book views it as a deliberate and systematic endeavor. It explores various health-related innovations, technologies, opportunities, and strategies, with a strong emphasis on improving the health of underprivileged individuals grappling with poverty and disadvantage. Each chapter addresses significant challenges in healthcare, particularly in rural and slum areas, while also discussing the integration of technology with healthcare system and its potential benefits. The book values the novelty, scientific rigor, and wit of ideas as a litmus test for their worth. Every chapter is introduced in a way that links innovation to the economy and concludes by relating it to societal well-being. Whenever possible, the presented ideas have been thoroughly tested and validated. It's only in recent years that the world has begun to pay close attention to health, innovation, and technology, making this work the first comprehensive and systematic exploration of the subject in the context of health.

Chandigarh, India — Varinder Garg

# CIBioD Odyssey: Innovative Story of CIBioD Journey

**ABOUT CIBioD:**

The Indian Council of Medical Research (ICMR) established the Center for Innovation and Bio Design (CIBioD) at PGIMER, Chandigarh, in 2019 to drive healthcare innovation. Located at a renowned medical research institution, CIBioD fosters innovation in medical devices, life sciences, and healthcare technology. It collaborates with academic institutions, government agencies, and private healthcare companies worldwide to support startups and ventures in healthcare. CIBioD provides infrastructure, mentorship, and research facilities to promote entrepreneurial initiatives in healthcare.

**ICMR-CIBioD's Principal Investigator:**
**Dr. Varinder Garg,**
**MBBS; MD (Radiology)**
**OSD to Union Health Minister**
**PGIMER, Chandigarh**

Dr. Varinder Garg earned his MBBS, MD (Radiology) from Government Medical College, Patiala, Punjab, and is currently OSD (Officer on special duty) to Union Health Minister, Government of India and President PGIMER, Chandigarh. He is Principal Investigator at ICMR-CIBioD which happens to be his brainchild.

**Co-principal Investigators of ICMR-CIBioD:**

**Dr. Surinder Rana** is Professor at the Department of Gastroenterology, PGIMER, Chandigarh

**Dr. Harish Kumar** is Professor at the Department of Computer Science and Engineering, University Institute of Engineering and Technology (UIET), Panjab University, Chandigarh

**Dr. Manoj Goyal is** Additional Professor at the Department of Neurology, PGIMER, Chandigarh

**Dr. Sakshi Kaushal** is Professor at the Department of Computer Science and Engineering, UIET, Panjab University, Chandigarh

**Our Mentors:**

**Dr. Rajiv Bahl**

**Director General, ICMR New Delhi**

Dr. Rajiv Bahl, a physician-scientist specialized in pediatrics and public health, has 30 years of experience in health research and policy translation. With an MD from the University of Delhi and a PhD from AIIMS, New Delhi, he received an Honorary Doctorate from the University of Bergen in 2022. He has led research at AIIMS and WHO.

**Sh. Rajinder Gupta**

**Chairman, Trident Group**

Sh. Rajinder Gupta, Founder and Chairman of Trident Limited, has led the company to become one of India's fastest-growing firms, with a compound annual growth rate of over 30%. A first-generation entrepreneur with over two decades of experience, he received the Padma Shri award in 2007 for his contributions to trade and industry.

**Dr. Nirmaljeet Singh Kalsi, IAS (Retd.)**

**Chairperson of National Council for Vocational Education and Training**

Dr. Nirmaljeet Singh Kalsi, Chairman of the National Council of Vocational Education and Training under India's Ministry of Skill Development, has over 35 years of public service experience. He has served in various roles, including as Punjab's Additional Chief Secretary and in the Ministry of Home Affairs. Dr. Kalsi holds degrees from IIT Roorkee, IIT Delhi, and Thapar University, with additional executive education from Harvard and Cambridge.

**Prof. Vivek Lal**

**Director, PGIMER Chandigarh**

Prof. Vivek Lal, with over 30 years of teaching experience, holds an MD and DM in Neurology from PGIMER Chandigarh. He has published over 170 articles in national and international journals and has led numerous research projects funded by ICMR, CSIO, and PGIMER. He is a member of several scientific bodies, including NANOS and the Indian Academy of Neurology.

**Prof. Rajeev Ahuja**

**Director, IIT Ropar**

Prof. Rajeev Ahuja, Appointed Director of IIT Ropar in April 2021, is also a Professor of Computational Materials Science at Uppsala University, Sweden. He earned his PhD from IIT Roorkee in 1992 and has published 1083 papers with over 41,000 citations, focusing on energy applications. He is widely recognized with numerous awards.

**Dr. KK Talwar**

**Ex-Director, PGIMER, Chandigarh**

Padma Bhushan Awardee Dr. Kewal Kishan Talwar is a renowned cardiologist and former chairman of the Medical Council of India. He led AIIMS and PGIMER's cardiology departments and introduced ICD therapy and Cardiac Resynchronization Therapy in South Asia, both featured in the LIMCA Book of Records. He has published extensively and received several honors, including the Dr. B.C. Roy Award.

**Advisory Board Members:**

1. Padma Bhushan, **Dr. KK Talwar,** Ex-Director, PGIMER, Chandigarh
2. Padma Shri **Prof Jagat Ram**, Ex-Director and Former Head, Department of Ophthalmology, PGIMER, Chandigarh
3. **Prof Arwind Rajwanshi,** Director, AIIMS, Rae Bareli
4. **Prof (Dr) YK Gupta**, President-AIIMS Bhopal, AIIMS Jammu/Medical advisor/Strategic Consultant
5. **Prof Meenu Singh**, Director AIIMS, Rishikesh
6. **Dr. Rajesh Gupta,** Professor and Head, Department of Surgical Gastroenterology, PGIMER, Chandigarh
7. **Dr. J Bamrah**, Chairman, British Association of Physicians of Indian Origin
8. **Dr. Akshay Kumar Saxena,** Professor, Department of Radio Diagnosis and Imaging, PGIMER, Chandigarh.
9. **Dr. Suchita Markan,** Scientist E and Mission In-Charge, Medical Device and Diagnostics Mission Secretariat (MDMS), Indian Council of Medical Research (ICMR)

# About Principal and Co-principal Investigators:

**PRINCIPAL INVESTIGATOR:**

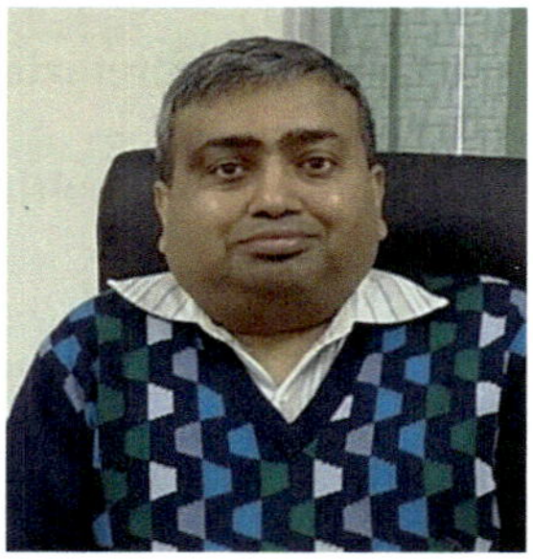

Dr. Varinder Garg, MBBS, MD (Radiology), serves as the Principal Investigator at ICMR-CIBioD, PGIMER, and as OSD to the Union Health Minister and President of PGIMER. With extensive experience in health planning and administration, he has been pivotal in advancing healthcare through innovative patents and the founding of the Society for Affordable Healthcare. His work includes strategic planning, patent development, and leadership in health technology initiatives.

| ICMR-CIBioD-Co-principal Investigator | About |
|---|---|
| **Dr. Surinder Rana** | Is Professor at the Department of Gastroenterology, PGIMER, Chandigarh. Multiple accolades have been bestowed on him including Don Wilson Award, Postgraduate grants by the European Society, Young Clinical Award, and Young Scientist Medal for significant contributions in research in gastroenterology. He has published many national and international papers |
| **Dr. Harish Kumar** | Is Professor in Computer Science and Engineering, UIET, and is Co-founder of Telecommunication Research Laboratory at Panjab University, Chandigarh. He is a researcher and enthusiastically engaging Professor with a proven record of completion of 10+ projects (Digital Kisan, CPSD, Satellite Based Identification of Active Fire Location funded by different industries/government) |

(continued)

| ICMR-CIBioD-Co-principal Investigator | About |
|---|---|
| **Dr. Manoj Goyal** | Is additional Professor in Neurology, PGIMER, Chandigarh. He completed his MBBS and MD from GMC, Patiala, and DM from the National Institute of Mental Health and Neurosciences, Bangalore. He is an enthusiastic researcher with 20+ years of experience with 135+ research publications |
| **Dr. Sakshi Kaushal** | Is Professor in Computer Science and Engineering, UIET, and is Co-founder of Telecommunication Research Laboratory at Panjab University, Chandigarh. With 18+ years of experience, her area of research includes Emerging Communication Networks Including 5G/IoT, M2M, Cloud, Tele-Health, AI/ML, etc. |

**Dr. Suchita Markan Scientist E**
**Mission-in-Charge & Member Secretary**
**Medical Device and Diagnostics Mission Secretariat (MDMS), Indian Council of Medical Research (ICMR)**
**Department of Health Research Ministry of Health and Family Welfare**
**Government of India**

Dr. Suchita Markan is a Scientist and Mission In-charge at the ICMR's Medical Device and Diagnostics Mission Secretariat. With over 15 years of expertise in public policy, intellectual property, and technology transfer in the medical device sector, she has led initiatives to promote innovation and entrepreneurship. An Emerging Leader in Biomedical Innovation, she holds a PhD from PGIMER, an executive management degree from IIM Lucknow, and is a Registered Technology Transfer Professional. Dr. Markan has numerous national and international publications and serves on various institutional committees.

# Acknowledgements

From the core of my heart, I am exceedingly thankful to Sh. JP Nadda ji, Honorable Health and Family Welfare Minister and President PGIMER, Chandigarh, for his blessings, inspiration, and motivation. His vision for indigenous medical technologies and affordable and accessible health care is a lighthouse. We were able to accomplish the CIBioD concept only with his blessings. I am grateful to Sh. Mansukh L Mandavia ji, Honorable Health and Family Welfare (HFW) Minister and President PGIMER, Chandigarh (2021–2024). He has been a great mentor to me and team CIBioD. I am grateful to Dr. Harshvardhan ji [Ex HFW Minister, Government of India (GoI), 2019–2024] and Dr. Jagat Ram (Ex Director PGIMER, Chandigarh) for their continuous guidance, encouragement, and support.

We are extremely grateful to MDMS-ICMR (Medical Device and Diagnostics Mission Secretariat—Indian Council of Medical Research; Grant no. 5/3/8/352/2019-ITR) for their support. This book is meant to start a debate and a discourse among all medical doctors, academic researchers, National/International collaborators, stakeholders, and policymakers who are interested in the long-term progressive evolution of our health system. We are also grateful to Dr. Rajiv Bahl, Director General, ICMR New Delhi and Dr. Vivek Lal, Director, PGIMER Chandigarh for providing support during the entire duration of this exercise. We would like to acknowledge doctors, researchers, and industry partners for their commitment, dedication, inspiration, and guidance that made this book possible.

We are grateful to all the Advisory Board members and mentors who contributed to this crucial piece of work, and we would also want to thank the following for their support/collaboration throughout the CIBioD journey.

- Sh. Rajindra Gupta, *Padma Shri, Chairman, Trident group*
- Dr. K.K. Talwar, *Padma Bhushan, Ex-Director, PGIMER, Chandigarh.*
- Prof. Jagat Ram, *Padma Shri, Ex-Director and Former Head, Ophthalmology, PGIMER, Chandigarh*
- Dr. Nirmaljeet Singh Kalsi, IAS (Retd.), *Chairperson of National Council for Vocational Education and Training*
- Dr. Balram Bhargava, Ex-DG, ICMR
- Prof. Y.K. Gupta, *President-AIIMS Bhopal, AIIMS Jammu/Medical advisor/ Strategic consultant*
- Prof. Arwind Rajwanshi, *Director, AIIMS, Rae Bareli*

- Dr. J.S. Bamrah, *National Chairman, British Association of Physicians of Indian Origin*
- Prof. Yash Paul Sharma, *Head, Department of cardiology, PGIMER, Chandigarh*
- Prof. Meenu Singh, *Executive Director and CEO, AIIMS Rishikesh*
- Prof. Surinder Rana, *Department of Gastroenterology, PGIMER, Chandigarh*
- Prof. Rajesh Gupta, *Head-Department of Surgical Gastroenterology, PGIMER, Chandigarh*
- Dr. Suchita Markan, *Mission In-charge, Medical Device and Diagnostics Mission Secretariat, Indian Council of Medical Research, New Delhi*
- Prof. Sanjay Bhadada, *Department of Endocrinology, PGIMER, Chandigarh*
- Dr. Manoj Goyal, *Department of Neurology, PGIMER, Chandigarh*
- Dr. Pankaj Aggarwal, *Department of Pediatric, PGIMER, Chandigarh*
- Dr. Aashima Arora, *Department of Obstetrics and Gynaecology, PGIMER, Chandigarh*
- Dr. Ajeet Kaushik, *Florida Poly-Tech University, Florida*
- Dr. Anirudda Malpani, *Chairman, Malpani Ventures, Funding Frugal Innovation in India*
- Dr. Anjali Agrawal, *Consultant Radiologist and Director New Delhi operations*
- Dr. Atharva Poundarik, *Department of Metallurgical and Materials Engineering, Indian Institute of Technology, Ropar*
- Dr. Basant Kumar, *Department of Cardiology, PGIMER, Chandigarh*
- Dr. Chirag Adatia, *Partner Mckinsey and Company, India*
- Dr. Girija Shankar Mohanty, *Department of Obstetrics and Gynaecology, PGIMER, Chandigarh*
- Dr. Harpreet Singh, *Department of Computer Science and Engineering, Thapar Institute of Engineering and Technology, Patiala*
- Dr. Karthik Vinay Mahesh, *Department of Neurology, PGIMER, Chandigarh*
- Dr. Kiran Jhangra, *Department of Anesthesia and Intensive Care PGIMER, Chandigarh*
- Dr. Mandeep Singh, *Department of Mechanical Engineering, Thapar Institute of Engineering and Technology, Patiala*
- Dr. Manjul Muraleedharan, *Department of Neuro-Otology, PGIMER, Chandigarh*
- Dr. Mayank Gurunani, *Associate Director-National University of Singapore*
- Dr. Meeta Mukherjee Verma, *Medical Device and Diagnostics Mission Secretariat, Indian Council of Medical Research, New Delhi*
- Dr. Minakshi Rohilla, *Department of Obstetrics and Gynaecology, PGIMER, Chandigarh*
- Dr. Monika Singh, *Northern India Institute of Fashion Technology, Mohali*
- Dr. Narender Kaloria, *Department of Anesthesia, PGIMER, Chandigarh*
- Dr. Naveen Naik B, *Department of Anesthesia and Intensive Care, PGIMER, Chandigarh*
- Dr. Neemu Hage, *AIIMS, Bibinagar*
- Dr. Neeraj Kumar Singh, *Deputy Librarian, AC Joshi Library, Panjab University, Chandigarh*

- Dr. Neeru Jindal, *Department of Electrical and Electronic Engineering, Thapar Institute of Engineering and Technology, Patiala*
- Dr. Nidhi Bidyut Panda, *Department of Pediatric, PGIMER, Chandigarh*
- Dr. Nisha Bhargava, *Principal—MCM DAV College, Chandigarh*
- Dr. Poonam Aggarwal Thakur, *Principal-Northern India Institute of Fashion Technology, Mohali*
- Dr. Prashant Singh Rana, *Department of Computer Science and Engineering, Thapar Institute of Engineering and Technology, Patiala*
- Dr. Ravinder Kumar Duvedi, *Department of Mechanical Engineering, Thapar Institute of Engineering and Technology, Patiala*
- Dr. Rohit Garg, *Director, Sri Venkteshwara Indo Global Medicare Private Limited*
- Dr. Sachin Gupta, *Director, Salus Healthcare Management Consultant*
- Dr. Sanjeev Kumar, *Department of Psychiatry, University of Toronto, Canada*
- Dr. Shiv Lal Soni, *Department of Anesthesia and Intensive Care, PGIMER, Chandigarh*
- Dr. Tarang Gianchandani, *CEO, HN Reliance Foundation Hospital, Mumbai*
- Dr. Vanita Jain, *Department of Obstetrics and Gynaecology, PGIMER, Chandigarh*
- Dr. Venkata Ganesh, *Department of Anesthesia, PGIMER, Chandigarh*
- Ms. Cheena Malhotra, *Centre for Innovation and Bio-Design, PGIMER, Chandigarh*
- Ms. Elizabeth G. (Liz) Clark, *MPH, International Health Expert, Based in Boston*
- Ms. Karuna Kanwar, *Incubation Manager, Technology Business Incubator Foundation, Indian Institute of Technology, Ropar*
- Prof Manish Modi, *Department of Neurology, PGIMER, Chandigarh*
- Prof. Akshay Kumar Saxena, *Department of Radiology, PGIMER, Chandigarh*
- Prof. Aman Sharma, *Department of Internal Medicine, PGIMER, Chandigarh*
- Prof. Anurag Snehi Ramavat, *Department of ENT, PGIMER, Chandigarh*
- Prof. Babita Ghai, *Department of Anesthesia, PGIMER, Chandigarh*
- Prof. Deepak Garg, *Director, NVIDIA-BU Research Center on Artificial Intelligence*
- Prof. Ganga Ram Chaudhary, *Department of Chemistry, Panjab University, Chandigarh*
- Prof. Gurpreet Kaur, *Department of Chemistry, Panjab University, Chandigarh*
- Prof. Gurpreet Singh, *Head-Department of General Surgery, PGIMER, Chandigarh*
- Prof. Raja Ramachandran, *Department of Nephrology, PGIMER, Chandigarh*
- Prof. Rakesh Sehgal (Retd.), *Department of Parasitology, PGIMER, Chandigarh*
- Prof. Ramandeep Singh Virk, *Department of ENT, PGIMER, Chandigarh*
- Prof. Sakshi Kaushal, *Department of Computer Science and Engineering, UIET (University Institute of Engineering and Technology), Panjab University, Chandigarh*
- Prof. Santosh Kumar, *Department of Urology, PGIMER, Chandigarh*

- Prof. Shankar Prinja, *Department of Community Medicine and School of Public Health, PGIMER, Chandigarh*
- Sh. Akhil Puri, *Director/NewCo Scale-Up/Operating Partner, Public Investment Fund*
- Sh. Neeraj Tayal, *Eminent Entrepreneur and Industrialist*
- Sh. Sushil Kumar Rana, *Medtech Expert and PhD Fellow—Chitkara University, Punjab*

# Introduction

Many people believe that innovation is a primary driver of economic progress. The primary impulse that propels and sustains the capitalist engine includes new consumer items, new methods of production or transportation, new markets, and new forces of industrial organization. The potential to create new products, processes, markets, or organizations is path dependent. Management of the innovation process is a difficult discipline to master since transforming a basic discovery into a commercial product, method, or service is a lengthy, high-risk, complicated, interactive, and non-linear process. Moreover, the ability of firms to initiate and sustain innovation is heavily influenced by the larger local and national context in which they operate. This is exactly why 'innovation within' necessitates a favorable 'context outside,' i.e., economic and social factors are crucial for an innovation to be successful. In terms of health, countries' economic progress can be achieved through development of new technologies, their dissemination, and attempts to build their own capacities. All this is achievable through continuous efforts and promotion of a collaborative framework. To achieve progressive development in the health sector, we need strategic intervention in infrastructure development, technological capacity formation, and human capital production.

# Contents

# Envisioning Digital Health Technology Innovations for 2025: Enhancing Digital Interventions in the Post-COVID-19 Era

1

Varinder Garg, Harish Kumar, Ramandeep Bansal, and Anupriya Bhardwaj

## 1.1 What Is at Risk? An 18-Month View of a Post-COVID World

The post-COVID-19 world is a landscape transformed by a global pandemic that challenged societies, economies, and healthcare systems in an unprecedented way. As we review this new era, it is clear that COVID-19 has left an indelible mark on our world, reshaping numerous aspects of our lives. One of the most significant lessons learned from the pandemic is the need for robust public health infrastructure. The governments worldwide have realized the importance of preparedness, timely responses, and vaccination campaigns. In the post-COVID world, public health takes center stage, with greater investments in research, surveillance, and healthcare accessibility [7]. The world of work underwent a revolution as remote work became the norm for many. This shift has profound implications for industries, employees, and the workplace. Hybrid work models, which combine in-office and remote work, provide a new level of flexibility and work–life balance. The pandemic accelerated the digital transformation across industries. E-commerce, telemedicine, and online education saw explosive growth. The reliance on digital tools and technologies is likely to persist, reshaping how we shop, receive healthcare, and learn [12].

V. Garg (✉)
ICMR-Centre for Innovation and Bio-Design (CIBioD), Postgraduate Institute of Medical Education and Research (PGIMER), Chandigarh, Chandigarh, India

H. Kumar
Department of Computer Science and Engineering, University Institute of Engineering and Technology (UIET) Panjab University, Chandigarh, Punjab, India

R. Bansal
Department of Obstetrics and Gynecology, PGIMER, Chandigarh, India

A. Bhardwaj
ICMR Center for Innovation and Bio-Design, PGIMER, Chandigarh, India

 
V. Garg et al. (eds.), *Innovations in Healthcare Technologies in India*,
https://doi.org/10.1007/978-981-97-0244-2_1

The travel and tourism industry was one of the most severely impacted sectors during the COVID-19 pandemic and is now experiencing a cautious revival [7]. Travel restrictions prompted a focus on sustainable and mindful tourism, with travelers seeking off-the-beaten-path destinations and eco-friendly options. The pandemic's economic impact was significant, with disruptions to businesses, job losses, and supply chain challenges. The governments deployed stimulus packages to support recovery efforts. As economies gradually rebound, discussions continue about long-term resilience and sustainable growth.

The COVID-19 pandemic had profound effects on mental health. Isolation, anxiety, and grief took a toll on individuals worldwide. The pandemic led to increased awareness and discussions about mental well-being, driving demand for accessible mental health services.

The pandemic underscored the importance of international cooperation. The rapid development and distribution of vaccines showed what a global collaboration can achieve. The calls for vaccine equity and preparedness for future health crises remain prominent on the global agenda. Lockdowns and reduced human activity had a positive impact on the environment, with decreased pollution and wildlife resurgence. This period prompted discussions about sustainable practices, including renewable energy, conservation, and responsible consumption.

Education faced immense challenges with the closure of schools. Remote learning exposed disparities in access and quality. In the post-COVID world, discussions about the future of education persist, with a focus on online and hybrid models, digital literacy, and educational equity. Disruptions in supply chains revealed vulnerabilities, leading to reassessments and potential shifts in manufacturing and logistics. Companies are exploring strategies to enhance resilience and adapt to changing global dynamics [12].

In conclusion, the post-COVID world is marked by resilience, adaptation, and transformation. Lessons learned during the pandemic have prompted societies, governments, and businesses to rethink their approaches and prioritize preparedness, flexibility, and sustainability. While challenges persist, the world is moving forward with a newfound awareness of the interconnectedness of our global community and the need for collaboration to address current and future crises. As we navigate this evolving landscape, the experiences of the pandemic continue to shape our decisions and priorities in the years to come.

## 1.2 Megatrends in Health and Wellness

The healthcare and wellness industry is on the verge of a significant transformation, fueled by breakthroughs in science, technology, and our knowledge of the human body. In this discussion, we will examine the major trends that are shaping the future of human evolution, ranging from augmented intelligence to digital biometrics, all in the pursuit of creating healthier, stronger, and more capable individuals. These megatrends are shown in Table 1.1 and Fig. 1.1.

**Table 1.1** Megatrends in health and wellness

| Megatrends | Description |
|---|---|
| Enhanced intelligence | In the near future, the convergence of artificial intelligence (AI) and human intelligence promises to unlock the full potential of our mental faculties. Brain-computer interfaces (BCIs) and neuro-enhancement technologies are leading this significant trend. BCIs will facilitate direct interaction between the brain and external devices, paving the way for accelerated learning, enhanced memory, and even the possibility of uploading and downloading thoughts and knowledge |
| Enhanced sensing | Human senses are also evolving, thanks to advancements in sensor technologies and biotechnology. Miniaturized sensors implanted in the body can provide enhanced sensory perception, from ultraviolet vision to infrared detection. These enhancements can not only aid in everyday life but also find applications in healthcare, security, and environmental monitoring |
| Disease-free body | The dream of a disease-free body is inching closer to reality, with gene editing techniques like CRISPR-Cas9 offering the potential to eliminate genetic diseases. Additionally, advancements in regenerative medicine and personalized healthcare will enable the repair and replacement of damaged or aging tissues, reducing the prevalence of chronic diseases |
| Sports optimization | Athletes of the future will benefit from advanced sports optimization techniques, combining genetic profiling, biomechanical analysis, and personalized training regimens. Wearable technology will continuously monitor an athlete's physiology, enabling real-time adjustments to maximize performance while minimizing the risk of injury |
| Digital hardware enhancement | The integration of technology into the human body will become a commonplace. Implantable devices, such as smart prosthetics and augmented reality contact lenses, will enhance our physical abilities and provide direct access to digital information, bridging the gap between man and machine |
| Enhanced strength | Advancements in genetic engineering and exoskeleton technology will empower individuals with superhuman strength and endurance. Exosuits can assist with heavy lifting and physically demanding tasks, while gene editing can optimize muscle growth and recovery |
| Increased attractiveness | The boundaries of beauty and attractiveness will expand with the help of genetic modification, cosmetic enhancements, and biotechnology. Tailored treatments will allow individuals to sculpt their appearance according to their preferences while maintaining health and well-being |
| Extreme aging | Anti-aging therapies are advancing rapidly, promising extended lifespans and prolonged youthful vitality. Telomere extension, cellular rejuvenation, and senescence reversal are among the strategies being explored to slow down the aging process |
| Optimized diet | Personalized nutrition, based on individual genetics and metabolic profiles, will revolutionize how we approach food. Precision diets will cater to specific dietary needs, improving overall health and preventing diet-related diseases |

(continued)

**Table 1.1** (continued)

| Megatrends | Description |
|---|---|
| Digital biometrics | Biometric data will be the cornerstone of healthcare and wellness in the future. Wearable devices and embedded sensors will continuously monitor vital signs, offering real-time health evaluations and early alerts for potential medical concerns |
| Ubiquitous and continuous monitoring | Health monitoring will extend beyond wearable devices. Smart environments, equipped with sensors and artificial intelligence (AI), will create a seamless, ubiquitous monitoring network. This will provide individuals with a holistic view of their health, enabling proactive interventions and lifestyle adjustments |

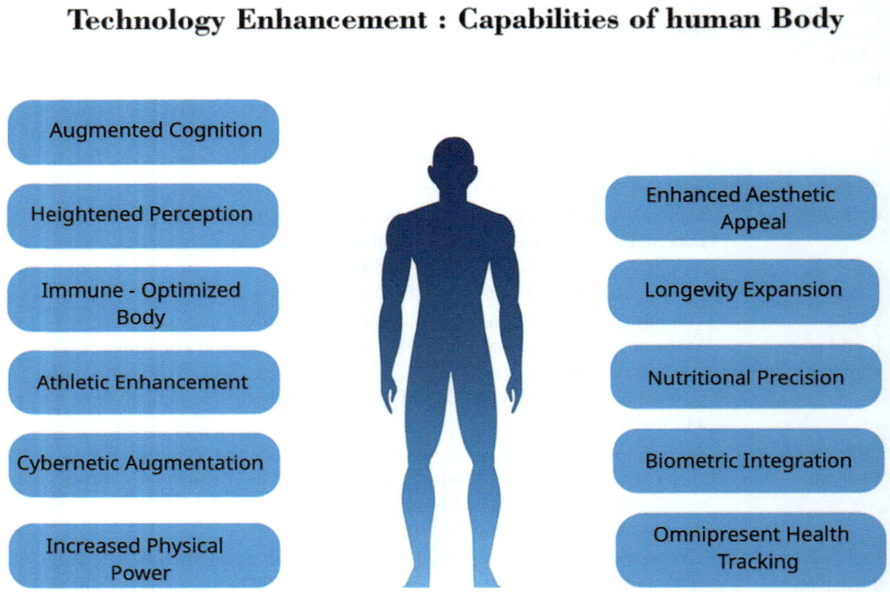


**Fig. 1.1** Megatrends in health and wellness

## 1.3 Technology-Induced Digital Disruption

### 1.3.1 Trends and Impacts

The convergence of technology and healthcare, often referred to as Health-Tech, is ushering in a transformative era. This digital disruption is driven by several key trends that leverage cutting-edge technologies, including artificial intelligence (AI) and machine learning (ML), big data analytics, Internet of Everything (IOE) and sensors, mobile technology, cloud computing, natural user interfaces, and ubiquitous connectivity. In this exploration, we will delve into these trends and their profound impacts on the healthcare landscape (Fig. 1.2).

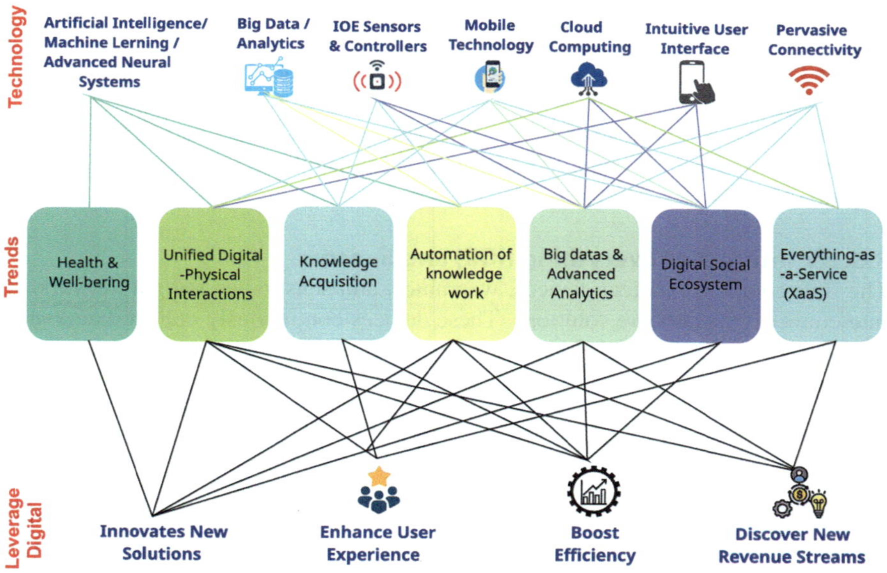


**Fig. 1.2** Some new technologies and their impact on healthcare

#### 1.3.1.1 Artificial Intelligence (AI) and Machine Learning (ML)

AI and ML have emerged as powerful tools in healthcare. They are highly effective at analyzing large volumes of medical data, ranging from patient records to research studies, to uncover valuable insights. AI-driven diagnostics, predictive analytics, and personalized treatment recommendations are revolutionizing patient care [2].

**Impact**

- AI can analyze medical images, such as X-rays and magnetic resonance images (MRIs), with incredible accuracy, aiding in early disease detection.
- ML algorithms can analyze genetic data to tailor treatment plans as per an individual's unique genetic makeup.
- ML models can forecast disease outbreaks, hospital resource needs, and patient-specific treatment outcomes, enhancing proactive care.

#### 1.3.1.2 Big Data Analytics

Healthcare generates an immense amount of data daily. Big data analytics tools can extract meaningful information from this data, enabling evidence-based decision-making. Researchers and healthcare providers benefit from comprehensive patient profiles and population health insights [5].

**Impact**

- Big data analytics accelerate medical research by identifying trends and correlations in vast datasets.
- Data-driven insights lead to improved patient care and better treatment strategies.
- Analyzing data can reveal inefficiencies in healthcare delivery, helping to reduce costs.

#### 1.3.1.3 Internet of Everything (IOE) and Sensors

The IOE connects medical devices, wearables, and sensors, creating a network of interconnected healthcare solutions. These devices continuously collect data, ranging from vital signs to medication adherence, fostering proactive and remote healthcare management [1].

**Impact**

- Patients with chronic conditions can be monitored remotely, reducing hospitalizations and improving the quality of life.
- Wearables and sensors can detect health issues early, enabling timely interventions.
- IOE enhances care coordination by connecting various healthcare devices and systems.

#### 1.3.1.4 Mobile Technology

Mobile technology, including smartphones and tablets, is ubiquitous. Mobile apps empower patients to access healthcare resources, schedule appointments, track their health, and communicate with healthcare providers. Mobile health (mHealth) applications improve patient engagement and self-care [22].

**Impact**

- Mobile apps enable individuals to actively manage their health through access to information and self-monitoring.
- Mobile devices facilitate telehealth consultations, increasing healthcare accessibility, especially in remote areas.
- Mobile platforms make it easy for patients to share health data with their healthcare providers.

#### 1.3.1.5 Cloud Computing

Cloud computing revolutionizes data storage, access, and sharing in healthcare. It facilitates secure and scalable storage of electronic health records (EHRs), medical images, and research data. Cloud-based healthcare systems offer flexibility and accessibility [17].

**Impacts**

- Cloud-based EHRs streamline healthcare workflows, reducing administrative overhead.
- Cloud providers invest heavily in security, ensuring patient data is protected.
- Researchers and healthcare providers can access and share data seamlessly, fostering collaboration.

#### 1.3.1.6 Natural User Interface (NUI)

NUI technologies, such as voice and gesture recognition, offer intuitive ways to interact with healthcare systems and devices. Voice assistants and gesture-controlled interfaces enhance accessibility for patients and healthcare professionals [8].

**Impact**

- NUI makes it easier for individuals with disabilities to access healthcare information and services.
- In the context of infection control (e.g., during pandemics), touchless interfaces minimize physical contact with devices.

#### 1.3.1.7 Ubiquitous Connectivity

The proliferation of high-speed, reliable internet connections ensures ubiquitous connectivity. This enables real-time data sharing, telehealth consultations, and the seamless integration of healthcare devices and systems [6].

**Impact**

- Healthcare providers can offer virtual consultations, extending care to remote or underserved areas.
- Continuous data exchange between devices, EHRs, and healthcare providers improves care coordination.
- Ubiquitous connectivity supports the scalability of digital health solutions.

### 1.3.2 Impacts on Healthcare Ecosystem

The digital disruption driven by these trends is reshaping the entire healthcare ecosystem. The changes include:

1. Patients are empowered with access to health information, remote monitoring, and personalized treatment plans.
2. AI-driven diagnostics enhance the speed and accuracy of disease detection.
3. Efficiency and cost savings: Digital solutions streamline healthcare workflows, reducing administrative overhead and minimizing errors. Wearable devices and

continuous monitoring enable early disease detection and proactive interventions.
4. Big data analytics and cloud computing facilitate medical research by providing access to vast datasets and collaboration tools.
5. As healthcare becomes more digital, robust security measures and privacy protections are crucial. Thus, regulatory bodies must adapt to evolving technologies to ensure patient safety and data security.

## 1.4 Digital Healthcare, Health Tech, and Wellness Trends

### 1.4.1 Telemedicine

Healthcare has been transformed by telemedicine, which allows patients and healthcare providers to conduct consultations remotely. It offers convenience, accessibility, and cost-effectiveness, particularly in underserved areas. The ability to consult with specialists without geographical constraints enhances patient care and reduces healthcare disparities [23].

### 1.4.2 VR in Healthcare

Virtual reality (VR) has found applications in healthcare, from pain management to medical training. VR environments can immerse patients in therapeutic experiences, reducing pain perception. Additionally, VR simulations aid medical professionals in refining their skills and practicing complex procedures in a risk-free environment [14].

### 1.4.3 Remote Monitoring, Critical Care

Critical care telemedicine and remote monitoring solutions are essential for continuously tracking patients' vital signs and delivering timely interventions. This technology is especially crucial for patients with chronic conditions or those recovering from surgeries, as it enables early detection of complications and reduces hospital readmissions [24].

### 1.4.4 Virtual Assistants and Chatbots

Virtual assistants and chatbots enhance patient engagement and support. They provide instant responses to health-related queries, medication reminders, and even mental health support. These AI-powered tools contribute to better patient education and adherence to treatment plans [26].

### 1.4.5 3D Organ Printing

Three-dimensional (3D) organ printing represents a groundbreaking advancement in healthcare. It holds the potential to create customized organs and tissues for transplantation, reducing the demand for donor organs and minimizing rejection risks. This technology is still in development but promises to revolutionize transplant medicine [15].

### 1.4.6 Artificial Intelligence

Artificial intelligence (AI) has wide-ranging applications in healthcare, from diagnostics to drug discovery. Machine learning algorithms are capable of interpreting medical images, forecasting disease outcomes, and streamlining administrative tasks, thereby improving the accuracy and efficiency of healthcare processes [2].

### 1.4.7 IOT Sensors and Devices

Internet of Things (IoT) sensors and devices collect real-time data from patients and medical equipment. Wearable devices, smartphones, and connected medical devices enable remote monitoring, early disease detection, and personalized treatment plans [1].

### 1.4.8 Digital Therapeutics

Digital therapeutics are software-based interventions designed to treat medical conditions. They offer nonpharmacological, evidence-based treatments for conditions like depression, substance abuse, and chronic diseases. These interventions are becoming an integral part of healthcare [27].

### 1.4.9 Genomics

The advances in genomics have led to personalized medicine. Genetic testing and analysis provide insights into an individual's susceptibility to diseases and their response to treatments. Genomic data is revolutionizing drug development and cancer treatment [20].

### 1.4.10 Data Science and Blockchain

Data science and blockchain technologies are transforming data management and security in healthcare. Data analytics enable researchers to extract valuable insights, while blockchain ensures the integrity and privacy of patient records and transactions [4].

### 1.4.11 Specialty Care

Specialty care telemedicine connects patients with specialized healthcare providers, regardless of geographic location. This improves access to expert opinions, reduces travel-related expenses, and reduces waiting times for specialized care [23].

### 1.4.12 Imaging and Other Diagnostics

Advances in medical imaging, including AI-enhanced interpretations, have improved diagnostic accuracy. The innovations in diagnostic tools and techniques, such as liquid biopsy for cancer detection, are enabling earlier and more precise diagnoses [25].

### 1.4.13 Pharma Supply Chain

Blockchain technology is being used to enhance transparency and traceability in the pharmaceutical supply chain. This helps in preventing counterfeit drugs, ensuring product quality, and improving the overall integrity of the pharmaceutical industry [4].

### 1.4.14 Primary Healthcare

Primary healthcare remains the cornerstone of healthcare delivery, focusing on preventive and basic healthcare services. In the era of digital disruption, technology is enhancing primary care through telemedicine, electronic health records (EHRs), and health information systems. These digital tools streamline patient data management, improve care coordination, and enable remote consultations, ensuring that individuals receive timely and accessible healthcare services [19].

### 1.4.15 Consumer Health, Fitness, and Wellness

Digital health and wellness solutions empower consumers to take control of their health. Mobile apps, wearables, and connected devices track fitness metrics, monitor vital signs, and provide personalized wellness recommendations. This trend encourages individuals to adopt healthier lifestyles, manage chronic conditions and engage in preventive care actively [13].

### 1.4.16 Nutrition and Mental Health

Digital disruption extends to nutrition and mental health. Mobile apps offer nutritional guidance, track dietary habits, and promote balanced eating. Mental health apps provide support, therapy and mindfulness exercises, making mental healthcare more accessible. These tools address the holistic well-being of individuals, recognizing the interconnectedness of physical and mental health [11, 16].

### 1.4.17 Clinical Efficiency Tools and IoT Sensors

Clinical efficiency is bolstered by technology. Clinical efficiency tools, including EHRs, digital prescriptions, and appointment scheduling apps, reduce administrative burdens. IoT sensors and smart devices in hospitals and homes monitor patient health continuously, enabling early intervention and reducing healthcare costs [1].

### 1.4.18 Drug Discovery Developments

In drug discovery, technology-driven advances are accelerating the development of novel treatments. Computational biology, AI-driven drug design, and high-throughput screening methods expedite the discovery and testing of potential drug candidates. This not only reduces the time and cost of drug development but also offers hope for addressing complex diseases [9].

### 1.4.19 Clinical Trials

Digital disruption is transforming the landscape of clinical trials. Virtual trials, wearable sensors, and electronic data capture streamline research processes. These innovations enhance patient recruitment, data accuracy, and trial efficiency, ultimately accelerating the development of new therapies [18].

### 1.4.20 Personalized Mobile Apps

Personalized mobile apps are revolutionizing healthcare. These apps cater to the health needs of an individual, offering targeted fitness routines, medication reminders, and chronic disease management tools. Personalization ensures that healthcare interventions align with each person's unique requirements [22].

### 1.4.21 Predictive Analysis and Risk Scoring

Predictive analysis and risk scoring leverage AI and big data to anticipate health outcomes. Algorithms analyze historical health data, identifying patients at risk for specific conditions. This allows for early interventions, personalized preventive care, and more effective resource allocation [4].

### 1.4.22 Hospital Decision Support Systems (DSSs), Administrative Tools, and Compliances

Healthcare institutions benefit from digital disruption through hospital DSSs and administrative tools. DSSs assist in clinical decision-making by providing real-time data insights. Administrative tools streamline billing, compliance reporting, and resource management resulting in better operational efficiency [21].

### 1.4.23 Insurance Benefits

Insurers harness technology to offer personalized insurance benefits. Telematics, wearable data, and health apps enable insurers to tailor policies to individual lifestyles and health behavior. This results in more accurate pricing and encourages policyholders to adopt healthier habits [10].

### 1.4.24 Video Marketing and Advanced Social Media

Video marketing and advanced social media strategies are transforming healthcare communication. Providers and pharmaceutical companies use engaging video content and social media platforms to disseminate health information, educate patients, and raise awareness. These approaches have the potential to improve health literacy and patient engagement.

## 1.5 Healthcare and Wellness Technologies

Some of the healthcare technologies include:

*Data Sciences:* This includes the use of data to monitor and prevent health problems, thereby improving diagnostic accuracy and efficiency, and providing better and directed therapeutic interventions. It also helps pharmaceutical research to find cures for rare and hither to untreatable illnesses.

*Chatbots:* Chatbots, known for their speed and seemingly intelligent responses, are increasingly replacing roles once held by humans. They significantly ease the burden on healthcare professionals by streamlining tasks and supporting patients by addressing medical questions, offering medication guidance, checking symptoms, and providing advice on nutrition and various health-related matters.

*Blockchain:* Blockchain technology has the potential to overhaul the entire digital marketing landscape by transforming data collection practices, improving the accuracy of digital display advertising, and enhancing transaction security.

*Telemedicine:* It is a powerful tool to provide healthcare services to people residing in remote and underserved areas.

*Personalized Digital Mobile Health Apps:* These apps are an excellent tool for delivering user-focused notifications, offering patients around the world relevant and tailored healthcare experiences.

## 1.6 Healthcare Around the World in 2025 (Fig. 1.3)

A connected ecosystem of sensors and devices, intricately woven into the fabric of an individual's daily life, plays an important role in revolutionizing healthcare. This digital tapestry serves as a vigilant guardian, capturing and measuring vital signs with unprecedented precision. These sensors offer a live glimpse into the body's internal processes, tracking everything from heart rate and blood pressure to glucose levels and oxygen saturation. Beyond mere monitoring, these devices possess the remarkable capability to identify diseases at their earliest stages. They serve as vigilant sentinels, detecting subtle deviations from baseline health patterns that

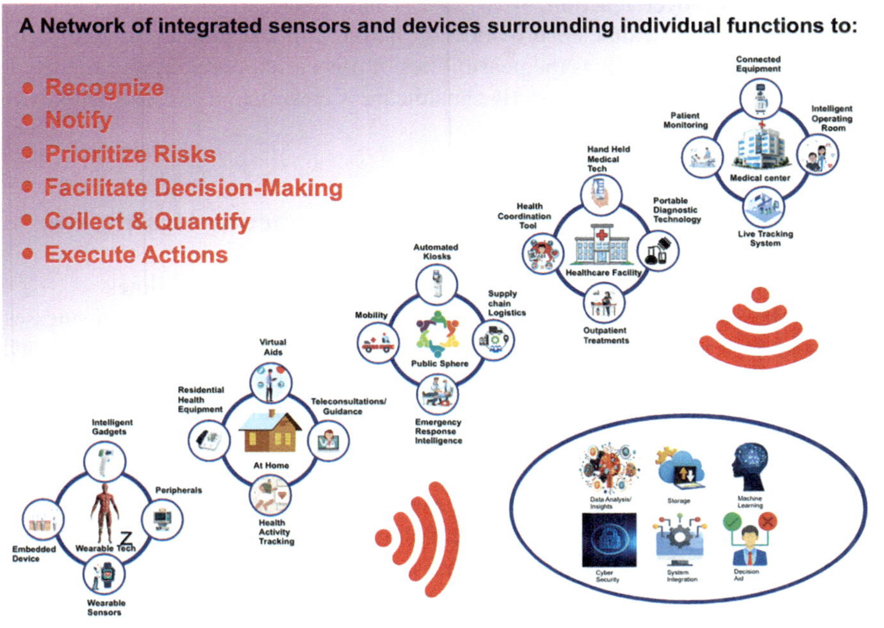


**Fig. 1.3** Healthcare in 2025

might escape human notice. For instance, irregular heart rhythms indicative of arrhythmias, elevated blood glucose levels signaling diabetes, or abnormal lung sounds hinting at respiratory issues can be promptly flagged for attention. Moreover, this connected ecosystem excels at risk stratification. By meticulously analyzing the wealth of data being gathered continuously, it identifies individuals at higher susceptibility to certain medical conditions. Whether it is recognizing the predisposition to heart disease based on genetic markers or assessing the risk of stroke through blood pressure trends, this technology empowers individuals and healthcare providers with the insights needed for proactive health management [1].

Note that this interconnected web of sensors and devices is not merely an observer; it is a decision-maker and an agent of action. With the assistance of advanced algorithms and artificial intelligence, it interprets the data it collects, generating actionable insights and recommendations. For instance, it might advise an individual to adjust their medication dosage based on real-time glucose readings or suggest a change in exercise routines to mitigate cardiovascular risks. Crucially, this ecosystem operates within the framework of a patient's healthcare plan, working in tandem with healthcare providers. It shares pertinent data seamlessly, ensuring that medical professionals are always in the loop. Physicians can remotely monitor their patients' health, receive automated alerts for critical conditions, and intervene promptly when necessary. In essence, this connected ecosystem is more than a collection of sensors and devices; it is a guardian of health, a vigilant identifier of diseases, a risk-stratification expert, a decision-support system, and a prompt responder. It transforms healthcare into a proactive, data-driven endeavor where prevention takes precedence over reaction. It empowers individuals to take charge of their health and engages healthcare providers as partners in the journey toward well-being. As the world embraces the possibilities of this digital transformation, the era of personalized, precise, and proactive healthcare is dawning, promising better outcomes and a healthier future for all [1].

## 1.7 Key Tech Trends of Sustainability Impacting Healthcare

- In the last 60 years, computing power has improved by 1 trillion times.
- From the social, mobile, analytics, and cloud (SMAC) paradigm, businesses must change to embrace emerging technologies such as blockchain technology, artificial intelligence (AI), and virtual and extended reality (VR and AR).
- The marketing landscape will be transformed as companies start analyzing consumer profiles in-depth, encompassing social, personal, health, financial, and employment data.
- The integration of 3D printing into healthcare could lead to breakthroughs in creating bionic body parts, while combining telemedicine with AI-driven diagnostic tools has the potential to overhaul how medical services are delivered.
- To keep pace with the technological advancements in 2020, businesses will need to invest in reskilling the next-generation workforce, focusing on areas like aug-

mented reality, virtual reality, the Internet of Things, blockchain, and artificial intelligence.

- AI-powered advancements, including IBM Watson, Oracle, and autonomous vehicles from companies such as Tesla, Uber, and Volvo, are projected to achieve higher levels of sophistication in the coming years.
- Business automation will unfold in three stages, namely algorithmic, augmentation, and autonomy, potentially leading to the gradual reduction of human involvement in automated retail environments.
- To seize real-time opportunities in "momentary markets," companies will need to enhance their customer analytics and advertising strategies.
- The advent of 5G is set to revolutionize connectivity by dramatically increasing network capacity, enabling billions of devices to connect, and offering lightning-fast speeds up to 10 gigabytes per second. However, as long-term evolution (LTE) continues to expand, it may complicate the widespread adoption and implementation of 5G technology.
- The rise of Facebook's cryptocurrency project, Libra, alongside the increasing popularity of digital payment platforms like Amazon Pay, will render conventional banking systems weaker.

In response to data privacy regulations, analytical approaches need to be modified by businesses to ensure the protection of user information.

## 1.8 Major Global Trends: The Impact of COVID-19

The impact of COVID-19 includes:

- *Serious Concerns About the Global Economy*: Major economies were in positive growth till 2019, but COVID-19 has changed it all. All major economies are in red.
- *Global Balance of Power Shifting*: The global power measured in terms of military, economic, political, and soft power is shifting from the Atlantic to the Indo-Pacific. China is returning to global power. China captured and cornered the global institutions (like the World Health Organization), corporates, natural resources, and markets. Although the USA is still the single strongest power in absolute terms, it is weakening in relative terms. Two most powerful countries, the USA and China, have veered from strategic engagement to open strategic competition: battle for military predominance in the Indo-Pacific; battle for technological dominance; battle of ideas; battle for economic supremacy and global leadership. The current trends also observe that Europe is beset by internal crises, Russia is still lethal, and India, Brazil, and Nigeria are rising slowly to global power.
- *Transnational Challenges:* These include climate change and environmental degradation, human trafficking, criminal and drug cartels, and cyber challenges.
- *Nationalism on the Rise*: There is a growing rise of nationalism in many countries including China, Japan, India, Russia, and the USA.

- *Nuclear Instability*: With the lapse of Intermediate-Range Nuclear Forces (INF) Treaty (1987), there is no limit on the intermediate range missiles.
- *USA Pulling Inward and No Longer Leading*: In the changing world scenario, the USA is seen to be pulling from many of its commitments including climate pact, Iran deal, United Nations (UN) agencies resulting in the weakening of many US alliances.

## 1.9 Prime Minister's Vision for "Atmanirbhar Bharat"

The Indian Prime Minister Narendra Modi has initiated several measures to advance the vision of Atmanirbhar Bharat [3]. These initiatives include:

- Launching the Self-Reliant India Movement to encourage national self-sufficiency.
- Defining the five key pillars that support Atmanirbhar Bharat: economy, infrastructure, system, dynamic demography, and demand.
- Introducing an extensive economic relief package amounting to ₹20 lakh crores, representing around 10% of the nation's GDP.
- Introducing a package aimed at supporting various sectors, including cottage industries, MSMEs (Micro, Small, and Medium Enterprises), laborers, the middle class, and larger industries.
- Implementing significant reforms across multiple sectors to accelerate the nation's journey toward self-reliance.
- Promoting the slogan "Vocal for Local" to encourage the adoption of local products and elevate them to a global level.

## References

1. Al-Kahtani MS, Khan F, Taekeun W. Application of internet of things and sensors in healthcare. Sensors. 2022;22(15):5738. https://doi.org/10.3390/s22155738.
2. Artificial intelligence and machine learning in healthcare. 2023. https://www.biomedcentral.com/collections/aiandmlinhealthcare.
3. Atmanirbhar Bharat Abhiyaan | Self-reliant India Campaign. Invest India. 2023. https://www.investindia.gov.in/atmanirbhar-bharat-abhiyaan.
4. Balamurugan B, Chilamkurti N, Beena TLA, Poongodi T. Blockchain and machine learning for e-healthcare systems. Institution of Engineering and Technology; 2020.
5. Batko K, Ślęzak A. The use of Big Data Analytics in healthcare. J Big Data. 2022;9(1) https://doi.org/10.1186/s40537-021-00553-4.
6. Da Silva Moreira ALC. The role of ubiquitous computing in the transformation of the healthcare system. IntechOpen eBooks. 2022; https://doi.org/10.5772/intechopen.98303.
7. Dynamics in healthcare post COVID-19. Deloitte. n.d. https://www2.deloitte.com/xe/en/pages/about-deloitte/articles/dynamic-evolution/dynamics-in-healthcare-post-covid-19.html.
8. GeeksforGeeks. What is a natural user interface? GeeksforGeeks. 2024. https://www.geeksforgeeks.org/what-is-a-natural-user-interface/.
9. Gep. Digital transformation in drug discovery and development. GEP. n.d.. https://www.gep.com/blog/mind/digital-transformation-in-drug-discovery-and-development.

10. Groene N, Schneck L. Covering digital health applications in the public insurance system: how to foster innovation in patient care while mitigating financial risks—evidence from Germany. Front Digital Health. 2023;5 https://doi.org/10.3389/fdgth.2023.1217479.
11. How is Digitalization Enhancing the Delivery of Mental Health Services? | Patricio V. Marquez. n.d. http://www.pvmarquez.com/digitalhealthformentalhealthcare.
12. Jazieh AR, Kozlakidis Z. Healthcare transformation in the post-Coronavirus pandemic era. Front Med. 2020;7 https://doi.org/10.3389/fmed.2020.00429.
13. Koh A, Swanepoel DW, Ling A, Ho BL, Tan SY, Lim J. Digital health promotion: promise and peril. Health Promot Int. 2021;36(Supplement_1):i70–80. https://doi.org/10.1093/heapro/daab134.
14. Kouijzer MMTE, Kip H, Bouman YHA, Kelders SM. Implementation of virtual reality in healthcare: a scoping review on the implementation process of virtual reality in various healthcare settings. Implement Sci Commun. 2023;4(1) https://doi.org/10.1186/s43058-023-00442-2.
15. Lam EHY, Yu F, Zhu S, Wang Z. 3D bioprinting for next-generation personalized medicine. Int J Mol Sci. 2023;24(7):6357. https://doi.org/10.3390/ijms24076357.
16. Limketkai BN, Mauldin K, Manitius N, Jalilian L, Salonen BR. The age of artificial intelligence: use of digital technology in clinical nutrition. Curr Surg Rep. 2021;9(7) https://doi.org/10.1007/s40137-021-00297-3.
17. Meir A. Applications of cloud computing in healthcare. Ridge Cloud. 2022. https://www.ridge.co/blog/cloud-computing-in-healthcare/.
18. Mitsi G, Grinnell T, Giordano S, Goodin T, Sanjar S, Marble E, Pikalov A. Implementing digital technologies in clinical trials: lessons learned. PubMed. 2022;19(4–6):65–9. https://pubmed.ncbi.nlm.nih.gov/35958972.
19. Neves AL, Burgers J. Digital technologies in primary care: implications for patient care and future research. Eur J Gen Pract. 2022;28(1):203–8. https://doi.org/10.1080/13814788.2022.2052041.
20. Nhgri. Genomics and medicine. 2019. Genome.gov. https://www.genome.gov/health/Genomics-and-Medicine.
21. Park Y, Kim YS, Yi B, Kim SM. Clinical decision support functions and digitalization of clinical documents of electronic medical record systems. Healthc Inf Res. 2019;25(2):115. https://doi.org/10.4258/hir.2019.25.2.115.
22. Sharma I. 11 benefits of using mobile technology in healthcare. Software and Technology Blog—TatvaSoft. 2023. https://www.tatvasoft.com/outsourcing/2022/05/mobile-technology-in-healthcare.html.
23. Tee-Melegrito RA. Telemedicine: What to know. 2022. https://www.medicalnewstoday.com/articles/telemedicine.
24. Thomas EJ, Lucke JF, Wueste L, Weavind L, Patel B. Association of telemedicine for remote monitoring of intensive care patients with mortality, complications, and length of stay. JAMA. 2009;302(24):2671. https://doi.org/10.1001/jama.2009.1902.
25. Tsao N. AI in Medical Diagnostics 2020-2030: image recognition, players, clinical applications, forecasts: IDTechEx. IDTechEx. 2020. https://www.idtechex.com/en/research-report/ai-in-medical-diagnostics-2020-2030-image-recognition-players-clinical-applications-forecasts/766.
26. Virtual Assistants and Chatbots | Healthcare Communications. Healthcare communications—patient communication software for the NHS. n.d. https://healthcare-communications.com/solutions/virtual-assistants-and-chatbots/.
27. Wikipedia contributors. Digital therapeutics. Wikipedia. 2024. https://en.wikipedia.org/wiki/Digital_therapeutics.

# Transforming Healthcare: Exploring the Potential of Futuristic Healthcare Delivery System

2

Varinder Garg, Cheena Malhotra, Harish Kumar, Anupriya Bhardwaj, Ramandeep Bansal, and Sujata Saini

## 2.1 Introduction

Over the years, the healthcare delivery system has been marked by numerous challenges that adversely impact the quality and accessibility of medical services. The late 1990s saw significant global health challenges, including the HIV/AIDS pandemic that continued to spread and devastate communities around the world. Many countries continue to struggle with high child and maternal mortality rates due to a lack of access to healthcare services and interventions. Communicable diseases like malaria, tuberculosis, and polio continue to remain as major health concerns in several regions. The last decade has witnessed improvement in global health outcomes, with advances in medical technology, better access to vaccines, and improved healthcare infrastructure. The introduction of antiretroviral therapy led to significant progress in managing HIV/AIDS, although challenges remain in terms of universal access to treatment. The efforts to combat malaria and polio saw considerable success, with reductions in their prevalence in many parts of the world. At the same time, noncommunicable diseases (NCDs) like heart disease, diabetes, and cancer have started gaining more attention owing to their increasing prevalence and impact on global health. Presently, Sustainable Development Goal 3 (SDG 3) for good health and well-being, adopted as part of the United Nations' 2030

V. Garg (✉)
ICMR-Centre for Innovation and Bio-Design (CIBioD), Postgraduate Institute of Medical Education and Research (PGIMER), Chandigarh, Chandigarh, India

C. Malhotra · A. Bhardwaj · S. Saini
ICMR Center for Innovation and Bio-Design, PGIMER, Chandigarh, India

H. Kumar
Department of Computer Science and Engineering, University Institute of Engineering and Technology (UIET) Panjab University, Chandigarh, Punjab, India

R. Bansal
Department of Obstetrics and Gynecology, PGIMER, Chandigarh, India



V. Garg et al. (eds.), *Innovations in Healthcare Technologies in India*,
https://doi.org/10.1007/978-981-97-0244-2_2

agenda for sustainable development, aims to ensure healthy lives and well-being for all at all ages. The goal addresses a wide range of health issues, including maternal and child health, infectious diseases, NCDs, mental health, and access to essential healthcare services. Progress toward SDG 3 requires efforts to strengthen healthcare systems, improve health infrastructure, enhance medical education and research, address health disparities between different populations, address the social determinants of health, promote health education, and ensure universal health coverage. Insufficient infrastructure, particularly in rural and underserved areas, has hindered the provision of adequate care to a significant portion of the population. The shortage of healthcare professionals, including doctors, nurses, and support staff, has stretched the existing workforce thin, leading to overburdened healthcare facilities and compromised patient outcomes. The lack of substantial government investment in the healthcare sector has resulted in limiting resources for public health initiatives, research, and improvement of medical services. As a result, marginalized communities face significant barriers to obtaining timely and appropriate medical attention. The rising out-of-pocket expenses and limited health insurance coverage have further exacerbated the financial burden on individuals, causing delays in seeking necessary treatment and leading to potential health complications. The decline in the healthcare delivery system necessitates urgent attention and comprehensive reforms to ensure that every individual can access quality healthcare without facing undue hardships.

The need for futuristic technologies in the healthcare domain stems from the ever-increasing complexities of medical challenges, the growing global population, and the potential to enhance healthcare efficiency. As societies evolve, so do the demands placed on healthcare systems, necessitating advances to meet the evolving needs. With the rising prevalence of chronic diseases, innovative wearable devices and remote monitoring technologies are needed to empower patients to manage their conditions proactively. These technologies provide real-time data to healthcare providers, enabling early intervention and personalized care plans, potentially reducing hospital admissions and healthcare costs [1]. Moreover, futuristic technologies, such as artificial intelligence (AI) and machine learning algorithms, have the potential to analyze vast amounts of medical data quickly and accurately. This can aid in disease prediction, drug discovery, and treatment optimization [2]. Additionally, telemedicine and virtual care platforms have gained prominence, especially during the COVID-19 pandemic, as they enable healthcare access to remote locations, enhance healthcare equity, and alleviate strain on overloaded healthcare systems [3]. In conclusion, futuristic technologies may play a crucial role in addressing the challenges faced by the healthcare domain and embracing these advances is essential to create a sustainable and efficient healthcare system that benefits individuals and communities worldwide.

There is a significant negative effect of noncommunicable and communicable diseases in India, ranging from high disease burden and mortality rates to economic losses, reduced productivity, and impacts on education, mental health, and social well-being. Through futuristic technologies such as artificial intelligence, blockchain technology, chatbots, IoMT, wearables, and robotics, we can reduce the morbidity and mortality due to NCD and CDs, thereby improving the overall health of Indian people.

## 2.2 Importance of Exploring Futuristic Healthcare Delivery Systems

In order to handle the constantly changing difficulties which the healthcare sector faces, it is imperative to explore the futuristic healthcare delivery methods. Innovative technologies can offer revolutionary solutions in view of the fast-changing demographics, rising prevalence of chronic diseases, and demand for more easily available and reasonably priced healthcare. Healthcare workers may improve resource allocation, expedite operations, and boost patient involvement by employing cutting-edge technologies like AI/ML, blockchain, IOMT, telemedicine, and remote monitoring devices. These technological advancements may result in more effective healthcare delivery, increased patient satisfaction, fewer medical errors, and better overall health for people and communities. Adopting newer delivery technologies can result in financial savings, resource optimization, and better quality of life.

The conventional healthcare models are not able to keep up with the rising demand for advanced healthcare services. By implementing technology-driven solutions, healthcare providers can automate monotonous operations, improve workflow streamlining and lower administrative costs. The gap between patients and medical experts can be bridged by employing telemedicine and remote monitoring technology in underserved and remote areas. The advanced healthcare delivery systems not only tackle the current healthcare problems but also provide the groundwork for a future healthcare ecosystem that is more patient-centered, robust, affordable, accessible, and sustainable. In order to provide a detailed overview of the current and forthcoming technological developments in the healthcare sector, this chapter on futuristic healthcare technologies inspects pioneering innovations and technologies that have the potential to completely transform healthcare delivery system, patient outcomes, and general medical practices. This chapter aims to provide an useful understanding of the transformative impact of these technologies on medical treatments, diagnostics, disease prevention, and patient care by exploring the recent developments in fields like artificial intelligence, IOMT, robotics, telemedicine, and wearable devices. The review aims to motivate healthcare professionals, stakeholders, policymakers, researchers, and readers to visualize a more effective, affordable, accessible, sustainable, and personalized healthcare settings generated by these groundbreaking technologies through an in-depth analysis of the current state and future prospects.

## 2.3 Overview of Emerging Technologies in Healthcare Sector

The healthcare sector has recently seen an outburst of new technologies which have the potential to change the scenario of patient care, boost patient outcomes, and speed up medical procedures. Two major examples of new technologies include AI and ML, which help in diagnosis, patient outcome predictions, and personalization of treatment regimens. Nowadays, healthcare workers are using AI-powered diagnostic technologies to precisely identify diseases including cancer, cardiovascular disorders, and neurological illnesses resulting in quick problem predictions, therapies, and better outcomes. AI assistances collaborated with robotics allow accurate and minimally invasive procedures thereby shortening the patient recovery times and reducing the recurrence of problems. Another groundbreaking innovation, the Internet of Medical Things (IoMT), allows connection of wearables and medical equipment over the internet. Gadgets (e.g., fitness trackers and smartwatches) continuously track patient's vitals, facilitating remote patient monitoring and enabling healthcare providers to deliver interventions more effectively, particularly for chronic illnesses. Furthermore, by collaborating data from several IoMT sources, medical personnel can make quick and accurate decisions, resulting in more individualized and focused treatment programs. Another technology called blockchain facilitates consistent and seamless data sharing across the healthcare providers while at the same time ensuring privacy and security of patient's medical data. This leads to safe and immutable record keeping resulting in better care coordination, fewer administrative hassles, and rapid and accurate processing of bills and claims. The advanced data analytics and big data applications play a critical role in decision-making leading to proper resource allocation and supply chain management. The newly available nano-scale devices have shown promise in diagnosis, monitoring, and management of diseases. Last but not least, three-dimensional (3D) printing allows the printing of living tissues and organs helping in the creation of customized limbs, prosthetics, and implants. All the above new technologies hold the potential to completely alter the healthcare sector. However, issues such as data privacy concerns, regulatory compliance, and equal access to these technologies must be addressed in order to fully utilize their transformative impact on healthcare [4, 5].

## 2.4 Artificial Intelligence in the Futuristic Healthcare Technology

The future of AI and ML in the healthcare domain is promising. It can revolutionize patient care, improve diagnostics, and enhance treatment outcomes. There are several studies discussing the future of AI and ML in healthcare. In one study, researchers created AI models using a single convolutional neural network (CNN), trained end-to-end from a dataset of 129,450 dermatological clinical images directly, using only pixels and disease labels as inputs [6]. They found that AI utilizing deep convolutional neural networks achieved dermatologist-level accuracy in diagnosing skin cancer.

Several other studies [7–12] have provided insights into the future of AI and ML in healthcare, discussing convergence of human and artificial intelligence and their potential impact on medical practice [7], including diagnosis (e.g., breast cancer) genomics and personalized medicine. However, the American Heart Association, while acknowledging the role of AI and ML in predicting and managing cardiovascular diseases, emphasized the need for ethical and responsible use of these technologies [11].

A potential challenge of AI implementation is that the widespread adoption of AI in healthcare needs the collection and analysis of vast amounts of patient data, raising concerns about data privacy and security. Protecting sensitive medical information from unauthorized access and potential breaches is crucial for maintaining patient trust and complying with data protection regulations [13, 14]. Accordingly, the implementation of AI in healthcare requires adherence to strict regulatory frameworks as well as compliance with medical device regulations, data protection laws, and ethical guidelines [15].

Other challenges include the integration of AI-enabled systems with existing healthcare infrastructure as well as training and convincing healthcare professionals to adopt AI technologies [7, 16].

## 2.5 Blockchain Technology in the Futuristic Healthcare Technology

Blockchain ensures secure and transparent data management. A nationwide blockchain network for electronic health records can improve health outcomes. Blockchain technology can streamline healthcare administration and billing by providing data security and privacy. Traditional healthcare systems often face challenges with data breaches and unauthorized access to sensitive patient information. Blockchain's decentralized and immutable nature ensures that patient data is securely stored and encrypted. Additionally, it allows patients to have more control over their data, granting access only to authorized parties, thereby improving patient trust and compliance [17]. In one study, blockchain was found to play a pivotal role in securing data from the Internet of Medical Things (IoMT) devices (such as wearable health monitors), reducing the risk of tampering or manipulation [18]. Blockchain-based solutions provide patients with unique cryptographic identity and streamline patient registrations. The capacity of blockchain to securely store large-scale genomic data may further facilitate accurate diagnostic and targeted therapy [19, 20].

In future, blockchain may transform the pharmaceutical supply chain by creating an immutable record of drug transactions, ensuring drug authenticity, reducing counterfeit drugs, and improving patient safety [21]. Blockchain-based smart contracts may help in automating administrative tasks such as claims processing, insurance verification, and billings, leading to cost reductions and increased efficiency in healthcare operations [22]. Blockchain has the capacity to revolutionize medical research by creating secure, transparent, and traceable platforms for data sharing among researchers. This will accelerate scientific discoveries and foster global collaboration while ensuring data privacy and patient consent [23]. This technology may streamline verification and storage of healthcare professional's credentials, licenses, and certifications resulting in quick boarding of qualified practitioners and increased trust in workforce [24]. Blockchain can facilitate secure telemedicine consultations and remote patient monitoring [25]. It provides transparency and tamper-resistant features which will reduce healthcare fraud by creating an auditable record of transactions and treatments, thereby reducing the likelihood of false claims [19]. All in all, the integration of blockchain technology in healthcare holds tremendous potential to transform healthcare delivery, improve patient outcomes, and drive innovation in the medical field.

## 2.6 Chatbots in Futuristic Healthcare Technology

Chatbots allow patients to communicate with specialist doctors using traditional methods, including phone calls, video calls, and messages. Through chatbots, engagement is enhanced, and medical personnel get more time and opportunity to concentrate on needy patients. A systematic review and meta-analysis revealed that chatbots play a crucial role in healthcare delivery by providing personalized and quick responses to patient's concerns. This improves patient engagement and satisfaction resulting in more adherence to treatment plans and better health outcomes [26]. AI-powered chatbots may triage patients by checking their symptoms and directing them to suitable healthcare faculty, thereby ensuring appropriate access to critical services [27]. Chatbots equipped with sensors and Internet of Things (IoT) devices enable continuous remote patient monitoring, allowing healthcare providers to collect real-time health data and intervene promptly in case of any abnormality [28].

Through data analysis and machine learning algorithms, chatbots can offer personalized treatment plans tailored to an individual patient's medical history, preferences, and lifestyle, thereby enhancing treatment efficacy and patient compliance [29]. Chatbots can also provide a nonjudgmental and confidential platform for individuals suffering from depression and seeking mental health support. They can offer therapeutic conversations, monitor emotional well-being, and detect early signs of mental illness, enabling timely intervention [30].

## 2.7 Internet of Medical Things (IOMT) in Futuristic Healthcare Technology

The IoMT enables continuous monitoring of patients, allowing healthcare workers to collect real-time data of vitals, symptoms of disease and medication adherence resulting in early detection of potential health issues and improved personalized care [31]. The IoMT devices integrated with AI algorithms can analyze vast amounts of patient data, leading to better diagnoses and treatment plans, thereby improving patient outcomes [32]. This has paved the way for wearable health devices such as fitness trackers, smartwatches, and glucose monitors which help individuals in controlling their health status and promote healthy behaviors [33]. IoMT facilitates telemedicine by enabling secure communication and data exchange between patients and healthcare professionals [34]. IoMT advanced solutions like smart pill dispensers and medication reminder apps help patients to take their prescribed medications at the right time, thereby reducing noncompliance and improving health outcomes [35].

## 2.8 Dry Biochemistry in the Futuristic Healthcare Technology

Dry biochemistry relies on sophisticated computational models for the prediction of protein interactions, enzyme functions, and drug interactions. It may help in quick drug discovery and personalized treatment plans [36]. When integrated with AI, dry biochemistry may help in drug development by analyzing big datasets and identifying potential drugs with higher efficacy and minimal side effects [2]. By analyzing an individual's genomic data and identifying specific molecular targets for treatment, dry biochemistry will facilitate precision medicine in the future, leading to personalized therapies [37]. Nano-sized drug delivery systems designed through dry biochemistry will allow targeted delivery of medications, which will help in minimizing side effects and enhancing drug efficacy [38].

Wearable devices developed through dry biochemistry will enable tracking of real-time health status and early detection of diseases [39, 40]. Futuristic healthcare systems will rely on integration of dry biochemistry data with electronic health records, enabling comprehensive patient profiling and better clinical decisions [41]. Dry biochemistry will help to identify novel applications for existing drugs and analyze potential synergies between different medications, leading to more efficient drug repurposing and combination therapies [42].

## 2.9 Wearable Devices and Health Tracking Apps in the Futuristic Healthcare Technology

Wearable devices are expected to play a significant role in healthcare in the future. These provide real-time, personalized health monitoring by allowing individuals to track their vital signs, sleep patterns, and overall well-being [43]. Advanced wearable devices with noninvasive diagnostic capabilities may help in the early detection of diseases. For example, smartwatches equipped with electrocardiogram sensors can help in diagnosis of cardiac arrhythmias [44]. Wearable devices allow for continuous glucose monitoring in diabetes promoting better diabetes control without the need for frequent finger pricks [45]. Future wearable devices are likely to incorporate drug delivery systems and administer medications based on real-time health data, thereby revolutionizing treatment for diseases such as Parkinson disease, diabetes, or chronic pain [46]. With advancements in AI, wearable devices will provide health insights by analyzing big data [7, 47]. Future wearables may even monitor mental well-being and measure stress levels by using heart rate variability/ other indicators as signs of anxiety or depression [48].

Wearable devices will integrate with telemedicine platforms for remote consultations with specialists. These will help patients to share real-time health data, resulting in better diagnosis and treatment [49]. For example, smart contact lenses have been developed which can monitor glucose levels, detect eye diseases, and provide augmented information about the surroundings of the user [50]. As wearable devices collect sensitive health data, futuristic wearables will prioritize security measures and data encryption as well [51].

## 2.10 Virtual and Augmented Reality in the Futuristic Healthcare Technology

Augmented reality (AR) and virtual reality (VR) simulations allow interactive training experiences for medical professionals. These technologies improve skill retention, learning outcomes and surgical performance [52]. AR and VR enable teleconsultations by providing real-time visualizations and interactions between healthcare providers and patients, resulting in better adherence to treatment plans [53, 54]. VR allows surgeons to practice and plan complex protocols before performing these on patients. By visualizing patient's anatomical data, surgeons can optimize surgical approaches and reduce complications [55]. VR-based distraction therapy is effective in managing pain during medical procedures and postoperative period and is shown to reduce the need for analgesics [56]. VR has shown promise in treating various mental health conditions, such as anxiety disorders and phobias [57]. AR- and VR-based rehabilitation programs (including gamified exercises) help in motor skill recovery and improve mobility for patients with neurological disorders or injuries [58]. AR overlays of medical data on 3D visualizations of organs help healthcare professionals in understanding complex medical information accurately [59]. VR-based simulations can be used to train healthcare workers on proper infection control protocols in the emergency departments, which are helpful in situations like pandemics [60]. AR applications can present patient health records in a visual way by which patients get a better understanding of their medical history and actively participate in decisions [61]. Major applications of VR/AR in medical education include training such as immersive anatomy visualization and education [62], simulated medical procedures and surgical training [63], remote collaborative learning and telementoring [64], patient empathy and communication skills training [65], and emergency and disaster management training [66].

## 2.11 Telemedicine and Remote Care in the Futuristic Healthcare Technology

Futuristic healthcare technology will enable patients to consult with doctors and specialists sitting at a remote place ensuring easy access to doctor's advice regardless of geographical location. Advanced wearable devices will allow real-time monitoring of patients by doctors sitting at a remote place [67]. AI algorithms will play a major role in interpreting imaging, laboratory results, and other diagnostic tests remotely [68]. The surgeons will be able to perform complex surgical procedures remotely with the advancements in robotics and haptic feedback systems, thereby reducing the need for patient travel [69].

The Internet of Things (IoT) will exquisitely integrate various wearable and medical devices to create an extensive health monitoring system. These interconnected devices will help healthcare professionals to get a holistic view of a patient's health status while sitting in a remote place [70]. Future healthcare technology will support remote rehabilitation programs for patients recovering from surgeries, injuries, or chronic conditions [71].

## 2.12 Big Data: Driven Healthcare in the Futuristic Healthcare Technology

To predict disease risks and diagnose illness at an early stage, big data analytics may help by holding an extensive amount of patient data including genomics, medical history, and lifestyle factors. This helps in improving treatment outcomes and reducing healthcare costs [72]. Big data analytics enables healthcare providers to tailor treatments based on individual's genetic makeup and unique health characteristics resulting in more effective medical interventions [73]. Big data analytics can process real-time patient data from monitoring systems or wearable devices and provide timely alerts to doctors and patients [74]. Large datasets allow healthcare organizations to identify patterns in community health allowing targeted interventions to improve community health [75]. Big data analytics hasten drug discovery by analyzing vast amounts of biomedical data thereby identifying potential drug candidates and optimizing clinical trials [76]. Through data analytics, healthcare institutions can optimize resource allocation, staff scheduling, the use of equipment, and bed availability, leading to better cost-effectiveness and operational efficiency [77]. Big data analytics can detect healthcare fraud by analyzing claims and data and identifying unusual patterns or suspicious activities [78]. Finally, these can help in designing personalized interventions to promote healthy behavior and improve patient engagement in their own care [79].

## 2.13 Robotics in the Futuristic Healthcare Technology

It is highly likely that in future robotics will enable precise and minimally invasive surgery resulting in better accuracy and dexterity with improved patient outcome and reduced time of recovery [80].

Robots can play a vital role in the care of the aged, assisting with medication reminders, daily tasks, and monitoring vital signs [81]. This will revolutionize rehabilitation and physical therapy by providing treatment programs in patient's own homes [82]. Nano-robotics can help in targeted drug delivery within the human body. These tiny robots can navigate through the bloodstream to deliver medications precisely to the affected areas, reducing side effects and increasing efficacy [83]. Robots equipped with UV-C lights will play a crucial role in infection control in hospitals and other healthcare facilities [84].

## 2.14 Ethical, Legal, and Social Implications

As healthcare technologies collect and analyze vast amounts of patient data, ensuring privacy and security becomes crucial. Every attempt shall be made to protect sensitive patient information from breaches and unauthorized access. While legal frameworks such as the General Data Protection Regulation (GDPR) in Europe and the Health Insurance Portability and Accountability Act (HIPAA) in the United States do address these concerns, continuous efforts are required to adapt to evolving technologies [85]. The adoption of healthcare technologies can exacerbate existing social disparities, creating a digital divide in access to care. Ethical considerations involve ensuring that underserved populations and vulnerable groups have equal access to technological advancements. Addressing the social determinants of health and promoting digital inclusion will be essential to prevent health inequality [86]. The use of advanced technologies (such as AI and ML) raises questions about informed consent and patient autonomy. Ethical considerations center on ensuring that patients are fully informed about how their data will be used and how decisions are made using AI algorithms. Upholding patient autonomy in decision-making processes and respecting their choices are crucial. Healthcare technologies that rely on algorithms may inadvertently perpetuate biases in diagnosis, treatment recommendations, and resource allocation. Ethical implications include the need to identify and mitigate algorithmic biases to ensure fairness and equity in healthcare decisions. Transparent and explainable AI models can address this concern. The adoption of futuristic healthcare technologies may impact the roles and responsibilities of healthcare professionals, leading to discussions about job displacement, retraining, and maintaining the human touch in patient care. Widespread adoption of futuristic healthcare technologies may require addressing societal concerns and ensuring public acceptance through transparent communication and engagement.

## 2.15 Conclusion

Overcoming the formidable challenge of delivering high-quality healthcare services is a constant endeavor, particularly in the face of rapid demographic shifts and evolving technologies. The multifaceted obstacles, ranging from resource limitations to workforce shortages, underscore the complexity of this mission. Adequate training and upskilling of healthcare professionals require substantial time and resources, further complicating matters. Even developed nations grapple with maintaining an optimal patient-to-medical and -paramedical personnel ratio. The global shortage of healthcare resources and professionals could be resolved through innovative technologies discussed above. While many regions continue to invest heavily in traditional healthcare systems, embracing unconventional policies, fostering innovations, and pioneering novel healthcare delivery models empowered by advanced technologies present a pathway to address some of these problems discussed in the preceding lines. New technologies may ensure continuous healthcare delivery, often at individuals' doorsteps, mitigating the burdens associated with

NCDs and mental health concerns. The integration of these technologies not only streamlines budgets but also champions environmental responsibility, sustainability, affordability, and accessibility. By harnessing the potential of these transformative advancements, the healthcare landscape can evolve into a more inclusive, resilient, and forward-looking realm, paving the way for a healthier global population. SDG 3 also focuses on ensuring healthy lives and promoting well-being for all at all ages. In India, this goal has led to significant improvements. It has facilitated better access to essential healthcare services, including maternal and child health, infectious disease control, and noncommunicable disease prevention. Additionally, SDG 3 has encouraged investments in healthcare infrastructure and technology, enhancing medical facilities. While challenges remain, the goal has driven positive changes in India's healthcare landscape, promoting healthier lives and more equitable care.

## References


1. Majumder S, Mondal T, Deen MJ. Wearable sensors for remote health monitoring. Sensors (Basel). 2017;17(1):130.
2. Paul D, Sanap G, Shenoy S, et al. Artificial intelligence in drug discovery and development. Drug Discov Today. 2021;26(1):80–93.
3. Doraiswamy S, Abraham A, Mamtani R, Cheema S. Use of telehealth during the COVID-19 pandemic: scoping review. J Med Internet Res. 2020;22(12):e24087.
4. Razdan S, Sharma S. Internet of medical things (IoMT): overview, emerging technologies and case studies. IETE Techn Rev. 2022;39(4):775–88.
5. Silvera-Tawil D, Hussain MS, Li J. Emerging technologies for precision health: an insight into sensing technologies for health and well-being. Smart Health. 2020;15:100100.
6. Esteva A, Kuprel B, Novoa RA, et al. Dermatologist-level classification of skin cancer with deep neural networks. Nature. 2017;542(7639):115–8.
7. Topol EJ. High-performance medicine: the convergence of human and artificial intelligence. Nat Med. 2019;25(1):44–56.
8. Rajkomar A, Oren E, Chen K, et al. Scalable and accurate deep learning with electronic health records. npj Digital Med. 2018;1:18.
9. Cruz-Roa A, Gilmore H, Basavanhally A, et al. Accurate and reproducible invasive breast cancer detection in whole-slide images: a deep learning approach for quantifying tumor extent. Sci Rep. 2017;7:46450.
10. Ravi D, Wong C, Deligianni F, et al. Deep learning for health informatics. IEEE J Biomed Health Inform. 2017;21(1):4–21.
11. Benjamin EJ, Virani SS, Callaway CW, et al. American Heart Association council on epidemiology and prevention statistics committee and stroke statistics subcommittee. Heart disease and stroke statistics-2018 Update: a report from the American Heart Association. Circulation. 2018;137(12):e67–e492.
12. Obermeyer Z, Emanuel EJ. Predicting the future—big data, machine learning, and clinical medicine. N Engl J Med. 2016;375(13):216–9.
13. Batko K, Ślęzak A. The use of big data analytics in healthcare. J Big Data. 2022:9–3.
14. Rajkomar A, Hardt M, Howell MD, et al. Ensuring fairness in machine learning to advance health equity. Ann Intern Med. 2018;169(12):866–72.
15. Food and Drug Administration. Proposed regulatory framework for modifications to artificial intelligence/machine learning-based software as a medical device. US department of health and human services. 2019. Downloaded from https://www.fda.gov/files/medical%20devices/published/US-FDA-Artificial-Intelligence-and-Machine-Learning-Discussion-Paper.pdf.

16. Reddy S, Winter J, Padmanabhan S. Artificial Intelligence in health care: opportunities and challenges. J Hosp Manage Health Policy. 2021;5:6812.
17. Roehrs A, da Costa CA, da Rosa Righi R. Omni PHR: a distributed architecture model to integrate personal health records. J Biomed Inform. 2017;71:70–81.
18. Fernández-Caramés TM, Fraga-Lamas P. A review on the use of blockchain for the internet of things. IEEEA. 2018;6:32979–3001.
19. Kuo TT, Kim HE, Ohno-Machado L. Blockchain distributed ledger technologies for biomedical and health care applications. J Am Med Inform Assoc. 2017;24(6):1211–20.
20. Benchoufi M, Porcher R, Ravaud P. Blockchain protocols in clinical trials: transparency and traceability of consent. F1000Res. 2017;23(6):66.
21. Yue X, Wang H, Jin D, Li M, Jiang W. Healthcare data gateways: found healthcare intelligence on blockchain with novel privacy risk control. J Med Syst. 2016;40(10):218.
22. Zhang P, Schmidt DC, White J, Lenz G. Blockchain technology use cases in healthcare. 2018. https://doi.org/10.1016/bs.adcom.2018.03.006.
23. Ichikawa D, Kashiyama M, Ueno T, et al. Blockchain distributed ledger technologies for biomedical and health care applications. J Am Med Inform Assoc. 2017;24(6):1211–20.
24. Hasselgren A, Kralevska K, Gligoroski D, et al. Blockchain in healthcare and health sciences—a scoping review. Int J Med Inform. 2020;134:104040.
25. Pahuja G, Sood SK. Blockchain based EHRs for healthcare: challenges and opportunities. In: 2018 IEEE 9th annual information technology, electronics and mobile communication conference (IEMCON). 2018, p. 71–6.
26. Singh B, Olds T, Brinsley J, et al. Systematic review and meta-analysis of the effectiveness of chatbots on lifestyle behaviors. npj Digit Med. 2013;6:118.
27. Aggarwal A, Tam CC, Wu D, et al. Artificial intelligence-based chatbots for promoting health behavioral changes: systematic review. J Med Internet Res. 2023;25:e40789.
28. Vaseleiou MV, Maglogiannis IG. Health chatbots in telemedicine: Intelligent dialog system for remote support. J Healthcare Eng. 2022:Article ID 4876512.
29. Habehh H, Gohel S. Machine learning in healthcare. Curr Genomics. 2021;22(4):291–300.
30. Fitzpatrick KK, Darcy A, Vierhile M. Delivering cognitive behavior therapy to young adults with symptoms of depression and anxiety using a fully automated conversational agent (Woebot): a randomized controlled trial. JMIR Ment Health. 2017;4(2):e19.
31. Qadri YA, Zikria YB, Vasilakos AV, Nauman A. The future of healthcare Internet of things: a survey of emerging technologies. IEEE Commun Surv Tutorials. 2020;22:1.
32. Akbarzadeh O, Baradaran M, Khosravi MR. IoT-based smart management of healthcare services in hospital buildings during COVID-19 and future pandemics. Wirel Commun Mob Comput. 2021;14 https://doi.org/10.1155/2021/5533161.
33. Alsalibi A, Shambour MK, Abu-Hashem M, et al. Internet of things in health care: a survey. In: Hybrid artificial intelligence and IoT in healthcare 2021, p. 165–200. https://doi.org/10.1007/978-981-16-2972-3_9.
34. Baig MM, GholamHosseini H, Moqeem AA, et al. A systematic review of wearable patient monitoring systems—current challenges and opportunities for clinical adoption. J Med Syst. 2017;41(7):115.
35. Peng Y, Wang H, Fang Q, et al. Effectiveness of mobile applications on medication adherence in adults with chronic diseases: a systematic review and meta-analysis. J Manag Care Spec Pharm. 2020;26(4):550–61.
36. Xia X. Bioinformatics and drug discovery. Curr Top Med Chem. 2017;17(15):1709–26.
37. AshleyEA.Theprecisionmedicineinitiative:anewnationaleffort.JAMA.2015;313(21):2119–20.
38. Zhang YN, Poon W, Tavares AJ, et al. Nanoparticle-liver interactions: cellular uptake and hepatobiliary elimination. J Control Release. 2016;240:332–48.
39. An G, Cockrell C. Drug development digital twins for drug discovery, testing and repurposing: a schema for requirements and development. Front Syst Biol. 2022;2:928387.
40. Jia W, Bandodkar AJ, Valdés-Ramírez G, et al. Electrochemical tattoo biosensors for real-time noninvasive lactate monitoring in human perspiration. Anal Chem. 2013;85(14):6553–60.

41. Li E, Clarke J, Neves AL, et al. Electronic health records, interoperability and patient safety in health systems of high-income countries: a systematic review protocol. BMJ Open. 2021;11(7):e044941.
42. Pushpakom S, Iorio F, Eyers PA, et al. Drug repurposing: progress, challenges and recommendations. Nat Rev Drug Discov. 2019;18(1):41–58.
43. Kher R, Patel D. A comprehensive review on wearable health monitoring systems. Open Biomed Eng J. 2021;15:213–25.
44. Tison GH, Sanchez JM, Ballinger B, et al. Passive detection of atrial fibrillation using a commercially available smartwatch. JAMA Cardiol. 2018;3(5):409–16.
45. Welsh JB, Gao P, Derdzinski M, et al. Accuracy, utilization, and effectiveness comparisons of different continuous glucose monitoring systems. Diabetes Technol Ther. 2019;21(3):128–32.
46. Lymberis A. Smart wearable systems for personalized health management: current R&D and future challenges. Annual Int Conf IEEE Eng Med Biol Proc. 2003;4:3716–9. https://doi.org/10.1109/IEMBS.2003.1280967.
47. Garrett B, Taverner T, Masinde W, et al. A rapid evidence assessment of immersive virtual reality as an adjunct therapy in acute pain management in clinical practice. Clin J Pain. 2014;30(12):1089–98.
48. Shatte ABR, Hutchinson DM, Teague SJ. Machine learning in mental health: a scoping review of methods and applications. Psychol Med. 2019;49(9):1426–48.
49. Dorsey ER, Topol EJ. State of telehealth. N Engl J Med. 2016;375(2):154–61.
50. Gmeinwieser K. Augmented reality contact lenses. Downloaded from https://www.diva-portal.org/smash/get/diva2:1441383/FULLTEXT01.pdf.
51. Bashir A, Mir A. Secure framework for internet of things based e-health system. Inter J E-Health Med Commun. 2019;10:16–29.
52. Kassutto SM, Baston C, Clancy C. Virtual, augmented, and alternate reality in medical education: socially distanced but fully immersed. ATS Sch. 2021;2(4):651–64.
53. Greenhalgh T, Vijayaraghavan S, Wherton J, et al. Virtual online consultations: advantages and limitations (VOCAL) study. BMJ Open. 2016;6(1):e009388.
54. Díaz Molina RJ, Castellar CC, Rigo JC, et al. Descriptive observational pilot study about the use of virtual reality (VR) in patients with inflammatory bowel disease (IBD) and biological treatment. J Crohn's Colitis. 2024;18(1):i1096.
55. Kim Y, Kim H, Kim YO. Virtual reality and augmented reality in plastic surgery: a review. Arch Plast Surg. 2017;44(3):179–87.
56. Gold JI, Kim SH, Kant AJ, et al. Effectiveness of virtual reality for pediatric pain distraction during I.V. placement. CyberPsychol Behav. 2006;9(2):207–12.
57. Freeman D, Haselton P, Freeman J, et al. Automated psychological therapy using immersive virtual reality for treatment of fear of heights: a single-blind, parallel-group, randomized controlled trial. Lancet Psychiatry. 2018;5(8):625–32.
58. Laver KE, Lange B, George S, et al. Virtual reality for stroke rehabilitation. Cochrane Database Syst Rev. 2017;11(11):CD008349.
59. Ventura S, Baños RM, Botella C. Virtual and augmented reality: new frontiers for clinical psychology [Internet]. State of the art virtual reality and augmented reality knowhow. InTech. 2018. Available from: https://doi.org/10.5772/intechopen.74344.
60. Theingi S, Leopold I, Ola T, et al. Virtual reality as a non-pharmacological adjunct to reduce the use of analgesics in hospitals. J Cogn Enhanc. 2022;6(1):108–13.
61. Bui DT, Barnett T, Hoang H, Chinthammit W. Usability of augmented reality technology in situational telementorship for managing clinical scenarios: quasi-experimental study. JMIR Med Educ. 2023;9:e47228.
62. Barrie M, Socha JJ, Mansour L, et al. Mixed reality in medical education: a narrative literature review. Proc Inter Symposium Human Factors Ergonomics Health Care. 2019;8(1):28–32.
63. Gurusamy K, Aggarwal R, Palanivelu L, Davidson B. Virtual reality training for surgical trainees in laparoscopic surgery. Cochrane Database Syst Rev. 2009;1:CD006575.

64. Sánchez-Margallo JA, de Miguel CP, Anzules RAF, Sanchez-Margallo FM. Application of mixed reality in medical training and surgical planning focused on minimally invasive surgery. Front Virtual Reality. 2021;2:2021.
65. Kamarudin B, Fadzil M, Nabil Z. Augmented reality, virtual reality and mixed reality in medical education: a comparative web of science scoping review. 2019. https://doi.org/10.20944/preprints201904.0323.v1.
66. Dubron K, Verbist M, Jacobs R, et al. Augmented and virtual reality for preoperative trauma planning, focusing on orbital reconstructions: a systematic review. J Clin Med. 2023;12(16):5203.
67. Ekeland AG, Bowes A, Flottorp S. Effectiveness of telemedicine: a systematic review of reviews. Int J Med Inform. 2010;79(11):736–71.
68. Rajkomar A, Dean J, Kohane I. Machine learning in medicine. N Engl J Med. 2019;380(14):1347–58.
69. Villavisanis DF, Kiani SN, Taub PJ, Marin ML. Impact of COVID-19 on global surgery: challenges and opportunities. Ann Surg Open. 2021;2(1):e046.
70. Rayan RA, Tsagkaris C, Romash I. The internet of things for healthcare: applications, selected cases and challenges. 2021. https://doi.org/10.1007/978-981-15-9897-5_1.
71. Tenforde AS, Hefner JE, Kodish-Wachs JE, et al. Telehealth in physical medicine and rehabilitation: a narrative review. PMR. 2017;9(5S):S51–8.
72. Hood L, Friend SH. Predictive, personalized, preventive, participatory (P4) cancer medicine. Nat Rev Clin Oncol. 2011;8(3):184–7.
73. Dash S, Shakyawar SK, Sharma M, et al. Big data in healthcare: management, analysis and future prospects. J Big Data. 2019;6:54.
74. Halamka JD. Early experiences with big data at an academic medical center. Health Aff (Millwood). 2014;33(7):1132–8.
75. Kindig D, Stoddart G. What is population health? Am J Public Health. 2003;93(3):380–3.
76. Duan Q, Flynn C, Niepel M, et al. LINCS canvas browser: interactive web app to query, browse and interrogate LINCS L1000 gene expression signatures. Nucleic Acids Res. 2014;42(Web Server issue):W449–60.
77. Lee SS, Singh SR, Suen L. Big data for better performance: a healthcare management model. Technol Forecast Soc Chang. 2014;87:149–62.
78. Spiros G, Parisis G, Vassilis P. Using big data analytics to detect fraud in healthcare provision. 2020:1–3. https://doi.org/10.1109/MECBME47393.2020.9265118.
79. Batko K, Ślęzak A. The use of big data analytics in healthcare. J Big Data. 2022;9(1):3.
80. Bhaskar S, Bradley S, Sakhamuri S, et al. Designing futuristic telemedicine using artificial intelligence and robotics in the COVID-19 era. Front Public Health. 2020;8:556789.
81. Koutentakis D, Pilozzi A, Huang X. Designing socially assistive robots for Alzheimer's disease and related dementia patients and their caregivers: where we are and where we are headed. Healthcare (Basel). 2020;8(2):73.
82. Volpe BT, Krebs HI, Hogan N, et al. A novel approach to stroke rehabilitation: robot-aided sensorimotor stimulation. Neurology. 2000;54(10):1938–44.
83. Upadhyay V, Sonawat M, Singh S, Merugu R. Nano robots in medicine: a review. Inter J Engr Tech Manag Res. 2020;4:27–37.
84. Piaggio D, Zarro M, Pagliara S, et al. The use of smart environments and robots for infection prevention control: a systematic literature review. Am J Infect Control. 2023;51(10):1175–81.
85. Filkins BL, Kim JY, Roberts B, et al. Privacy and security in the era of digital health: what should translational researchers know and do about it? Am J Transl Res. 2016;8(3):1560–80.
86. Burr C, Taddeo M, Floridi L. The ethics of digital well-being: a thematic review. Sci Eng Ethics. 2020;26(4):2313–43.

# ICMR-CIBioD Telehealth Kiosk: Futuristic Healthcare Delivery Ecosystem

# 3

Varinder Garg, Shankar Prinja, Harish Kumar, Basant Kumar, Manoj Goyal, Raja Ramachandran, Ramandeep Bansal, Sujata Saini, Paras Sharma, Anupriya Bhardwaj, and Ritika Mahajan

## 3.1 Background Information and Rationale

Digital health technology [including though not limited to, mobile health (mHealth), health information technology (HIT), telehealth, and telemedicine] has been endorsed by the Indian government to overcome the deficits in healthcare delivery system. Its immediate target is to strengthen primary healthcare while continuing to move toward attaining its ultimate goal, i.e., "to transit the health system to a gate-keeping paradigm." The main barrier in accomplishing the above goal is the

V. Garg (✉)
ICMR-Centre for Innovation and Bio-Design (CIBioD), Postgraduate Institute of Medical Education and Research (PGIMER), Chandigarh, Chandigarh, India

S. Saini · P. Sharma · A. Bhardwaj · R. Mahajan
ICMR Center for Innovation and Bio-Design, PGIMER, Chandigarh, India

S. Prinja
Department of Community Medicine and School of Public Health, PGIMER, Chandigarh, India

H. Kumar
Department of Computer Science and Engineering, University Institute of Engineering and Technology (UIET) Panjab University, Chandigarh, Punjab, India

B. Kumar
Department of Cardiology, PGIMER, Chandigarh, India

M. Goyal
Department of Neurology, Postgraduate Institute of Medical Education and Research (PGIMER), Chandigarh, Chandigarh, India

R. Ramachandran
Department of Nephrology, PGIMER, Chandigarh, India

R. Bansal
Department of Obstetrics and Gynecology, PGIMER, Chandigarh, India



V. Garg et al. (eds.), *Innovations in Healthcare Technologies in India*,
https://doi.org/10.1007/978-981-97-0244-2_3

disparity in medical resources between urban and rural populations. Despite 75 years of independence, the vast rural population of our nation continues to suffer from a lack of quality healthcare which may deteriorate further as the present-day medical practitioners retire and young healthcare workers move to urban areas as they get allured by the attractive options in urban regions. Digital health technologies may address this growing gap by providing better diagnostic and therapeutic services in rural areas. However, there is lack of quality evidence on cost-effectiveness and the overall efficacy of the available tools for applying digital health in rural areas. Also, there is no quality data on potential behavioral and institutional barriers that may drive a wedge between the potential of these tools and expected outcomes.

A major barrier to ensuring quality healthcare in rural areas, which needs to be countered actively, is the myth that "noncommunicable diseases (NCDs) are diseases of urban areas." Rural population, accounting for approximately 68% of Indian people, has seen a major shift in disease pattern in the last two decades. As per the Government of India (GOI) report, deaths in rural India due to NCDs (40%) match those due to communicable diseases (40%). A follow-up study in rural India spanning years 2010–2013 reported NCDs to be accounting for 47% of all mortality, compared to 30% by communicable, maternal, perinatal, and nutritional etiologies combined. Thus, NCDs have become a healthcare priority even among people residing in rural areas.

Currently, the world is witnessing an increase in incidence and spread of communicable diseases (CDs). Besides health, CDs pose a threat to the economy, development, and security. During the past few decades, more than 30 new infectious disease have been detected across the world. The epidemics/pandemics caused by these CDs result in lots of suffering and create a situation of panic and concern to health and economy, accounting for 26% of annual deaths in the world and an annual loss of approximately 0.5 billion Disability-adjusted life years (DALYs). India, being a developing country, suffers the most from morbidity and mortality related to CDs, which account for approximately 50% of the country's disease burden. Many of these emerging infections are zoonotic. Thus, a lack of proper sanitation and hygiene and the limited availability of safe water put India at risk of further epidemics. In the recent past, India has witnessed an increase in cases of drug-resistant malaria, tuberculosis, HIV-TB co-infections, epidemics of avian influenza, and the list goes on. Be it diphtheria (1980), cholera (1992), plague (1994), Nipah virus (1999), H1N1 (2010), or coronavirus (2020), these CDs had and will continue to test the credibility of health infrastructure and services.

During pandemic like situations (COVID-19), it becomes hard for the doctors and hospitals to manage patients with other CDs and NCDs. During such times, delivery of healthcare through telemedicine has been considered as ideal by various stakeholders in healthcare including the World Bank and the World Health Organization (WHO) [1]. According to the WHO, telemedicine can reduce the impacts of limited healthcare workforce and long hours spent on routine healthcare in clinics thereby promoting efficiency and reducing stress on healthcare workers. It ensures scheduling flexibility, speed, timeliness, and easy delivery of health services through mobile applications and other technological devices shared by clinicians and patients, limiting regular physical contact that could otherwise increase transmission of CDs.

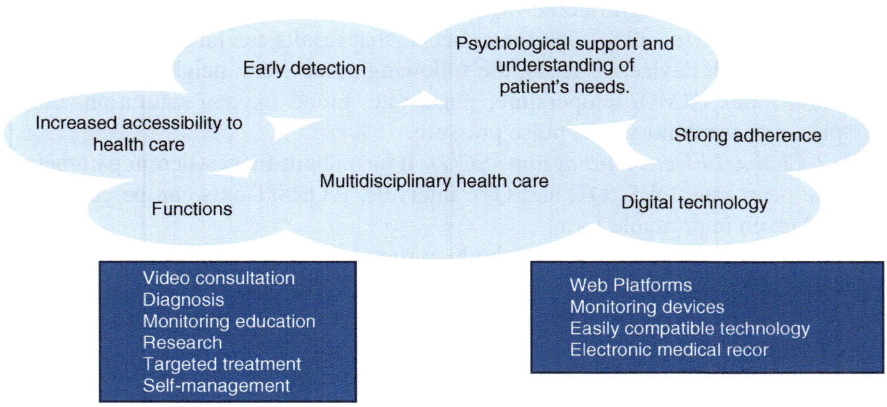


**Fig. 3.1** Advantages of telemedicine-based healthcare

India is the second most populous country in the world with population of more than 130 crores [2]. The number of doctors to cater to this enormous population is much less and thus ensuring adequate and equitable distribution of healthcare services is a big challenge. Adding to this mismatch is the recent trend of concentration of healthcare facilities in the cities and towns (including 75% of the population of doctors), away from rural India, where 68.84% of national population lives [2]. In 2020, the COVID-19 pandemic has added unprecedented burden on an already burdened healthcare system in our country [3]. Telemedicine is an important tool that can combat this mismatch and improve the delivery of healthcare services through usage of information and communication technologies for exchange of valid information in diagnosis, treatment and prevention of disease and injuries, research and evaluation, and for the continuing education of healthcare providers. This is depicted in Fig. 3.1.

## 3.2 Description of the Investigational Product: Tele-Master Kiosk 201

To provide telehealth services, we at CIBioD have developed Tele-Master Kiosk 201 (TM 201), specifications of which are given as follows:

### 3.2.1 Name

The name of this system is Tele-Master Kiosk 201 (TM 201).

### 3.2.2 Facilities Available

The features available in this kiosk are as follows:

1. Video conferencing facility for video teleconsultation.

2. Data transfer through Internet with server space for data storage and dedicated software with machine–cloud interface so that results can be autofetched.
3. It has inbuilt devices to check the following parameters: height, weight, body mass index (BMI), temperature, pulse rate, blood oxygen saturation, blood pressure, respiratory rate, pulse pressure.
4. *12-Channel Electrocardiogram (ECG):* It has inbuilt ECG wherein parameters like heart rate, QRS, QT, and QTc intervals, P/QRS/T axis can be calculated and given in printable form.
5. *Digital Spirometer:* It has an inbuilt spirometer to enable specialists to assess respiratory pathologies in real-time during teleconsultation.
6. *Digital Stethoscope:* It enables physicians to perform virtual auscultation during teleconsultation.
7. Vision assessment.
8. *Otoscope:* An inbuilt otoscope enables specialists to visualize and examine ear canal and ear drum.
9. *Dermoscope:* It is a noninvasive, diagnostic tool to visualize subtle skin lesions and subsurface skin structures.
10. *Rapid Card Tests:* This test kit enables the diagnosis of pregnancy, malaria, dengue, typhoid, chikungunya, blood grouping, and HIV.
11. It has an inbuilt point-of-care diagnostic lab which can perform 85+ biochemistry tests. It consists of *(a) urine analyzer (semiautomatic)* which allows the complete assessment of urine (protein, sugar, bilirubin, specific gravity, urobilinogen, nitrate, pH, ketone, blood, ascorbic acid, and leukocytes) and *(b) blood analyzer (semiautomatic)* which allows blood tests to be done (Fig. 3.2).

In a nutshell, telehealth kiosk is a health ATM with integrated diagnostic lab along with hardware–cloud interface. These kiosks provide point-of-care diagnostic and video consultation services to the rural population at their first contact. TM 201 can automatically measure ten noninvasive clinical parameters with the ability to perform more than 80 blood tests at spot. The acquisition of clinical and laboratory data is automatic, and data can be stored in cloud. TM 201 has a 19″ touch screen LED display with a user-friendly module. It also has an inbuilt 12-channel ECG and digital spirometer. In combination, all the above facilities make TM 201 an excellent platform to provide teleconsultation services. It is an innovative, robust, comprehensive, and easy-to-install telemedicine clinic with an artificial intelligence (AI)-enabled real-time data management platform.

## 3.3 Testing of Tele-Master 201 Kiosk in Real World

Three Tele-Master 201 Kiosk units have been installed by the ICMR Center for Innovation and Bio-Design (CIBioD) in Himachal Pradesh's Awah Devi (District: Hamirpur), Thana Kalan (District: Una), and Thunag (District: Mandi). We further decided to test their efficacy in real-life situation.

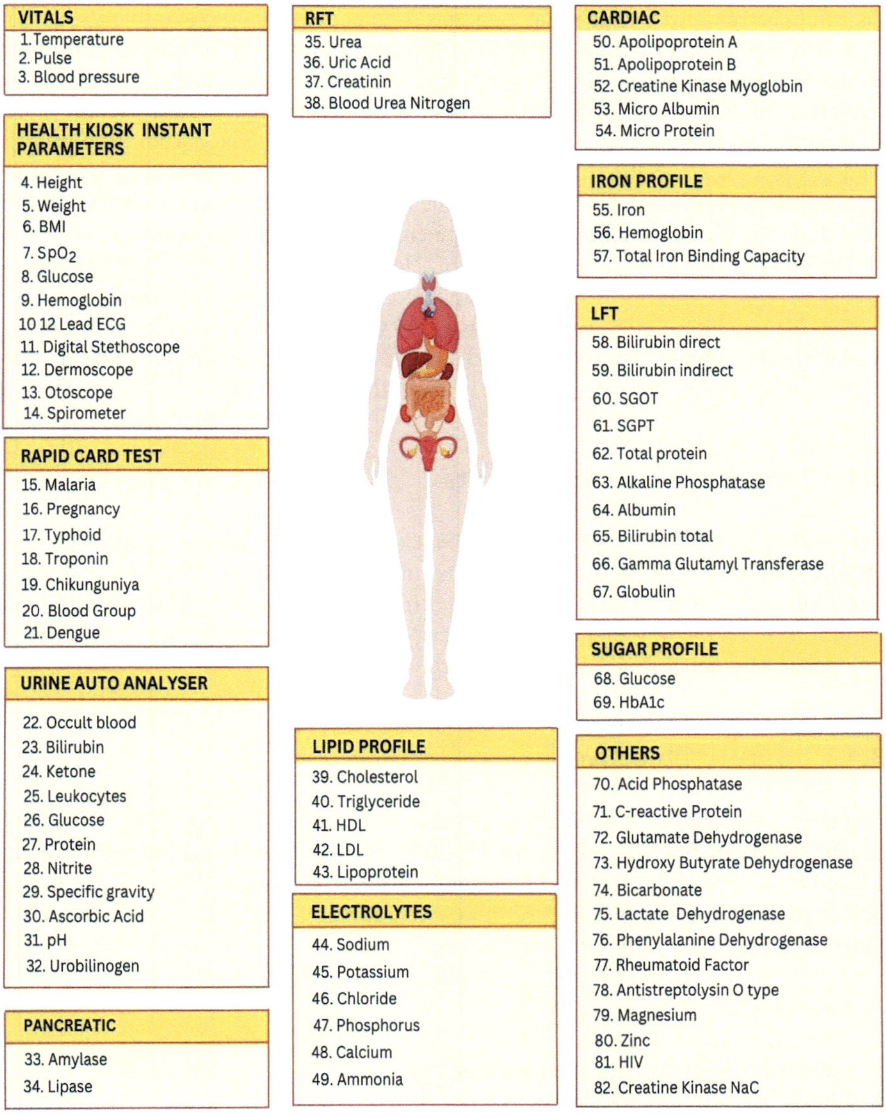


**Fig. 3.2** Blood tests which can be performed in TM 201

## 3.3.1 Rationale for Testing

Regular hospital visits are expensive, particularly in rural areas, due to travel costs. Furthermore, it becomes impossible to visit health centers due to travel restrictions imposed during difficult times such as COVID-19 pandemic. Fortunately, medical visits can be reduced through telemedicine. Telemedicine can streamline the workflow of hospitals and clinics and allows for easy monitoring of patients on treatment. Another important, though often ignored advantage of telemedicine, is the reduction in health sector–related emission of greenhouse gases. Health Care Without Harm had estimated that the healthcare-related global carbon footprint to be 2 gigaton of carbon dioxide equivalents, equating to 4.4% of global carbon dioxide emission. Health-related transport alone accounts for approximately 7% of this emission. Telemedicine can help to reduce emission of greenhouse gases.

Despite the abovementioned benefits of telemedicine, it is surprising that there is a lack of data regarding efficacy, acceptance, and utility of telemedicine in real world. We conducted surveys at various sites (where we have installed our kiosks) to determine efficacy, acceptance, and utility of telemedicine in real world. The methodology and results are provided in the following sections:

## 3.4 Methodology and Results

*The Indian Council of Medical Research Center for Innovation and Bio-Design (ICMR-CIBioD)* in association with its incubated startups, *Sri Venkteshwara Indoglobal Medicare (SVIG)* and *Nirogya Life Line Foundation (NLLF)* along with inputs from Tata Communication (GloHeal) started telemedicine services at three villages in Himachal Pradesh as mentioned earlier.

### 3.4.1 Survey Objective

A survey was conducted between July 3 and 21, 2023, in Thunag village of Mandi district, between July 23 and August 15, 2023, in Una district, and between August 18 and September 12, 2023, in Hamirpur district of Himachal Pradesh. The major objective of this survey was to determine the grading of telehealth kiosk as rated by users in terms of the following parameters:

1. Ease of use
2. Appearance/look & feel
3. Accessibility to basic health checkup
4. Interaction with doctor/staff
5. Any difficulty faced in giving sample
6. Speed of service
7. Report delivery

The survey was conducted through "Patient Feedback Form for Telehealth Kiosk."

### 3.4.2 Survey Report (Thunag-Mandi District) (Tables 3.1 and 3.2; Figs. 3.3 and 3.4)

In total, 205 patients of all ages, who used telehealth kiosk, gave their feedback between July 3 and 21, 2023, in terms of the abovementioned parameters. The patients had to mark between 1 and 5: 1 being "Dissatisfied"; 2 being "Slightly Satisfied"; 3 being "Moderately Satisfied"; 4 being "Very Satisfied"; and 5 being "Completely Satisfied." The outcome of the survey is as follows:

*Ease of Use:* Out of 205 patients, 163 (79.51%) patients were completely satisfied with ease of use and 42 (20.49%) patients were very satisfied. None of the patients found any difficulty in using the machine.

*Appearance/Look & Feel:* 161 (78.54%) patients were completely satisfied, whereas 44 (21.46%) patients were very satisfied with the appearance of TM 201.

*Accessibility to Basic Health Checkup:* 163 (79.51%) rated TM 201 telehealth kiosk as accessible to basic health checkup with complete satisfaction, while 42 (20.49%) patients were very satisfied.

*Interaction with Doctor/Staff:* 160 (78.05%) patients were completely satisfied on this parameter, 44 (21.46%) were very satisfied, while 1 (0.49%) patient was moderately satisfied.

*Any Difficulty Faced in Giving Sample:* 164 (80%) patients did not find any difficulty while giving the sample and were completely satisfied, while 41 (20%) patients were very satisfied.

*Speed of Service:* 152 (74.15%) patients were completely satisfied, 47 (22.93%) were very satisfied, while 6 (2.93%) patients were moderately satisfied.

*Report Delivery:* 163 (79.51%) patients were completely satisfied, and 42 (20.49%) patients were very satisfied.

Overall, 100% of the patients were satisfied with the telehealth kiosk and its uses, accessibility, and affordability.

Feedback regarding functioning of TM 201 was also obtained from ten medical practitioners who operated telehealth kiosks on July 10, 2023, in Thunag village in terms of the following parameters:

1. Product quality
2. Product design
3. Effectiveness/time saving features
4. Ease of use
5. Easy to set up
6. Result outcome
7. Software display/user-friendliness
8. Usage preference over existing gold standards
9. Data transmission
10. Doctor consultation
11. Speed of service

**Table 3.1** Description of feedback forms in Thunag village

| Survey analysis of patient feedback form for telehealth kiosk | | | | | | | | | | |
|---|---|---|---|---|---|---|---|---|---|---|
| **State** | **Total patients** | **Village** | | | | | | | | |
| Himachal Pradesh | 205 | Thunag | | | | | | | | |
| **Particulars** | **Score 1/5** | **% of total patients** | **Score 2/5** | **% of total patients** | **Score 3/5** | **% of total patients** | **Score 4/5** | **% of total patients** | **Score 5/5** | **% of total patients** |
| Ease of use | 0.00 | 0.00% | 0.00 | 0.00% | 0.00 | 0.00% | 42.00 | 20.49% | 163.00 | 79.51% |
| Appearance/ look & feel | 0.00 | 0.00% | 0.00 | 0.00% | 0.00 | 0.00% | 44.00 | 21.46% | 161.00 | 78.54% |
| Accessibility to basic health checkup | 0.00 | 0.00% | 0.00 | 0.00% | 0.00 | 0.00% | 42.00 | 20.49% | 163.00 | 79.51% |
| Interaction with doctors/staff | 0.00 | 0.00% | 0.00 | 0.00% | 1.00 | 0.49% | 44.00 | 21.46% | 160.00 | 78.05% |
| Any difficulty faced in giving sample | 0.00 | 0.00% | 0.00 | 0.00% | 0.00 | 0.00% | 41.00 | 20.00% | 164.00 | 80.00% |
| Speed of service | 0.00 | 0.00% | 0.00 | 0.00% | 6.00 | 2.93% | 47.00 | 22.93% | 152.00 | 74.15% |
| Report delivery | 0.00 | 0.00% | 0.00 | 0.00% | 0.00 | 0.00% | 42.00 | 20.49% | 163.00 | 79.51% |
| **Particulars** | **Score 1/5** | **Mean% of total patients** | **Score 2/5** | **Mean% of total patients** | **Score 3/5** | **Mean% of total patients** | **Score 4/5** | **Mean% of total patients** | **Score 5/5** | **Mean% of total patients** |
| Weighted average of scoring/patient | 0 | 0.00% | 0 | 0.00% | 1 | 0.49% | 44 | 21.46% | 161 | 78.54% |

**Table 3.2** Rating scores at Thunag village

| Details | Score 1/5 | Score 2/5 | Score 3/5 | Score 4/5 | Score 5/5 |
|---|---|---|---|---|---|
| No. of patients | 0 | 0 | 1 | 43 | 161 |
| % of total | 0.00% | 0.00% | 0.49% | 21.05% | 78.47% |

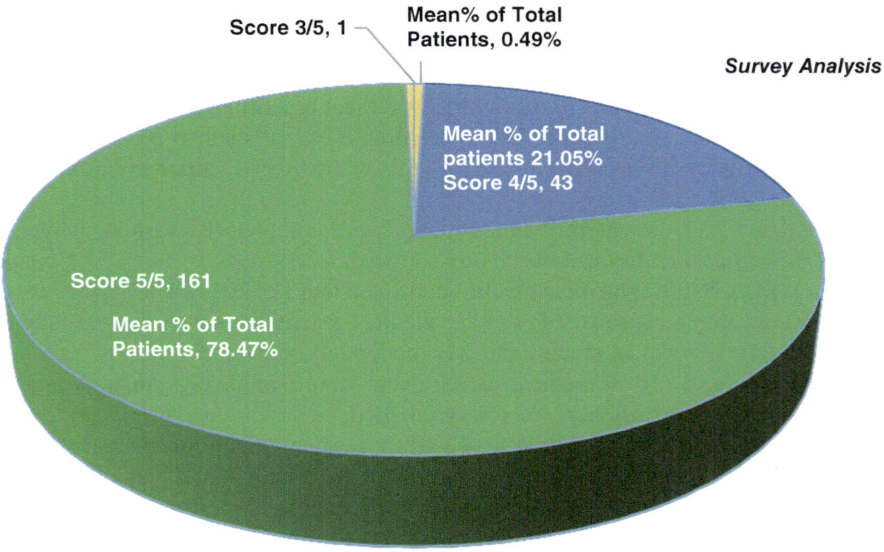


**Fig. 3.3** Pie chart showing results of the survey (Thunag village)

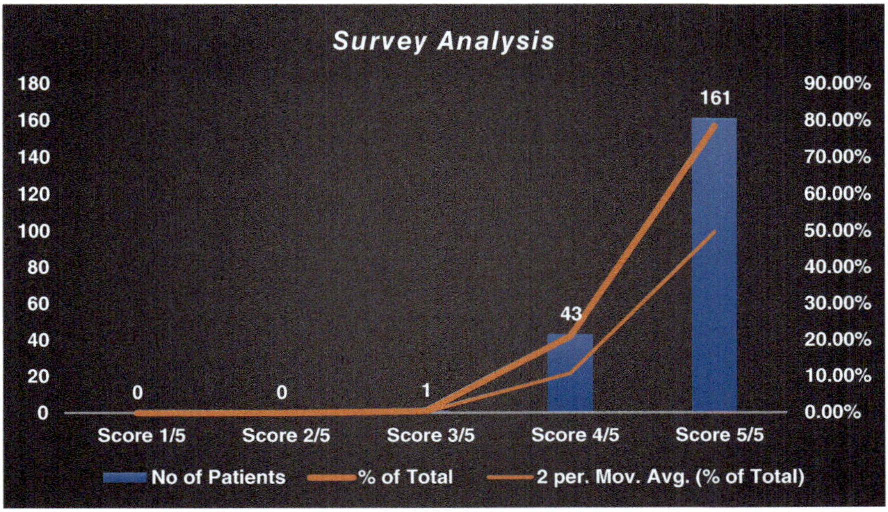


**Fig. 3.4** Graphic depiction of the results of the survey

The medical practitioners had to mark between 1 and 5; 1 being "Dissatisfied"; 2 being "Slightly Satisfied"; 3 being "Moderately Satisfied"; 4 being "Very Satisfied"; and 5 being "Completely Satisfied." The following was the outcome of the survey:

*Product Quality:* All 10 (100%) medical practitioners were completely satisfied with the quality of Telehealth Kiosk.

*Product Design:* 9 (90%) medical practitioners were completely satisfied, while 1 (10%) medical practitioner was very satisfied.

*Effectiveness/Time Saving Feature:* 3 (30%) medical practitioners rated TM 201 to be effective and time saving and were completely satisfied; 6 (60%) medical practitioners were very satisfied, while 1 (10%) medical practitioner was moderately satisfied.

*Ease of Use:* 7 (70%) medical practitioners were completely satisfied, while 3 (30%) medical practitioners were very satisfied.

*Easy to Set Up:* 5 (50%) medical practitioners rated that TM 201 can be set up easily and were completely satisfied; 4 (40%) medical practitioners were very satisfied, while 1 (10%) medical practitioner was moderately satisfied.

*Result Outcome:* 5 (50%) medical practitioners were completely satisfied, and 5 (50%) medical practitioners were very satisfied.

*Software Display/User-Friendliness: 4* (40%) medical practitioners were completely satisfied with the software display of telehealth kiosk, while 6 (60%) medical practitioners were very satisfied.

*Usage Preference over Gold Standards:*2 (20%) medical practitioners were completely satisfied on this parameter, 5 (50%) were very satisfied, whereas 3 (30%) medical practitioners were moderately satisfied.

*Data Transmission:* 4 (40%) medical practitioners were completely satisfied, and (60%) medical practitioners were very satisfied.

*Doctor Consultation:* 4 (40%) medical practitioners were completely satisfied, 4 (40%) were very satisfied, whereas 2 (20%) medical practitioners were moderately satisfied.

*Speed of Service:* 3 (30%) medical practitioners were completely satisfied, 6 (60%) were very satisfied, whereas 1 (10%) medical practitioner was moderately satisfied.

Overall, 40% of the medical practitioners were completely satisfied with telehealth kiosk and its uses, accessibility, and affordability, 50% of the medical practitioners were very satisfied, and 10% of medical practitioners were moderately satisfied with overall functioning of TM 201.

Seven medical practitioners recommended for the installation of telehealth kiosk, one medical practitioner said that it could probably be installed, while two medical practitioners were not sure about the same.

All 10 medical practitioners were satisfied with telehealth kiosk.

### 3.4.3 Survey Report (Una District) (Tables 3.3 and 3.4; Figs. 3.5 and 3.6)

In total, 102 patients of all ages used Telehealth Kiosk and gave their feedback between July 23 and August 15, 2023, as determined by parameters mentioned earlier. The patients had to mark between 1 and 5; 1 being "Dissatisfied"; 2 being "Slightly Satisfied"; 3 being "Moderately Satisfied"; 4 being "Very Satisfied"; and 5 being "Completely Satisfied." The results of the survey are given below:

*Ease of Use:* 41 (40.20%) patients rated TM 201 easy to use and were completely satisfied while 61 (59.80%) patients were very satisfied. Not a single patient found difficulty in using the machine.

*Appearance/Look & Feel:* 41 (40.20%) patients were completely satisfied, whereas 61 (59.80%) patients were very satisfied.

*Accessibility to Basic Health Checkup:* 41 (40.20%) patients rated TM 201 as being accessible to basic health checkup and were completely satisfied, whereas 61 (59.80%) patients were very satisfied.

*Interaction with Doctor/Staff:* 41 (40.20%) patients were completely satisfied, and 61 (59.80%) patients were very satisfied.

*Any Difficulty Faced in Giving Sample:* 41 (40.20%) patients found no difficulty and were completely satisfied, while 61 (59.80%) patients were very satisfied.

*Speed of Service:* 41 (40.20%) patients were completely satisfied, 51 (50.00%) were very satisfied, while 10 (9.80%) patients were moderately satisfied.

*Report Delivery:* 41 (40.20%) patients were completely satisfied while 61 (59.80%) patients were very satisfied.

Overall, 100% of the patients were satisfied with the telehealth kiosk and its uses, accessibility, and affordability.

### 3.4.4 Survey Report (Hamirpur District) (Tables 3.5 and 3.6; Figs. 3.7 and 3.8)

In total, 103 patients including young and geriatric patients used telehealth kiosk and gave their feedback between August 18 and September 12, 2023, in terms of the above given parameters. The patients had to mark between 1 and 5; 1 being "Dissatisfied"; 2 being "Slightly Satisfied"; 3 being "Moderately Satisfied"; 4 being "Very Satisfied"; and 5 being "Completely Satisfied." The following was the outcome of the survey:

*Ease of Use:* 54 (52.43%) patients rated TM 201 easy to use and were completely satisfied, while 49 (47.57%) patients were very satisfied. Not a single patient found any difficulty in using the machine.

*Appearance/Look & Feel:* 54 (52.43%) patients were completely satisfied, and 49 patients (47.57%) were very satisfied.

**Table 3.3** Depiction of feedback forms for telehealth kiosk (Una district)

| Survey analysis of patient feedback form for telehealth kiosk | | | | | | | | | | |
|---|---|---|---|---|---|---|---|---|---|---|
| **State** | **Total patients** | **District** | | | | | | | | |
| Himachal Pradesh | 102 | Una | | | | | | | | |
| **Particulars** | **Score 1/5** | **% of total patients** | **Score 2/5** | **% of total patients** | **Score 3/5** | **% of total patients** | **Score 4/5** | **% of total patients** | **Score 5/5** | **% of total patients** |
| Ease of use | 0.00 | 0.00% | 0.00 | 0.00% | 0.00 | 0.00% | 61.00 | 59.80% | 41.00 | 40.20% |
| Appearance/look & feel | 0.00 | 0.00% | 0.00 | 0.00% | 0.00 | 0.00% | 61.00 | 59.80% | 41.00 | 40.20% |
| Accessibility to basic health checkup | 0.00 | 0.00% | 0.00 | 0.00% | 0.00 | 0.00% | 61.00 | 59.80% | 41.00 | 40.20% |
| Interaction with doctors/staff | 0.00 | 0.00% | 0.00 | 0.00% | 0.00 | 0.00% | 61.00 | 59.80% | 41.00 | 40.20% |
| Any difficulty faced in giving sample | 0.00 | 0.00% | 0.00 | 0.00% | 0.00 | 0.00% | 61.00 | 59.80% | 41.00 | 40.20% |
| Speed of service | 0.00 | 0.00% | 0.00 | 0.00% | 10.00 | 9.80% | 51.00 | 50.00% | 41.00 | 40.20% |
| Report delivery | 0.00 | 0.00% | 0.00 | 0.00% | 0.00 | 0.00% | 61.00 | 59.80% | 41.00 | 40.20% |

**Table 3.4** Average scoring given by patients at Una district

| Particulars | Score 1/5 | Score 2/5 | Score 3/5 | Score 4/5 | Score 5/5 |
|---|---|---|---|---|---|
| Weighted average of scoring/ patient | 0 | 0 | 1 | 60 | 41 |
| Mean% of total patients | 0.00% | 0.00% | 1.40% | 58.40% | 40.20% |

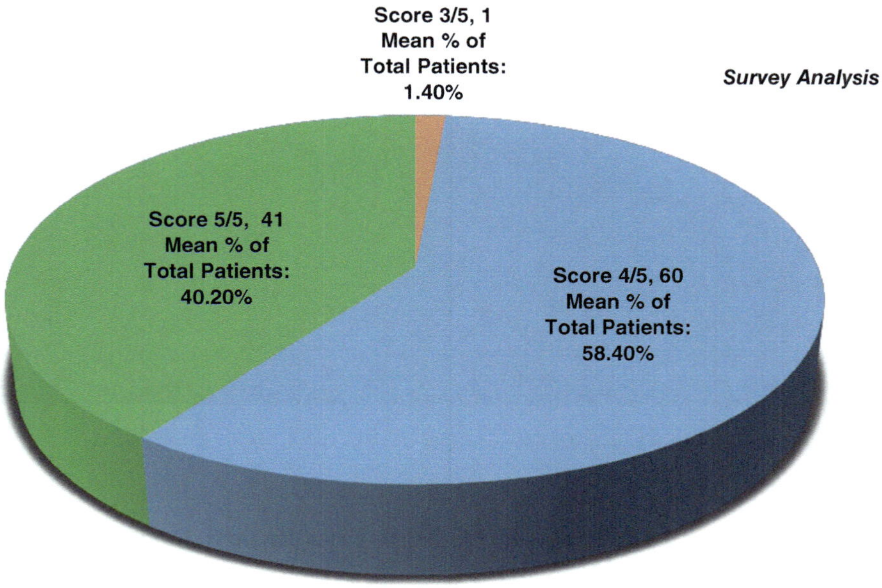


**Fig. 3.5** Pie chart showing results of survey at Una district

*Accessibility to Basic Health Checkup:* 55 (53.40%) patients were completely satisfied, and 48 (46.60%) patients were very satisfied.

*Interaction with Doctor/Staff:* 54 (52.43%) patients were completely satisfied, and 49 (47.57%) patients were very satisfied.

*Any Difficulty Faced in Giving Sample:* 55 (53.40%) patients did not find any difficulty while giving the sample and completely satisfied, 47 (45.63%) were very satisfied, while 1 (0.97%) patient was moderately satisfied.

*Speed of Service:* 55 (53.40%) patients were completely satisfied, 47 (45.63%) were very satisfied, while 1 (0.97%) patient was moderately satisfied.

*Report Delivery:* 54 (52.43%) patients were completely satisfied and 49 (47.57%) patients were very satisfied.

Overall, 100% of the patients were satisfied with the telehealth kiosk and its uses, accessibility, and affordability.

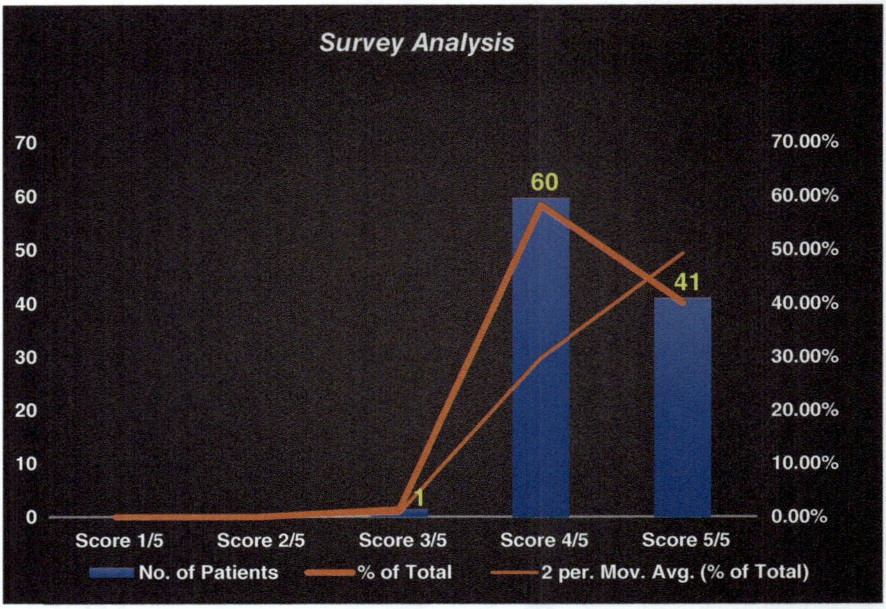


**Fig. 3.6** Graphical depiction of the survey results

## 3.5 Studies Conducted at PGIMER, Chandigarh, Regarding the Use of Telemedicine

To provide more insight into the need for telemedicine, we conducted a survey at three departments (cardiology, nephrology, and neurology) of PGIMER, Chandigarh. A total of 246 patients ($n = 67$ for nephrology department; $n = 89$ for neurology department; $n = 90$ for cardiology department) coming from different parts of India were enrolled in the study. About 57% of patients were men and 43% of patients were women. Overall, 17.9% of patients did not have any serious illness as rated by the treating doctor, 31.3% has moderately serious illness, while 50.8% of patients had serious disease. Of the patients, 34.1% visited the treating unit for the first time, while 65.9% came for a follow-up. Of the patients, 28.4% were not advised on any investigations, 33.4% were advised to undergo some tests, while 38.2% were evaluated extensively. About 55.28% of patients were advised to use telemedicine for follow-up testing rather than visiting the hospital. Among various departments, 53.93% of patients attending neurology department, 73.4% of patients attending nephrology department, and 51.11% of patients visiting the cardiology department were advised to use telemedicine for follow-up rather than come in person. These results are summarized in Fig. 3.9.

Overall, the results of our surveys suggest the following:

**Table 3.5** Data of feedback forms of survey in Hamirpur district

| Survey analysis of patient feedback form for telehealth kiosk | | | | | | | | | | |
|---|---|---|---|---|---|---|---|---|---|---|
| **State** | **Total patients** | **District** | | | | | | | | |
| Himachal Pradesh | 103 | Hamirpur | | | | | | | | |
| **Particulars** | **Score 1/5** | **% of total patients** | **Score 2/5** | **% of total patients** | **Score 3/5** | **% of total patients** | **Score 4/5** | **% of total patients** | **Score 5/5** | **% of total patients** |
| Ease of use | 0.00 | 0.00% | 0.00 | 0.00% | 0.00 | 0.00% | 49.00 | 47.57% | 54.00 | 52.43% |
| Appearance/look & feel | 0.00 | 0.00% | 0.00 | 0.00% | 0.00 | 0.00% | 49.00 | 47.57% | 54.00 | 52.43% |
| Accessibility to basic health checkup | 0.00 | 0.00% | 0.00 | 0.00% | 0.00 | 0.00% | 48.00 | 46.60% | 55.00 | 53.40% |
| Interaction with doctors/staff | 0.00 | 0.00% | 0.00 | 0.00% | 0.00 | 0.00% | 49.00 | 47.57% | 54.00 | 52.43% |
| Any difficulty faced in giving sample | 0.00 | 0.00% | 0.00 | 0.00% | 1.00 | 0.97% | 47.00 | 45.63% | 55.00 | 53.40% |
| Speed of service | 0.00 | 0.00% | 0.00 | 0.00% | 1.00 | 0.97% | 47.00 | 45.63% | 55.00 | 53.40% |
| Report delivery | 0.00 | 0.00% | 0.00 | 0.00% | 0.00 | 0.00% | 49.00 | 47.57% | 54.00 | 52.43% |

**Table 3.6** Scores given by patients at Hamirpur district

| Particulars | Score 1/5 | Score 2/5 | Score 3/5 | Score 4/5 | Score 5/5 |
|---|---|---|---|---|---|
| Weighted average of scoring/ patient | 0 | 0 | 1 | 48 | 54 |
| Mean% of total patients | 0.00% | 0.00% | 0.97% | 46.88% | 52.84% |

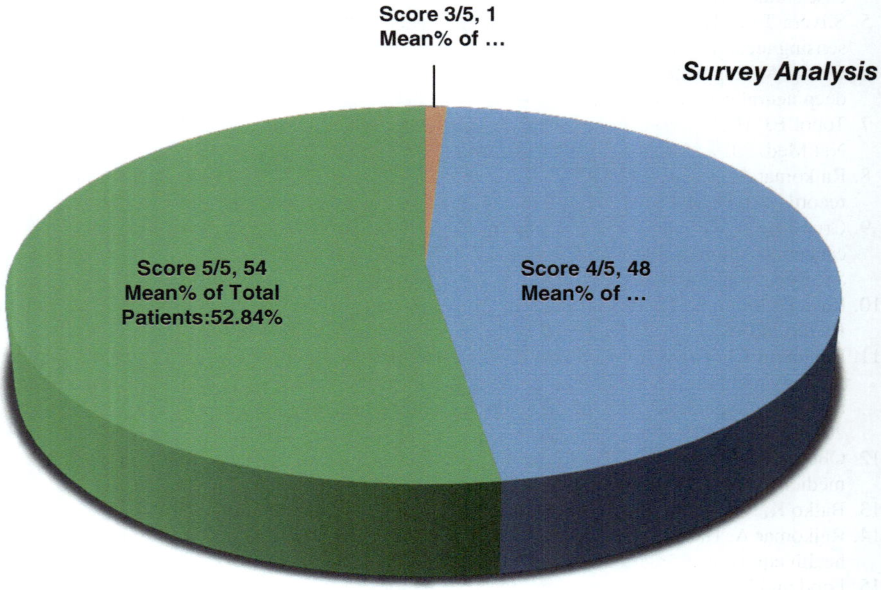


**Fig. 3.7** Pie chart showing results of survey at Hamirpur district

1. Telemedicine can be used for ongoing management of chronic diseases such as hypertension, diabetes mellitus, particularly during a time when social distancing is encouraged.
2. Telemedicine can serve as a safe and effective alternative to in-person care.
3. Telemedicine can be used for providing psychological support to patients and their family members without getting exposed to the infection.

## 3.6 Review of Literature and Discussion

Several authors have suggested that telemedicine can be an effective alternative to conventional healthcare and can connect healthcare providers to patients living in geographically disparate locations [4, 5]. In medicine, teleconsultation can be used for prevention, diagnosis, consultation, evaluation, monitoring, mentoring, treatment, follow-up, and rehabilitation [6, 7]. Telemedicine, as a broad specialty, includes several subcategories such as telepsychiatry, teledermatology, teleradiology,

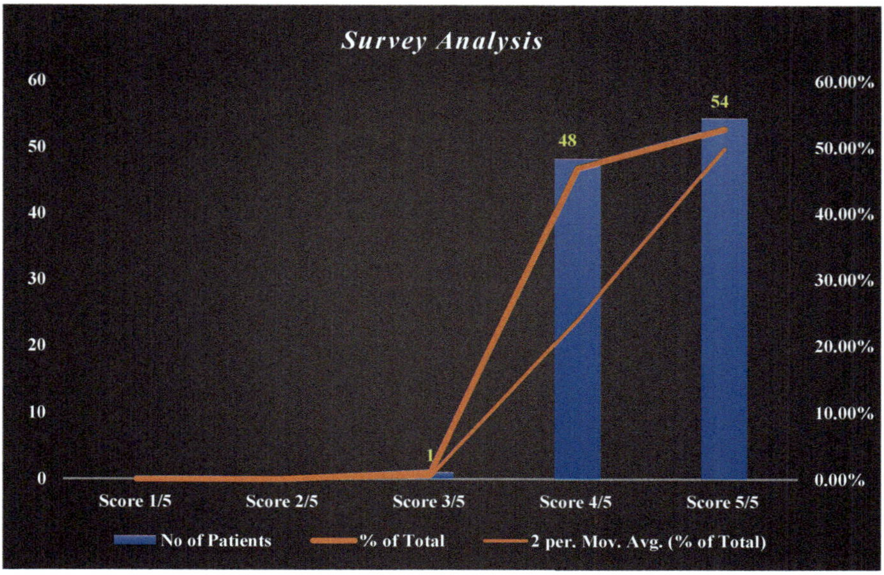


**Fig. 3.8** Graphical representation of survey conducted at Hamirpur district

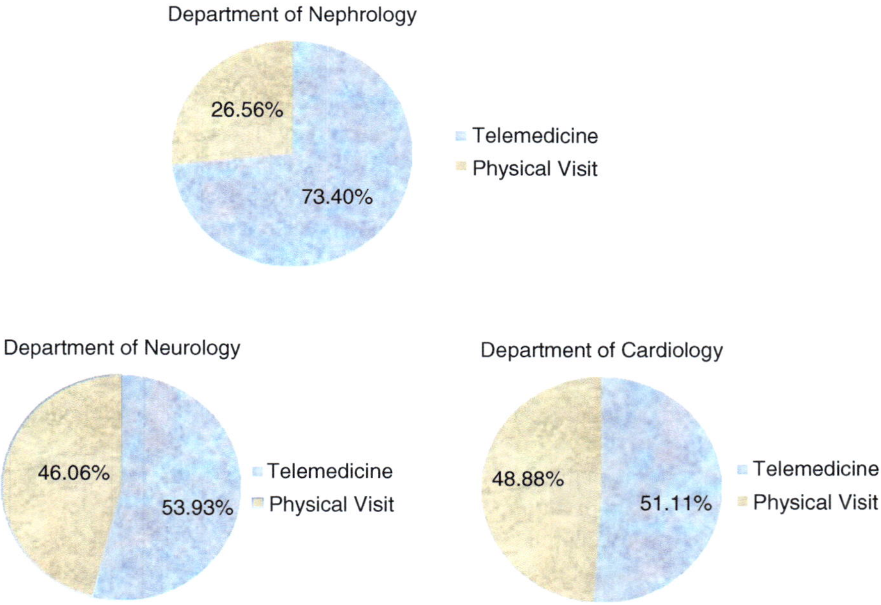


**Fig. 3.9** Pie charts showing results of survey at PGIMER, Chandigarh

telepathology, telerehabilitation, and tele-education [8, 9], all of which use specific techniques. For instance, telepathology provides pathology services from a distance using video imaging visualizations [10]. Teleradiology involves transmission of radiological images (e.g., X-rays, CT, and MRI) at a distance for interpretation [11]. Telerehabilitation, on the other hand, relies on patient examination through video assessment [12, 13].

Telemedicine plays a key role in healthcare by increasing accessibility of healthcare especially in rural communities [14]. Its use has significantly increased in recent years as suggested by increase in the number of published studies from 56 in 1992 to 3861 studies in 2015 [15, 16]. Also, there is an increase in the number of systemic reviews focusing on subject of telemedicine and its branches such as telepsychiatry [17], teledermatology [18], and telepathology [19].

Though the number of studies on telemedicine has increased dramatically over the years, there is still no definite evidence on its clinical and economic benefits. Also, there is no data as to the degree of patient satisfaction [20–24]. Also, most of data regarding use of telemedicine has emerged from developed nations such as the United States, Australia, United Kingdom, Canada, and China [25].

## 3.7 Future Plan at CIBioD

In the light of preceding discussion, primary healthcare can be boosted by telemedicine to realize the goal of universal health coverage. At ICMR-CIBioD, we are committed to developing futuristic healthcare delivery ecosystem with the deployment of cutting-edge technologies. This ecosystem will not only provide quality primary healthcare with point-of-care diagnostics in an affordable, accessible, and sustainable manner, but it will also generate high quality data. This data will pave the way for wider application of AI, machine learning (ML), deep learning (DL), virtual reality (VR), augmented reality (AR), chatbot, and precision medicine, with an aim to fulfill the unmet healthcare needs.

We aim to improve services, for communicable and noncommunicable diseases, and for both rural and urban populations. We hope that, in future, telemedicine will be used increasingly to achieve the following goals:

1. To promote diagnosis and treatment of communicable and non-communicable diseases.
2. To effectively implement national programs to achieve the "Sustainable Development Goals 3" in future.
3. To improve treatment adherence among patients.
4. To synchronize all our data under the National Digital Health Mission.
5. To build capacity of primary healthcare teams to deliver essential health services with support from technology and integration with NPCDCS (National Programme for Prevention and Control of Cancer, Diabetes, Cardiovascular Diseases and Stroke).

6. To explore opportunities for integrating the teleconsultation model with other sectors involved in healthcare.
7. To promote social stability by reducing travel expenditure, time and out-of-pocket expenses.
8. To reduce carbon footprint due to health-related travel of the patients and their attendants.

## References


1. Akintunde TY, Akintunde OD, Musa TH, et al. Expanding telemedicine to reduce the burden on the healthcare systems and poverty in Africa for a post-coronavirus disease 2019 (COVID-19) pandemic reformation. Glob Health J. 2021;5(3):128–34.
2. Census of India. GOI. 2012. [Last accessed on 2020 May 06]. Available from: http://censusindia.gov.in.
3. Agarwal N, Jain P, Pathak R, Gupta R. Telemedicine in India: a tool for transforming health care in the era of COVID-19 pandemic. J Educ Health Promot. 2020;28:190.
4. AlDossary S, Martin-Khan MG, Bradford NK, Smith AC. A systematic review of the methodologies used to evaluate telemedicine service initiatives in hospital facilities. Int J Med Inform. 2017;97:171–94.
5. Alves DS, Times VC, da Silva ÉMA, et al. Advances in obstetric telemonitoring: a systematic review. Int J Med Inform. 2020;134:104004.
6. Amatya B, Galea MP, Kesselring J, Khan F. Effectiveness of telerehabilitation interventions in persons with multiple sclerosis: a systematic review. Mult Scler Relat Disord. 2015;4(4):358–69.
7. Appleby E, Gill ST, Hayes LK, et al. Effectiveness of telerehabilitation in the management of adults with stroke: a systematic review. PLoS One. 2019;14(11):e0225150.
8. Backhaus A, Agha Z, Maglione ML, et al. Videoconferencing psychotherapy: a systematic review. Psychol Serv. 2012;9(2):111–31.
9. Banbury A, Nancarrow S, Dart J, et al. Telehealth interventions delivering home-based support group videoconferencing: systematic review. J Med Internet Res. 2018;20(2):e25.
10. Baron J, McBain H, Newman S. The impact of mobile monitoring technologies on glycosylated hemoglobin in diabetes: a systematic review. J Diabetes Sci Technol. 2012;6(5):1185–96.
11. Bashi N, Karunanithi M, Fatehi F, et al. Remote monitoring of patients with heart failure: an overview of systematic reviews. J Med Internet Res. 2017;19(1):e18.
12. Bashshur RL, Howell JD, Krupinski EA, et al. The empirical foundations of telemedicine interventions in primary care. Telemed J E Health. 2016;22(5):342–75.
13. Batastini AB, King CM, Morgan RD, McDaniel B. Telepsychological services with criminal justice and substance abuse clients: a systematic review and meta-analysis. Psychol Serv. 2016;13(1):20–30.
14. Batsis JA, DiMilia PR, Seo LM, et al. Effectiveness of ambulatory telemedicine care in older adults: a systematic review. J Am Geriatr Soc. 2019;67(8):1737–49.
15. Berryhill MB, Halli-Tierney A, Culmer N, et al. Videoconferencing psychological therapy and anxiety: a systematic review. Fam Pract. 2019;36(1):53–63.
16. Bittner AK, Wykstra SL, Yoshinaga PD, Li T. Telerehabilitation for people with low vision. Cochrane Database Syst Rev. 2015;8:CD011019.
17. Blank L, Coster J, O'Cathain A, et al. The appropriateness of, and compliance with, telephone triage decisions: a systematic review and narrative synthesis. J Adv Nurs. 2012;68(12):2610–21.

18. Bolton CE, Waters CS, Peirce S, Elwyn G, EPSRC and MRC Grand Challenge Team. Insufficient evidence of benefit: a systematic review of home telemonitoring for COPD. J Eval Clin Pract. 2011;17(6):1216–22.
19. Brearly TW, Shura RD, Martindale SL, et al. Neuropsychological test administration by videoconference: a systematic review and meta-analysis. Neuropsychol Rev. 2017;27(2):174–86.
20. Brons M, Koudstaal S, Asselbergs FW. Algorithms used in telemonitoring programmes for patients with chronic heart failure: a systematic review. Eur J Cardiovasc Nurs. 2018;17(7):580–8.
21. Bruce AF, Mallow JA, Theeke LA. The use of teledermoscopy in the accurate identification of cancerous skin lesions in the adult population: a systematic review. J Telemed Telecare. 2018;24(2):75–83.
22. Buekers J, De Boever P, Vaes AW, et al. Oxygen saturation measurements in telemonitoring of patients with COPD: a systematic review. Expert Rev Respir Med. 2018;12(2):113–23.
23. Bush ML, Thompson R, Irungu C, Ayugi J. The role of telemedicine in auditory rehabilitation: a systematic review. Otol Neurotol. 2016;37(10):1466–74.
24. Carrasqueiro S, Oliveira M, Encarnação P. Evaluation of telephone triage and advice services: a systematic review on methods, metrics and results. Stud Health Technol Inform. 2011;169:407–11.
25. Goharinejad S, Hajesmaeel-Gohari S, Jannati N, et al. Review of systematic reviews in the field of telemedicine. Med J Islam Repub Iran. 2021;35:184.

# Health Technology Assessment of Center for Innovation and Bio-Design (CIBioD)

4

Shankar Prinja

## 4.1 Introduction

Health technology assessment (HTA) is a comprehensive process that draws from various disciplines to analyze the implications of health technologies across healthcare, societal, financial, and ethical dimensions. This methodical and impartial approach aims to inform the development of policies that prioritize the patient's safety and efficacy while striving to deliver the highest possible value [9]. In recent years, healthcare has seen significant improvements due to the development and use of various medical treatments and technologies. These include drugs that combat viruses, prevent blood clots, manage diabetes and high blood pressure, and treat rheumatic conditions. Additionally, innovations in vaccines, personalized medicine through pharmacogenomics, targeted therapies for cancer, and cardiac rhythm management have played a crucial role. The advances in diagnostic imaging, less invasive surgical techniques, joint replacement procedures, pain management, and infection control practices, and the integration of health information technology have further enhanced patient care and outcomes.

In a nutshell, HTA helps the following stakeholders:

**Salient Features**

- Clinicians and Patients: To ensure that healthcare treatments are chosen and applied based on the specific clinical needs and situations of each patient.
- Healthcare professional organizations regarding a technology's involvement in clinical procedures or practice standards.

S. Prinja (✉)
Department of Community Medicine and School of Public Health, PGIMER, Chandigarh, India



V. Garg et al. (eds.), *Innovations in Healthcare Technologies in India*,
https://doi.org/10.1007/978-981-97-0244-2_4

- Hospitals, networks, and collective purchasing groups in making well-informed decisions about technology acquisition and implementation.
- Standard-Setting Bodies for guiding organizations involved in establishing standards for the manufacture, performance, and use of health technologies.
- Government Health Officials in supporting the deployment and execution of national health initiatives, including vaccination efforts, health assessments, and environmental safety programs.
- Policymakers and other political leaders on providing guidance on advancements in technology, investment in research, regulatory frameworks, and the financing and provision of healthcare services.
- Product development and marketing considerations for healthcare technology businesses.
- Investors and Business Entities on offering insights into funding opportunities, strategic business transactions such as mergers and asset sales, and dealings related to companies in the healthcare sector.
- Research Organizations in highlighting areas where current data is lacking and identifying sectors with insufficient attention in healthcare.

## 4.2 Health Technology Assessment in India (HTAIn)

As part of the 15th Financial Commission framework, the Health Technology Assessment in India (HTAIn) was set up. It operates as a component within the broader "Human Resource and Capacity Building" scheme. Endorsed by the Department of Health Research (DHR) and the Ministry of Health & Family Welfare (MoHFW), HTAIn seeks to advance clear and data-driven decision-making in healthcare. This program is dedicated to reviewing a range of healthcare innovations—such as drugs, medical equipment, and healthcare initiatives—by evaluating their efficiency, effectiveness, and fairness. Its primary objectives are to enable well-informed choices, maximize the use of constrained healthcare funds, improve patient care quality, and reduce personal healthcare costs for patients.

## 4.3 Goals and Importance of HTAIn

The objectives of HTAIn are as follows:

- Conduct assessments aimed at minimizing personal health expenses and addressing disparities.
- Share research outcomes and policy recommendations to educate the public, enabling them to make more informed health choices.
- Establish and implement processes for evaluating both emerging and established health innovations with a transparent and comprehensive approach.
- Systematically gather and analyze data to ensure it is reliable, accessible, relevant, and useful for shaping health-related decisions.

- Improve healthcare choices at national and regional levels by providing reliable, data-driven insights.
- Evaluate health programs and technological solutions using detailed information on resource allocation, expenses, efficacy, and safety.

## 4.4 HTA Resource Centers in India [2]

The resource centers are established in the following places:

1. Post-Graduate Institute of Medical Education and Research (PGIMER), Chandigarh
2. Indian Institute of Technology (IIT), Delhi
3. All India Institute of Medical Sciences (AIIMS), Jodhpur
4. Indian Institute of Public Health (IIPH), Gandhinagar
5. National Institute of Virology (NIV), Pune
6. National Institute for Research in Reproductive Health (NIRRH), Mumbai
7. National Centre for Disease Informatics and Research (NCDIR), Karnataka
8. Indian Institute of Science (IISc), Bengaluru
9. Sree Chitra Tirunal Institute for Medical Sciences and Technology (SCTIMST), Trivandrum
10. Jawaharlal Institute of Postgraduate Medical Education and Research (JIPMER), Puducherry
11. National Institute for Research in Tuberculosis (NIRT), Chennai
12. National Institute of Epidemiology (NIE), Chennai
13. Indian Institute of Public Health (IIPH), Hyderabad
14. Kalam Institute of Technology (KIT), Hyderabad
15. Regional Medical Research Center (RMRC), Bhubaneswar
16. Indian Institute of Public Health (IIPH), Shillong
17. State Cancer Institute and King George Medical University (KGMU), Lucknow
18. All India Institute of Medical Sciences (AIIMS), Rishikesh
19. Institute of Medical Sciences, Banaras Hindu University (BHU), Varanasi
20. Dr. Rajendra Prasad Government Medical College (RPGMC), Kangra

## 4.5 ICMR-CIBioD (Indian Council of Medical Research-Center for Innovation and Bio-Design)

The CIBioD telemedicine kiosk with point-of-care diagnostics is a significant advancement in healthcare technology, offering standardized diagnostic capabilities. It is an innovative, robust, comprehensive, easy-to-install telemedicine clinic—which is an all-in-one diagnostic lab and specialists' consultation hub, with an artificial intelligence (AI)-enabled real-time data management platform. It is installed in three districts of Himachal Pradesh, namely Hamirpur (Awah Devi),

Una (Thana Kalan), and Mandi (Thunag Village). Its salient features are summarized below:

**Salient Features**

- Employs standardized medical devices and digital health infrastructure, ensuring the reliability and consistency of diagnostic tests.
- Kiosk offers clinically effective estimates at a cost-effective price and has the potential to offer further cost savings due to regular health check-ups and early disease detection.
- Kiosk promotes preventive care.
- Kiosk has the potential to reduce the burden of chronic diseases and the associated healthcare costs.
- Patients can access medical services without the need for extensive travel, saving transportation costs and time. Thus, it has the potential to improve healthcare access and quality while reducing the financial burden on individuals and healthcare systems.
- Kiosk can reduce the burden on tertiary care center which has a higher unit cost of delivering diagnostic services.
- Kiosk's initial setup and operational costs are relatively low, in comparison to building and maintaining traditional healthcare facilities.

### 4.5.1 Background

In the multifaceted landscape of Indian healthcare with its vast geographic spread and demographics, there is an urgent need for innovative solutions to bridge the gap in access to healthcare between rural and urban populations. In rural areas, the availability of healthcare facilities and specialized care is limited, resulting in delayed and/or inadequate treatment. Telemedicine, along with point-of-care diagnostic services at primary health center (PHC) level, may help to bridge this gap to a great extent. The use of telemedicine may usher in a new era of healthcare delivery in rural areas through timely and comprehensive evaluation of health along with immediate initiation of treatment if needed. This transformative shift in delivery and accessibility of healthcare may help to reach the ultimate goal of ensuring that every individual regardless of their geographical location or socioeconomic status has access to high-quality healthcare.

The telehealth kiosk (TM-103) equipped with point-of-care diagnostic facilities, developed at ICMR-funded CIBioD, represents an innovative solution to provide telehealth services in remote areas. It focuses on improving healthcare accessibility, providing timely and comprehensive health screening and thereby expediting the initiation of treatment. Its point-of-care diagnostic services can provide information about blood glucose and hemoglobin levels, spirometric assessment of pulmonary function tests, and information about blood pressure, body temperature, oxygen saturation, cardiac status, and body composition, among many others. It has inbuilt autoanalyzer which allows clinical validation of various measurements, thereby enhancing reliability of diagnostic results. It has an inbuilt stethoscope which allows for transmission of cardiac sounds to the attending physician. Our kiosk is functional in three PHCs in the state of Himachal Pradesh and is linked to tertiary care center (Department of Cardiology at PGIMER, Chandigarh), thereby working as what is called a hub (represented by tertiary care center) and spoke (represented by PHCs) model.

The Department of Community Medicine and School of Public Health at PGIMER, Chandigarh, a leading tertiary care institute in North India, carried out rapid health technology assessment (HTA) of ICMR-CIBioD telemedicine kiosk. The objective was to evaluate its safety, efficacy in diagnostic testing, and potential to reduce healthcare services–related costs.

### 4.5.2 Methodology

We undertook a rapid literature review to collect all the existing evidence regarding the overall effectiveness and cost-effectiveness of the kiosk and its individual components such as glucometer, spirometer, hemoglobinometer, and digital stethoscope. We searched the PubMed database to identify studies with regard to effectiveness of kiosk and its costs and health-related outcomes. To study the effectiveness, we collected data from relevant randomized controlled trials (RCTs) and well-conducted observational studies which compared the effectiveness of diagnostic devices used in CIBioD Kiosk with similar devices based on other technologies. The effectiveness parameters were measured by sensitivity, specificity, and accuracy.

To evaluate cost-effectiveness, we identified economic evaluations which compared costs and effects of diagnostic devices integrated into CIBioD kiosk with their standard counterparts or routinely used comparators. As far as possible, the Indian economic evaluations were identified to determine cost-effectiveness. If Indian studies were not available, we used evidence from other countries and adapted it to generate Indian-specific results. The adaptation process involved two steps. First, the cost was adjusted to account for differences in healthcare prices between the reference country and India, using purchasing power parity (PPP) adjusted gross domestic product (GDP) per capita data for India and the reference country. Additionally, adjustments were also made to account for inflation in healthcare costs over time. Second, health outcomes and quality adjusted life year (QALY) adjustments were made to adjust disparities in life expectancy between the reference country and India. The adapted costs and QALYs were then used to calculate the adjusted incremental cost-effectiveness ratio (IECRs) for different components of CIBioD kiosk. The data on PPP-adjusted GDP per capita and life expectancy were sourced from the website of the World Bank.

## 4.6 Results

### 4.6.1 Safety and Effectiveness

The kiosk incorporates a range of safety devices with high sensitivity and specificity, making it a trustworthy tool for accurate medical assessments. The urine analysis module of kiosk is certified with ISO 9001, TUV, ISO13845, and CE. It has a sensitivity of 99.6% and specificity of 99%, indicating its ability to reliably detect urinary abnormalities. For a similar point-of-care diagnostic device, the sensitivity and specificity were 96% and 98%, respectively [1]. The hemoglobin-testing component has a turn-around time of under 30 s with accuracy rates of around 98%. The coefficient of variation for the reproducibility was <3%, reflecting the consistent and reliable nature of the results. The sensitivity and specificity of the results of the glucometer are more than 80% and 90%, respectively. The time taken to determine blood glucose is just 5 seconds, allowing for efficient management of even diabetic emergencies. The spirometer, which utilizes a bidirectional turbine cartridge and infrared interruption technology, has an accuracy of ±1%. Though its sensitivity for detection of asthma is lower (21%), the specificity is 90%. Its $SpO_2$ module has a high accuracy with sensitivity and specificity of 92% and 90%, respectively.

The infrared thermometer is ideal for noncontact temperature measurement. It has a sensitivity of 80% and a specificity of 92% [2]. The electronic stethoscope has a sensitivity of 60% and a specificity of 95%. A cross-sectional study undertaken at our center to compare the e-stethoscope with conventional stethoscope suggested that an e-stethoscope is equally effective in interpreting the cardiac sounds as a conventional stethoscope. Other studies [3–5] have reported similar results. ECG module also has high accuracy and allows for a reasonable assessment of cardiac health of the patient. The accuracy of the body composition analysis (BCA) module is 98%. These results are summarized in Table 4.1.

### 4.6.2 Cost-Effectiveness

The cost-effectiveness of the glucometer component of the kiosk was calculated by adapting the findings from a cost-effective analysis conducted in Poland [6].

**Table 4.1** Sensitivity and specificity of various diagnostic tests used in telemedicine kiosk

| Parameter | Sensitivity | Specificity |
|---|---|---|
| Glucometer | 80% | 90% |
| Hemoglobinometer | 80% | 80% |
| Infrared thermometer | 80% | 92% |
| Spirometer | 21% | 90% |
| Oximeter | 92% | 90% |
| Urine analysis | 99.6% | 99% |
| Electronic stethoscope | 60% | 95% |

**Table 4.2** Summary of cost-effectiveness of various components of CIBioD kiosk

| Kiosk component | Comparator | Incremental cost-effectiveness ratio |
|---|---|---|
| Glucometer (automatic coded glucometer) | Non-coded manual glucometer | INR (Indian National Rupee) 42,561 per QALY (quality adjusted life year) gained |
| Hemoglobinometer (reflectance photometry) | Sahli's hemoglobinometer | INR 30.8 per anemia case diagnosed |
| ECG (Electrocardiography) (12-lead portable ECG) | Conventional ECG | INR 2299 per life year saved |

The study suggested that coded glucometer used in our kiosk was associated with cost-saving when compared to non-coded glucometer. After adapting these results for India, a coded glucometer was found to be cost-saving in the Indian context also with an incremental cost-effectiveness ratio (ICER) of Indian National Rupees (INR) 42,561 per QALY gained. Similarly, an Indian economic evaluation undertaken to compare different types of hemoglobinometers suggested that reflectance photometry–based hemoglobinometers are cost-effective with an ICER of INR 30.8 per anemia case diagnosed when compared with conventional Sahli's hemoglobinometer [7]. Another economic evaluation undertaken to evaluate the cost-effectiveness of the use of a 12-lead ECG machine at the PHC level suggested it to be cost-effective with ICER of INR 2299 per life year saved [8]. These results are summarized in Table 4.2.

## 4.7 Conclusion

The CIBioD telemedicine kiosk with point-of-care diagnostics is a significant advancement in healthcare, offering good diagnostic services. It uses standardized medical devices and digital health infrastructure, ensuring reliability and consistency of diagnostic results.

The results of rapid assessment of our kiosk suggest that it offers clinically effective estimates at a cost-effective price. It provides rapid results and, at the same time, it offers cost savings due to the following reasons. First, by enabling regular health check-ups and early disease detection, the kiosk promotes preventive care, thereby reducing the burden of chronic diseases and the associated healthcare costs. Second, the patients can access medical services without the need for travel, thereby saving transportation costs and time. Third, it reduces the burden on tertiary care centers which have higher per unit cost of diagnostic services. Also, the kiosk's initial setup and operational costs are low, in comparison to building and maintaining traditional healthcare facilities.

As telemedicine continues to gain prominence, our kiosk has the potential to improve healthcare access and quality while reducing the financial burden on individuals and the healthcare system. Further studies and long-term evaluations are recommended to assess its sustained impact and scalability in diverse healthcare settings.

## References

1. McTaggart MP, Newall RG, Hirst JA, et al. Diagnostic accuracy of point-of-care tests for detecting albuminuria: a systematic review and meta-analysis. Ann Intern Med. 2014;160(8):550–7.
2. Aggarwal N, Garg M, Dwarakanathan V, et al. Diagnostic accuracy of non-contact infrared thermometers and thermal scanners: A systematic review and meta-analysis. J Travel Med. 2020;27(8):taaa193.
3. Kelmenson DA, Heath JK, Ball SA, et al. Prototype electronic stethoscope vs. conventional stethoscope for auscultation of heart sounds. J Med Eng Technol. 2014;38(6):307–10.
4. Høyte H, Jensen T, Gjesdal K. Cardiac auscultation training of medical students: a comparison of electronic sensor-based and acoustic stethoscopes. BMC Med Educ. 2005;5(1):14.
5. Fragasso G, Cuko A, Spoladore R, et al. Validation of remote cardiopulmonary examination in patients with heart failure with a videophone-based system. J Car Failure. 2007;13:281–6.
6. Holko P, Kawalec P. Cost effectiveness and cost utility of the noncoding blood glucose meter CONTOUR TS. Diabetes Metab Syndr Obes. 2011;4:79–88.
7. Neogi SB, Sharma J, Pandey S, et al. Diagnostic accuracy of point-of-care devices for detection of anemia in community settings in India. BMC Health Serv Res. 2020;20(1):468.
8. Shah K, Pandya A, Kotwani P, et al. Cost-effectiveness of portable electrocardiogram for screening cardiovascular diseases at a primary health center in Ahmedabad district, India. Front Public Health. 2021;9:753443.
9. Goodman CS. Introduction to health technology assessment. Bethesda: National Library of Medicine (US); 2014.

# Revolutionizing Healthcare Access: Exploring the Potential of Telehealth Kiosks

5

Varinder Garg, Suchita Markan, Cheena Malhotra, Anupriya Bhardwaj, Ramandeep Bansal, Sujata Saini, and Saana Chaudhary

## 5.1 Introduction

An important norm for a civilized society is to ensure that each of its members has access to affordable and good quality healthcare. It ensures improvement in the health status of the population resulting in improvement in the economy of the nation. However, there are inherent problems in the healthcare (e.g., inadequate infrastructure, high prevalence of unqualified medical quacks) which hinders the provision of proper health services especially in isolated and rural areas. The shortage of healthcare workers, coupled with a large number of patients, results in long waiting times for treatment. This coupled with high cost of private healthcare services eventually forces many patients to stop therapy for chronic diseases.

The shortage of health staff is higher in developing nations including India. According to a recent World Health Organization (WHO) report, India will need at least 1.8 million additional physicians, nurses, and midwives by 2030 in order to reach the benchmark of 44.5 health professionals per 10,000 people [1]. However, at the current growth rates, the projected density of the skilled health personnel is not expected to change by 2030.

There is a significant difference in the availability of healthcare workers and facilities, first between urban and rural locations and second between the public and

V. Garg (✉)
ICMR-Centre for Innovation and Bio-Design (CIBioD), Postgraduate Institute of Medical Education and Research (PGIMER), Chandigarh, Chandigarh, India

C. Malhotra · A. Bhardwaj · S. Saini · S. Chaudhary
ICMR Center for Innovation and Bio-Design, PGIMER, Chandigarh, India

S. Markan
MDMS-ICMR, New Delhi, India

R. Bansal
Department of Obstetrics and Gynecology, PGIMER, Chandigarh, India



V. Garg et al. (eds.), *Innovations in Healthcare Technologies in India*,
https://doi.org/10.1007/978-981-97-0244-2_5

private sectors. About 33% of the country's health professionals reside in rural areas which account for 66% of the country's overall population. The majority of health staff is employed in private sector, which provides for 60% of inpatient and 70% of outpatient care [2]. This increases the cost of healthcare. Given the shortage of professionals in India, particularly in auxiliary public institutions, there is a significant discrepancy in health services offered by the private and public sectors. In community health facilities across India, there is a deficit of 79% for surgeons, 70% for gynecologists, and 78% for pediatricians [3]. Needless to say, there is a vast difference between the need and supply of healthcare services in India.

Telemedicine is a viable option to narrow down these service delivery gaps and provide medical treatment even during epidemics. We have developed a telehealth clinic that serves both as comprehensive diagnostic lab and a hub for specialist consultation. It includes artificial intelligence (AI) technology for real-time data management. Our telemedicine kiosks have the potential to help in achieving the Sustainable Development Goal 3 (SDG3) of ensuring healthy lives, promoting well-being for all, and generating employment opportunities. By leveraging telemedicine and telehealth kiosks, we can bridge the gap in healthcare service delivery, bring healthcare services closer to communities, and improve access to quality healthcare. Our kiosk has the potential to revolutionize healthcare delivery, making it more efficient, affordable, and inclusive.

According to the information provided by the National Medical Commission (NMC), there are 13,08,009 doctors registered with the state medical councils and the National Medical Commission as of June 2022. The doctor (both practicing allopathic medicine and 6.5 lakh AYUSH doctors practicing traditional medicine) to patient ratio in our country is 1:834, which is better than the WHO standard of 1:1000 [4]. More than 75% of the healthcare infrastructure is concentrated in metro cities, where only 27% of the country's population resides. Accordingly, approximately 73% of the Indian population which resides in rural areas does not have access to even basic medical facilities. There is a lack of approximately 3000 doctors in primary health centers which has increased by more than 200% in the last decade [5]. Most of the doctors are employed in private sector, which is not affordable for common population of India [6]. In rural India, only 11% of subcenters, 13% of primary health centers (PHCs), and 16% of community health centers (CHCs) meet the Indian Public Health Standards (IPHS). In 2019, 9.6% of the 24,855 PHCs in India had no doctors, 38.4% were without laboratory technician, and 23.9% were without pharmacist [7, 8]. There are only 1.5 hospital beds per 1000 population.

India is facing a lot of healthcare–related challenges. Changing lifestyles and environment has led to a rise in various communicable (CDs; tuberculosis, leprosy, HIV) and noncommunicable diseases (NCDs; cardiovascular illnesses, chronic respiratory diseases, cancers, and diabetes). The WHO hopes to eliminate tuberculosis only by the year 2050 due mainly to lack of doctors, infrastructure, and other paramedical staff who can actually handle this dreadful disease [9]. According to the International Diabetes Federation (IDF), worldwide 537 million individuals suffer from diabetes, a number which is set to increase to 783 million by 2045. These numbers underscore the need to implement cost-effective measures for care of diabetes [10].

Communicable diseases (CDs) account for 26% of annual deaths in the world and 30% of 1.49 billion disability-adjusted life years (DALYs) which are lost annually. India, being a developing country suffers the most due to morbidity and mortality created by CDs [11]. However, NCDs are not far behind. A recent report released by the India State-Level Disease Burden Initiative shows that three of the top five leading causes of DALYs lost in India were NCDs: coronary artery disease, chronic lung diseases, and stroke. It is estimated that India is likely to lose $4.58 trillion before 2030 due to NCDs [12]. Our telehealth kiosk has the potential to effectively manage NCDs and CDs through early detection, appropriate management, treatment adherence, and better compliance with reduced carbon footprint and enhanced social stability, without putting any extra burden on the patients and the state.

## 5.2 History of Telehealth Kiosks

Telemedicine has been used for decades, with origins in the twentieth century [13]. The best-known telemedicine program, the Extension for Community Healthcare Outcomes (ECHO), was developed by the University of New Mexico Healthcare Center for managing hepatitis C and helped to deliver specialty medical care [14]. Telemedicine has been utilized by the US military for several years. The Walter Reed National Medical Center offers chronic pain consultations to remote military training force (MTF) since 2009. In recent years, telemedicine is being used to treat mental health issues (including opioid-use related problems) in people residing in remote areas [15, 16].

With the rise of the COVID-19 pandemic, telemedicine became very popular. The clinicians and patients adapted to a novel way of medical care. During the pandemic, telemedicine provided a connection between patients and clinicians while maintaining social distancing and avoiding infection transmission [17]. Whether telemedicine will continue in the post-pandemic world depends on many factors. Some of these factors are related to patients, some to the consultants and their practices, and some are related to money reimbursements.

Health kiosks can be installed anywhere. Another example of telehealth kiosks includes health point, a community-based touchscreen kiosk developed and evaluated in Glasgow in 1989 [18]. Nicholas et al. [19, 20] provided data regarding the utility of touchscreen health kiosks located throughout the United Kingdom. They examined the use of a sample of 20 kiosks over three and half years and identified four patterns of use over time. These were a declining pattern, a stable pattern, an increasing pattern, and a no-trend pattern. Porter et al. [2004] [21] developed an asthma kiosk designed to address five critical issues for patient-centered technology to promote guideline-based care in the emergency department (ED). These issues included the following: (i) Develop front-end interface for patient-driven data capture that fits physical and logistical challenges of the ED setting; (ii) implement an interface that is neutral to patient's technology-based experience or medical expertise; (iii) create an architecture for the display and capture of medication data for asthma; (iv) implement a rules-based approach to link parent-derived data to "Best

Practice Guidelines Recommendations" in pediatric asthma; and (v) create output that encourages "activated and informed" patients and "prepared and proactive" providers. Some kiosks such as Wellpoint also included blood pressure, body fat, and body mass index measurements. These have been installed in occupational health settings [22]. Recently, a study on the "Retail Outlet Health Kiosk Hypertension Trial (ROKHYT)" supported the use of text-messaging intervention to improve control of hypertension [23]. In another study, a card-based telehealth kiosk system implemented in a community setting reduced the costs of installing and maintaining individual systems. However, most of the studies on telehealth kiosks have addressed user acceptance of telehealth systems in the context of home residences, and there is a lack of data on their use in community-based systems [24].

Despite successes in efforts to integrate HIV (human immunodeficiency virus) testing into medical kiosks, challenges remain. Kiosk-facilitated self-testing is one novel approach to improve HIV testing. One study recruited emergency department patients, aged between 18 and 64 years, to evaluate the use of tablet-based kiosks to guide the patients to conduct their own point-of-care HIV tests followed by the standard-of-care HIV tests by healthcare workers. Both tests were OraQuick Advance tests. The results showed that patients were comfortable using HIV-testing kiosk [25, 26]. Another study evaluated the role of kiosk as an automated patient history intake device (APHID). Here, the authors used an approach to assess the utility of patient-facing medication reconciliation and allergy review (MRAR) kiosk [27]. Still later, kiosks were developed and used to support self-management strategies for chronic kidney disease [28] and to promote sexual health and prevent sexually transmitted infections and unwanted pregnancies [29]. One study evaluated the efficacy of Guangdong Second Provincial General Hospital's Digital Health Kiosk program, wherein Dingbei telemedicine platform was used to connect rural clinicians to physicians in upper-level health facilities. They reported that the use of telemedicine resulted in better healthcare utilization, more patient satisfaction, decreased out-of-pocket costs, and improved health outcomes [30]. Still later, teleophthalmology was found to give promising results in the diagnosis and management of ophthalmological diseases. Remidio, a proprietary, offline, smartphone-based, automated system of analysis of retinal images can be used to detect referable diabetic retinopathy (RDR) through images taken by a minimally trained healthcare worker with Remidio non-mydriatic fundus (a smartphone-based, non-mydriatic retinal camera) on phone [31, 32].

Two smart walk-in clinics have been prepared by the Center for Innovation and Bio-Design (CIBioD), namely Health Kiosk 101 and Health Kiosk 201, which have systems such as 12-lead electrocardiography, spirometer, blood pressure, body mass index, and weight measurements, rapid strip-based tests, hemoglobinometer, biochemistry analysis, vision assessment, pulse oximeter, digital stethoscope, body temperature measurement, height sensor, otoscope, urine strip test, glucose meter, and dermascope (Fig. 5.1).

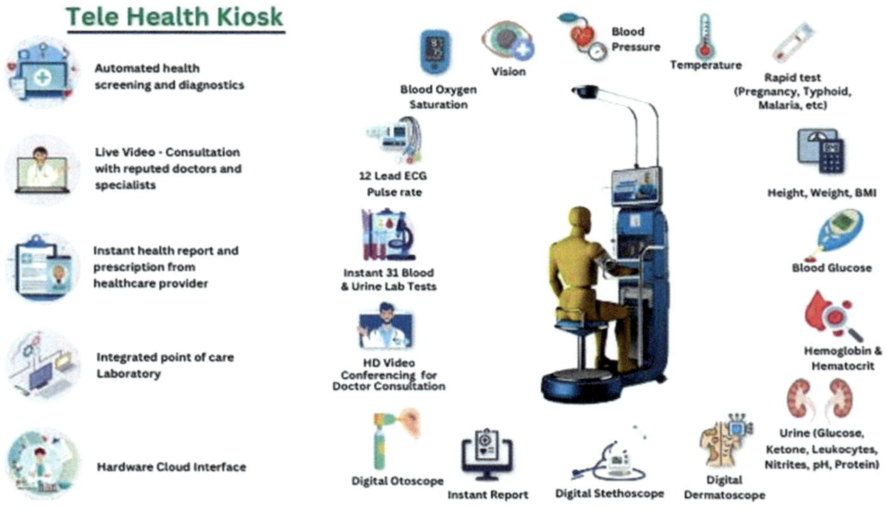


**Fig. 5.1** Representation of telehealth kiosk developed by CIBioD

## 5.3 Estimated Healthcare Kiosk Market in India

It is estimated that, if one healthcare kiosk serves 15,000 people, it will need 59,865 kiosks to cater to approximately 90 crore rural people, while for the urban slum population, assuming that one kiosk can serve 30,000 people, we will need 5655 kiosks. This is supposed to generate employment opportunities for 151,351 people. For a small kiosk without integrated lab, we require one comprehensive health officer (CHO) per machine. There are about 6,64,369 villages in India. If we install one such machine per village, then it will provide employment to around 6,64,369 rural people across the country.

## 5.4 CIBioD Telehealth Kiosk

Telehealth kiosk is an electronic machine that allows patients to connect with healthcare professionals. The ICMR Center for Innovation and Bio-Design (CIBioD), PGIMER, Chandigarh, has upgraded the primary healthcare system with telehealth kiosks (Fig. 5.1). Our telehealth kiosks are equipped with medical devices and communication tools to enable virtual consultations and monitoring. We have devised two kiosk models, i.e., TELEMASTER (TM) 201 (telehealth kiosk with integrated biochemistry lab) and TM 101 (telehealth kiosk without integrated biochemistry lab) which can be integrated into TM 201 in a hub and spoke manner. TM 201 has a built-in, diagnostic lab with a hardware-cloud interface. Our kiosks can provide a point-of-care diagnosis and teleconsultation services to the rural, marginal population at their first point of contact and can measure ten noninvasive body parameters automatically. In addition, more than 85 biochemistry tests/parameters can be performed in the kiosk itself. From the vital acquisition to the lab tests, the entire process is automated and data is stored in the cloud storage. Our kiosk has a 19" LED display with a touchscreen and user-friendly module. A 12-channel electrocardiogram (ECG) and a digital spirometer are also integrated with the kiosk. All these facilities make it a human error-free virtual platform to provide point-of-care diagnostics and teleconsultation services anywhere. It is an innovative, robust, comprehensive, easy-to-install, and -operate telemedicine clinic which can decongest the tertiary care centers and strengthen the primary healthcare system. This kiosk bridges the gap in service delivery and allows uninterrupted services even during situations like epidemics. Our telehealth kiosk consists of automatic height and weight measurement system, noninvasive automatic pressure measurement (NIBP), contactless thermometer for body temperature measurement, pulse oximeter rate and $SpO_2$ measurements, digital stethoscope device, 12-lead ECG integrated devices with built-in thermal printer, spirometer device for lung functions testing, urine analyzer, biochemistry analyzer, dermoscope, otoscope, glucometer, hemoglobinometer, diagnostic tests for dengue, typhoid, malaria, HIV, and pregnancy, and finally measurement systems for urine glucose, urine bilirubin, urine ketone, urine blood, urine pH, urine protein, urine urobilinogen, urine nitrite, and leukocyte. The design patent on the telehealth kiosk has been granted by the Indian Patent Office, Government of India, with design number 346372-001. The procedure to operate our kiosk is shown in Fig. 5.2.

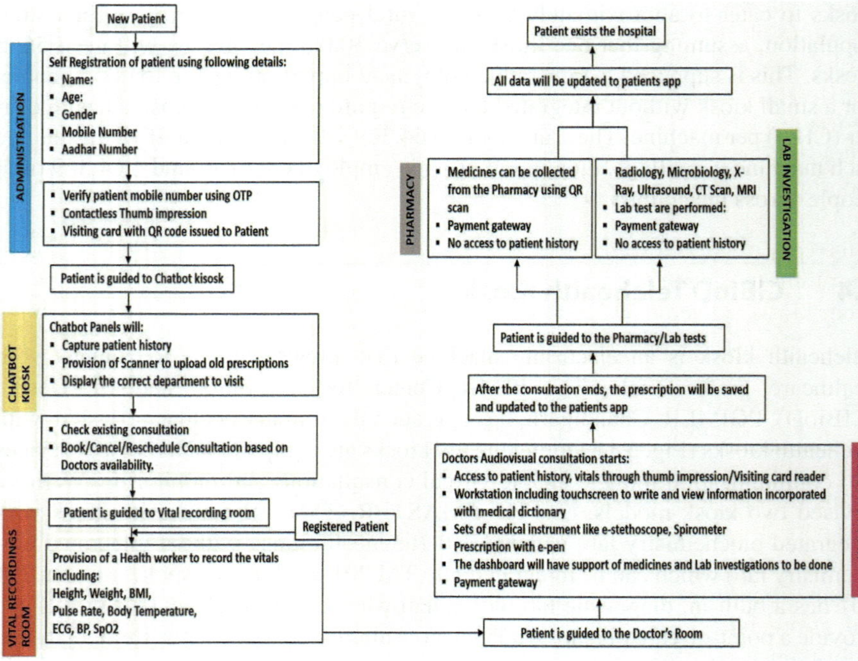


**Fig. 5.2** Flow diagram showing the whole procedure of the operation of a telehealth kiosk

## 5.5 Telehealth Kiosk Incorporates an Advanced AI System

All the gadgets and devices integrated into our telehealth kiosk meet the gold standards, ensuring the highest level of accuracy and reliability. The seamless hardware–software interfacing enables automatic data fetching, eliminating the need for manual entry and reducing the chances of errors. As an example, ECG interpretation is based on an AI-based module which captures 500 samples/s/channel. The signal captured is then interpreted on the basis of an algorithm developed after being trained on Massachusetts Institute of Technology–Beth Israel Hospital (MIT-BIH) databases. The ECG signal is also stored in the kiosk in a secured proprietary format. Spirometry interpretation is based on an AI algorithm which contains prediction equations both for adults and children. The AI-based algorithm evaluates the patient as per their age and sex and selects suitable equations for computation of predicted norms making a basis for interpretation of patient's results. The algorithms used in all integrated devices are AI-enabled in such a way that any malfunctioning device can be auto-detected. The clinical data (patient identification, history, and vitals) and investigations (like ECG, spirometry, blood, and urine tests) are fed and auto-fetched by various devices and equipment in futuristic healthcare delivery (FHCD) kiosk. The entire system has secured data transmission and encrypted data storage. All the devices comply with IEC 60601 standard. The signals fetched from the devices are collected into numerical, visual, and audio formats. We have developed specific software, the components of which are loaded on the medical devices performing the tests and the computing device of the kiosk. This software organizes and stores all the data fed and fetched by all the devices. The data captured in the kiosk can be accessed only through the authenticated credentials (login ID and password). Different levels of hierarchy authorizations (like lab technician and doctor) are used to access the data. Biomedical signals captured by the devices integrated with kiosks are in analog form which are amplified, processed, and then converted into digital format and transmitted to the FHCD kiosk in a proprietary encrypted format. The audio and image data are stored in wave and jpg format, respectively. In the case of data from a biochemistry analyzer (BCA), the BCA has 48 different algorithms to capture the parameters of a blood sample. The basic software features of our kiosk is given in Fig. 5.3.

## 5.6 Insights Gained from Our Experience

The results from patients' feedback form for telehealth kiosk (see Chap. 3 for details) reveals that more than 80% of users gave our kiosk a five-star rating (one star: poor; five star: best) on various parameters (such as appearance of kiosk, convenience of use, accessibility of basic health checkup, ease of giving blood tests and getting report, satisfaction of interaction with medical personnel, speed of service, and affordability), while approximately 20% gave it four-star rating. Only one (0.49%) patient gave a three-star rating to interaction with medical personnel,

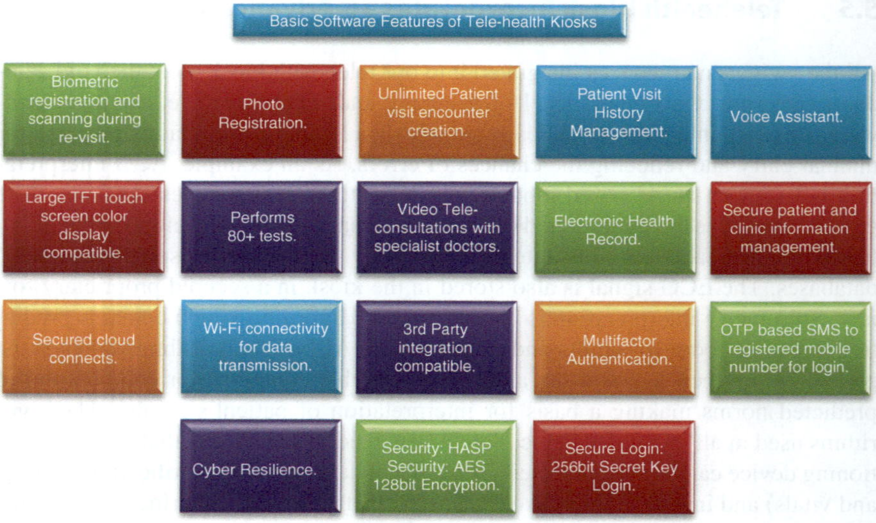


**Fig. 5.3** Basic software features of telehealth kiosks

while six (2.93%) gave three-star rating to speed of service. Similarly, most medical practitioners gave either a four- or five-star rating to our kiosk (refer to Chap. 3 for detailed results).

## 5.7 Conclusion

The use of telemedicine through the deployment of telehealth kiosks at primary health centers appears to have potential for further improvement in healthcare with many advantages such as affordability, accessibility, timely diagnosis, and initiation of treatment for populations which traditionally do not have quick access to healthcare. It allows adherence to treatment and good follow-up, effective implementation of national programs to achieve the SDG3, reduction of human errors, and better synchronization of health data through national health information management system (HIMS) and national digital health mission. It provides opportunities for the promotion of social stability by reducing travel expenditure and saving time and out-of-pocket expenses, along with reduction in the carbon footprint associated with health-related travels.

## References

1. Health workforce in India: where to invest, how much and why? Downloaded from: https://cdn.who.int/media/docs/default-source/searo/india/publications/health-workforce-in-india-where-to-invest%2D%2Dhow-much-and-why.pdf?sfvrsn=8ae98d85_2.
2. Karan A, Negandhi H, Hussain S, et al. Size, composition and distribution of health workforce in India: why, and where to invest? Hum Resour Health. 2021;19(1):39.

3. Ojha DK, Rawat A, Saha A, et al. 2019–2020. Downloaded from: https://hmis.nhp.gov.in/downloadfile?filepath=publications/Rural-HealthStatistics/RHS%202019-20.pdf.
4. India's doctor population ratio 1:834: Minister. Downloaded from https://timesofindia.indiatimes.com/india/indias-doctor-population-ratio-1834-minister/articleshow/105930987.cms.
5. Bajaj S. Digital health for all: importance of digital healthcare in India. Downloaded from: https://timesofindia.indiatimes.com/blogs/voices/digital-health-for-all-importance-of-digital-healthcare-in-india/.
6. Kasthuri A. Challenges to healthcare in India—the five A's. Ind J Comm Med. 2018;43(3):141–3.
7. Alexander A. India's rural public health facilities need urgent fixing. Downloaded from: https://www.livemint.com/Opinion/bMq6hKmYWKXd7P0tM3piaO/Indias-rural-public-health-facilities-need-urgent-fixing.html.
8. Health equity. Downloaded from: https://www2.deloitte.com/content/dam/Deloitte/pt/Documents/life-sciences-health-care/health-equity.pdf.
9. WHO aims to eliminate TB by 2050. Downloaded from: https://www.biospectrumasia.com/analysis/53/2196/who-aims-to-eliminate-tb-by-2050.html.
10. Diabetes now affects 1 in 10 adults worldwide. Downloaded from: https://idf.org/news/diabetes-now-affects-one-in-10-adults-worldwide/.
11. Dikid T, Jain SK, Sharma A, et al. Emerging & re-emerging infections in India: an overview. Ind J Med Res. 2013;138(1):19–31.
12. Bloom DE, Cafiero-Fonseca ET, Candeias V, et al. Economics of non-communicable diseases in India: the costs and returns on investment of interventions to promote healthy living and prevent, treat, and manage NCDs. World Economic Forum: Harvard School of Public Health; 2014.
13. Kim T, Zuckerman JE. Realizing the potential of telemedicine in global health. J Glob Health. 2019;9(2):020307.
14. Arora S, Kalishman S, Thornton K, et al. Expanding access to hepatitis C virus treatment—extension for community healthcare outcomes (ECHO) project: disruptive innovation in specialty care. Hepatology. 2010;52(3):1124–33.
15. Barnett ML, Ray KN, Souza J, et al. Trends in telemedicine use in a large commercially insured population, 2005–2017. J Am Med Assoc. 2018;320:2147e9.
16. Rubin R. Using telemedicine to treat opioid use disorder in rural areas. J Am Med Assoc. 2019;322(11):1029–31.
17. Eccleston C, Blyth FM, Dear BF, et al. Managing patients with chronic pain during the COVID-19 outbreak. Pain. 2020;161:889e93.
18. Jones RB, McLachlan K. HEALTHPOINT: a public access health information system. In: Richards B, editor. Current perspectives in health computing. Weybridge: BJHC Books; 1990. p. 5–69.
19. Nicholas D, Huntington P, Williams P. Health kiosk use: a national comparative study. Aslib Proceedings. 2001;53(4):130–40.
20. Nicholas D, Huntington P, Williams P. Three years of digital consumer health information: a longitudinal study of the touch screen health kiosk. Information Process Manag. 2003;39(3):479–502.
21. Porter SC, Cai Z, Gribbons W, et al. The asthma kiosk: a patient-centered technology for collaborative decision support in the emergency department. J Am Med Inform Assoc. 2004;11(6):458–67.
22. Jones R. The role of health kiosks in 2009: literature and informant review. Int J Environ Res Public Health. 2009;6(6):1818–55.
23. Shea S, Thompson JL, Schwartz JE, et al. The retail outlet health kiosk hypertension trial (ROKHYT): pilot results. Am J Hypertension. 2022;35(1):103–10.
24. Demiris G, Thompson H, Boquet J, et al. Older adults' acceptance of a community-based telehealth wellness system. Informatics Health Social Care. 2013;38(1):27–36.

25. Gaydos CA, Solis M, Hsieh YH, et al. 2013. Use of tablet-based kiosks in the emergency department to guide patient HIV self-testing with a point-of-care oral fluid test. Inter J STD AIDS. 2013;24(9):716–21.
26. Lewis MK, Hsieh YH, Gaydos CA, et al. Informed consent for opt-in HIV testing via tablet kiosk: an assessment of patient comprehension and acceptability. Inter J STD AIDS. 2013;28(13):1292–8.
27. Lesselroth B, Adams K, Tallett S, et al. Usability evaluation of a medication reconciliation and allergy review (MRAR) kiosk: a methodological approach for analyzing user interactions. Stud Health Technol Inform. 2015;218:61–7.
28. Ong SW, Jassal SV, Porter E, et al. Using an electronic self-management tool to support patients with chronic kidney disease (CKD): a CKD clinic self-care model. Semin Dial. 2013;26(2):195–202.
29. Shafii T, Benson SK, Morrison DM, et al. Results from e-KISS: electronic-KIOSK intervention for safer sex: a pilot randomized controlled trial of an interactive computer-based intervention for sexual health in adolescents and young adults. PLoS One. 2019;14(1):e0209064.
30. Cheng W, Zhang Z, Hoelzer S, et al. Evaluation of a village-based digital health kiosks program: a protocol for a cluster randomized clinical trial. Digit Health. 2022;8:20552076221129100.
31. Agrawal T, Agarwal M. Teleophthalmology and its impact-an eye disease pattern analysis in central India's hot spot during COVID-19 pandemic. Indian J Clin Exp Ophthalmol. 2020;6(4):522–6.
32. Natarajan S, Jain A, Krishnan R, et al. Diagnostic accuracy of community-based diabetic retinopathy screening with an offline artificial intelligence system on a smartphone. JAMA Ophthalmol. 2019;137(10):1182–8.

# Comparison of E-stethoscope with Conventional Stethoscope and Its Validation

6

Varinder Garg, Suchita Markan, Basant Kumar, Sujata Saini, and Ritika Mahajan

## 6.1 Introduction

Cardiovascular illnesses continue to remain as the leading causes of mortality. Cardiovascular diseases were responsible for three out of every ten deaths in 2012, killing 17.5 million people worldwide [1, 2]. One of the ways to decrease this mortality is early diagnosis and relevant treatment. Some of the available diagnostic measures for cardiac diseases include electrocardiogram (ECG), echocardiogram, and imaging (both computed tomography [CT] and magnetic resonance imaging) of the heart. Electrocardiograms are ubiquitously available, easy to use, and inexpensive. However, it may not always succeed in diagnosing the presence of structural heart valve anomalies [3]. Echocardiogram, computed tomography (CT) scan and magnetic resonance imaging provide high quality data but are costly and need qualified personnel both for carrying out the tests and for their interpretation, limiting their availability only to big hospitals in major cities [4–8].

Heart auscultation by stethoscope has long been used as a screening tool for early detection of heart disorders [9]. A phonocardiogram (PCG) is a high-fidelity plot of the normal and abnormal heart sounds (HS) obtained by a phonocardiograph. Despite its low cost and simple operation, auscultation of the heart is constrained by three facts. First, a high level of selective sensitivity in a stethoscope

V. Garg (✉)
ICMR-Centre for Innovation and Bio-Design (CIBioD), Postgraduate Institute of Medical Education and Research (PGIMER), Chandigarh, Chandigarh, India

S. Saini · R. Mahajan
ICMR Center for Innovation and Bio-Design, PGIMER, Chandigarh, India

S. Markan
MDMS-ICMR, New Delhi, India

B. Kumar
Department of Cardiology, PGIMER, Chandigarh, India



V. Garg et al. (eds.), *Innovations in Healthcare Technologies in India*,
https://doi.org/10.1007/978-981-97-0244-2_6

(or the sensor used in the stethoscope) is essential as heart sounds (HS) contain a mixture of low-amplitude, high-frequency (HF), and low-frequency (LF), high-amplitude acoustic waves. Second, noise-corrupted HS data obtained with a stethoscope can make it difficult to accurately diagnose heart problems. Third, interpretation of HS is heavily dependent on the listener's training, expertise, and hearing capacity. A new field called "computer-aided auscultation" has emerged with the introduction of electronic stethoscopes (e-stethoscope). The acoustic-based automatic diagnosis of cardiac dysfunction through an electronic stethoscope has gained a lot of attention in recent years thanks to technological advancements in areas like acoustic sensor design, advanced digital signal processing, and computer-based machine learning.

Cardiac sounds represent acoustic signals resulting from the mechanical activity of the heart. These signals can be captured electronically and processed using the right electrical circuits. These can be transmitted electronically and can be heard by medical experts sitting hundreds of kilometers away for correct interpretation and diagnosis of cardiac dysfunction.

We at the Center for Innovation and Bio-Design (CIBioD) have prepared an electronic stethoscope which is a small-sized battery-operated handy device with easy-to-read Light emitting diode (LED) indicator lights. It transmits auscultatory waves to cell phones and speakers via Bluetooth thereby allowing medical experts to interpret them while sitting at a distance. Our electronic stethoscope has AI-enabled automatic interpretation of heart sounds thereby improving results of auscultation. It is included in both our telehealth kiosks TM 101 and TM 201.

We further planned a study to determine the utility of e-stethoscope in listening to and interpreting heart sounds when compared to conventional stethoscope.

## 6.2 Methodology

This study was conducted in 202 patients (men = 66%, females = 34%), attending out-patient department (OPD) or in-patient department (IPD) at the Department of Cardiology at PGIMER, Chandigarh. Cardiac auscultation was carried out by a cardiologist using both traditional (3M, Littmann, Classic III) and electronic stethoscopes. The auscultation was done in a typical patient room and physicians were allowed to perform more auscultations at a specific location until they were satisfied with the sound quality. All the patients underwent echocardiography after cardiac auscultation. The study was approved by the institutional ethics committee (IECs) (approval number IEC-03/2022-2335) and written informed consent was obtained from all the subjects before inclusion in the study.

Each valve was analyzed separately. The study investigators recorded all the normal and abnormal heart sounds separately using both conventional and electronic stethoscopes. All the findings were recorded meticulously. The results of auscultation were then compared with echocardiographic results.

## 6.3 Results

This study included 202 patients, 133 men and 69 women. The most common reasons for hospitalization included dyspnea, chest pain, and abnormal electrocardiogram. The most common valvular abnormality on echocardiography was due to mitral regurgitation. Reasons for hospitalization or consultation with the cardiologist are given in Table 6.1.

When compared, there is no statistically significant difference in the interpretation of cardiac sounds and murmurs when heard through an electronic stethoscope or a conventional stethoscope.

## 6.4 Conclusion

CIBioD invented electronic stethoscope that is simple to use and can detect both normal and abnormal heart sounds with as much efficiency as a conventional stethoscope with some advantages as follows:

(a) Electronic stethoscopes can be used from a distance of 5–6 m, which can be used to maintain social distances especially during a pandemic.
(b) Data can be stored in cloud for future comparisons.

**Table 6.1** Medical reasons for consultation in cardiology department

| S. no. | Medical reasons | Number of patients ($n = 202$) |
|---|---|---|
| 1 | Mild MR (mitral regurgitation) | 31 |
| 2 | Mild AR (aortic regurgitation) | 10 |
| 3 | Mild TR (tricuspid regurgitation) | 6 |
| 4 | Mild AS (aortic stenosis) | 3 |
| 5 | Mild LVH (left ventricular hypertrophy) | 15 |
| 6 | Mild PAH (pulmonary artery hypertension) | 3 |
| 7 | Mod AR | 18 |
| 8 | Mod AS | 2 |
| 9 | Mod TR | 2 |
| 10 | Mod MS (mitral stenosis) | 3 |
| 11 | Mod-Severe MR | 2 |
| 12 | Severe AS | 6 |
| 13 | Severe MS/TR | 14 |
| 14 | Ejection fraction (EF) $\leq 40\%$ | 41 |
| 15 | Ejection fraction (EF) $> 40\%$ | 46 |
| 16 | Others (aortic valve replacement = 1; trivial AR and TR = 2 each; global left ventricle hypokinesia = 9, hypokinesia in distribution of left anterior descending coronary artery territory = 3; coronary artery disease = 2) | 19 |

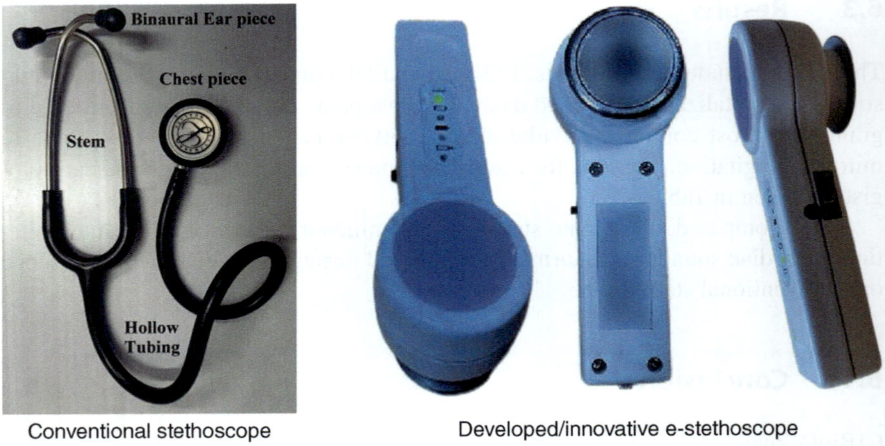


**Fig. 6.1** Conventional and electronic stethoscopes

The major disadvantages are the possibility of connectivity problem and background noise in the kiosk.

The conventional and electronic stethoscopes are given in Fig. 6.1.

## References


1. The top 10 causes of death. http://www.who.int/mediacentre/factsheets/fs310/en/index2.html. Accessed 30 Mar 2015.
2. Morsi YS. Tissue engineering of the aortic heart valve: fundamentals and developments. New York: Nova Science Publishers; 2012.
3. Molcer PS, Kecskes I, Delic V, et al. Examination of formant frequencies for further classification of heart murmurs. In: Proceedings of the international symposium on intelligent systems and informatics; 2010, p. 575–8.
4. How is heart disease diagnosed? http://www.nhlbi.nih.gov/health/health-topics/topics/hdw/diagnosis.html. Accessed 30 Mar 2015.
5. Zhong L, Zhang JM, Zhao XD, et al. Automatic localization of the left ventricle from cardiac cine magnetic resonance imaging: a new spectrum-based computer-aided tool. PLoS One. 2014;9(4):e92382.
6. Tan ML, Su Y, Lim CW, et al. A geometrical approach for automatic shape restoration of the left ventricle. PLoS One. 2013;8(7):e68615.
7. Lim CW, Su Y, Yeo SY, et al. Automatic 4D reconstruction of patient- specific cardiac mesh with 1-to-1 vertex correspondence from segmented contours lines. PLoS One. 2013;9(4):e93747.
8. Cui HF, Wang DS, Wan M, et al. Coronary artery segmentation via hessian filter and curve skeleton extraction. In: Proceeding of 36th international conference IEEE engineering in medicine and biology society (EMBS); 2014.
9. Ericson B. Heart sounds and murmurs: a practical guide. Saint Louis: Mosby Year Book Inc.; 1997.

# 7 Assisted Rambler for the Older Population (Particularly Suffering from Paraplegia)

Manoj Goyal, Karthik Vinay Mahesh, Varinder Garg, Siddhant Mukherjee, Sujata Saini, and Ashita Joshi

## 7.1 Introduction

Maintaining freedom and a good quality of life requires mobility (gait and turning). Gait and turning deficits are invariable accompaniments of advancing age. The profile of older people has changed dramatically over the years as a result of the rapidly changing socioeconomic and demographic scenario, medical science advancement, increased literacy rate, rapid industrialization, migration of younger population, growing popularity of nuclear families, and the breakdown of the joint family system. People have longer life spans than ever before, and at the age of 60, they can expect to live for another 25–30 years. This implies that they will spend nearly a third of their lives in old age. In addition, gait and turning deficits are common among people with neurological diseases resulting in falls, often with disastrous consequences. The common neurological disorders which cause gait problems include parkinsonian syndromes, stroke, multiple sclerosis, tumors, and central nervous system trauma, especially spinal cord injuries [1–7].

Nothing disables a person more than paraplegia, a medical illness characterized by impairment in motor function of the lower extremities. Patients with paraplegia are unable to move their legs, feet, and even their abdomen on their own. Usually, paraplegia in isolation results from lesions of the spinal cord including trauma, neoplasms,

M. Goyal (✉) · K. V. Mahesh
Department of Neurology, Postgraduate Institute of Medical Education and Research (PGIMER), Chandigarh, Chandigarh, India

V. Garg
ICMR-Centre for Innovation and Bio-Design (CIBioD), Postgraduate Institute of Medical Education and Research (PGIMER), Chandigarh, Chandigarh, India

S. Mukherjee · S. Saini · A. Joshi
ICMR Center for Innovation and Bio-Design, PGIMER, Chandigarh, India

 
V. Garg et al. (eds.), *Innovations in Healthcare Technologies in India*,
https://doi.org/10.1007/978-981-97-0244-2_7

demyelinating disorders such as multiple sclerosis, and involvement of cord secondary to vertebral pathologies such as caries of the spine. Every year, about 250,000–500,000 people around the world suffer from spinal cord injury resulting in temporary or permanent impairment in sensory and motor functions of lower extremities alone or in combination with upper extremities [4]. Despite the fact that India has the world's second-largest population, exact data regarding spinal cord injuries is not available [5].

The other common causes of gait problems include parkinsonian syndromes and gait disorders which accompany normal aging. India has more than 100 million elderly people, accounting for 8.6% of the country's total population. The estimated number of patients with Parkinson disease in India is approximately 5.8 lakh, amounting to a crude prevalence rate of 6 to 53/100,000 and a prevalence rate of 247/100,000 for people over the age of 60. In addition, as people age, their mobility deteriorates. The commonest mobility problems in the elderly are related to balance such as imbalance while walking, trouble getting out of a chair, and difficulty in climbing up or down stairs. All these have a significant impact on the lives of elderly people.

The above-mentioned problem presents a more serious issue in developing countries. Developing nations such as India, Pakistan, Bangladesh, and Sri Lanka all have the same problem: a large population with an alarmingly low number of experienced and educated neuro-rehabilitation professionals. Of the 1.4 billion people in India, 70% reside in rural regions and 30% live in poverty, with no access to rehabilitation services. Even in metropolitan regions where private medical services are available, the number of experienced and trained rehabilitation specialists is insufficient to meet the population's needs. Although rehabilitation is now widely acknowledged as a vital necessity for the general public, there remains an enormous gap between the demand for and provision of rehabilitative services. Only a few well-equipped contemporary rehabilitation institutions and experienced individual therapists are currently attempting to cover this vast gap.

At ICMR-CIBioD, we are developing a rambler with assistive technology that will serve as a tool for elderly or disabled people, particularly those suffering from paraplegia, Parkinson's disease, balance and coordination issues, and who require additional support to maintain equilibrium. Our aim is to enable the patient to achieve maximum independence in terms of walking using the residual force potential of the muscles. Our assisted rambler is inexpensive. It has numerous built-in features like sensors, an autonomous braking system that uses a gyroscope and an accelerometer, and an adjustable cushion handle. This rambler will assist patients in receiving physiotherapy in-house. Its inexpensive nature will reduce the cost of frequent physiotherapy sessions. It can be produced in mass and transported easily for widespread availability. It can handle a weight of 150 kg.

Approximately 1% of the world's population, translating into an absolute number of 80 million people, uses a wheelchair. Although the quality of wheelchairs has greatly improved over time, patients still have few options for movement. Patients who use wheelchairs are more likely to develop urinary tract, intestinal, cardiovascular, metabolic, and skin disorders because of lack of movement. This increases morbidity, cost of care, and mortality [8].

A paraplegic walker is an assistive device designed to let paraplegic individuals walk independently. It has navigation and balancing control systems. The navigation panel features built-in algorithms and high torques with four degrees of freedom on each side to assist the patient in moving around on the floor. The balance system uses gyroscopic sensors, force sensors, and encoders to synchronize the patient's balance and movement [9]. Several assistive devices have been used for years to provide mobility to people with paraplegia. Swivel walkers have been used by paraplegic individuals for more than 10 years. This device provides three-point fixation at hips, knees, and ankles, ensuring the patient's intrinsic stability. A pair of swiveling footplates located beneath the body frame offers extrinsic stabilization. Ambulation is accomplished by swaying the trunk sideways, causing the frame to swivel forward on the ground footplate. However, it is not appropriate for every paraplegic patient with disadvantages of slow mobility, comparative metabolic inefficiency, discomfort while getting into and out of the standing position, and poor efficiency on uneven surfaces [10]. Stallard and Major [11] reviewed utility of widely prescribed orthoses with reciprocal walking systems. They concluded that despite the availability of numerous orthoses for paraplegic individuals, their cost, efficacy, and clinical feasibility are all debatable. Another major problem for paraplegic patients is the transition from sitting to standing position. Patients with paraplegia often rely on their upper extremities for proper support during sit-to-stand transition. A vertical lift walker is a nonelectrical gadget that aids in the transition from sitting to standing. However, it lacks sensors and an autonomous braking mechanism [12].

Medical ramblers offer advantages over regular walkers because these have wheels on all four legs. They do not require elevating, while ordinary walkers and two-wheeled walkers must be gently elevated off the ground. They go more easily on rough terrain than regular walkers. They include built-in seating as well. At ICMR-CIBioD, we have developed an assisted rambler which is detailed in the following sections:

## 7.2 Study Product: Medical Rambler

We have developed an assisted rambler for people suffering from paraplegia and gait problems due to various illnesses including (though not limited to) spinal cord injury, multiple sclerosis, and Parkinson's disease. Its design is developed in a way that facilitates an elderly individual with lower hip and knee pain (e.g., for people suffering from painful illnesses of knee and hip joints such as osteoarthritis or rheumatoid arthritis). It incorporates infrared sensors and human detection sensors connected with a message-based buzzer system (placed at the front end of the rambler) which can be turned on/off based on the discretion of the user or the user's guardian. It will help in alerting the nearby individuals whenever the user needs to be given immediate assistance, for instance during a fall. It also has built-in sensors which can alert the user with impaired vision about upcoming obstacles. Our device is sturdy to support the patient's weight and it can withstand 150 kg of weight of the patient. It has an automated braking system using gyroscope and accelerometer to help paraplegic patients to avoid falls. The sensor bag of the rambler is sleek and

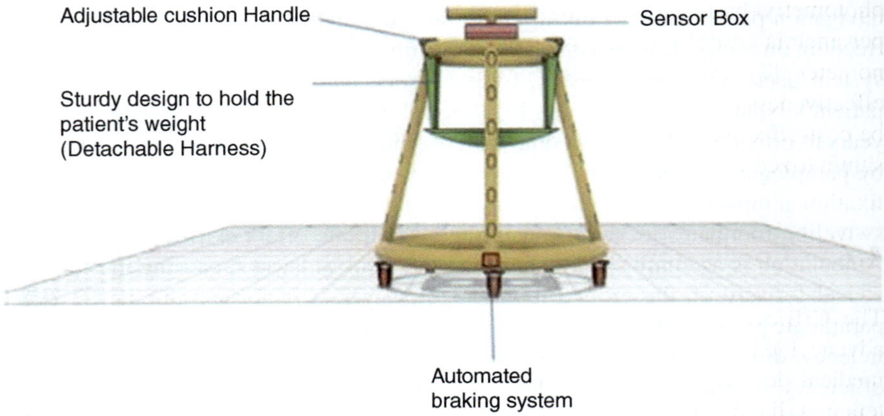


**Fig. 7.1** Front view of the developed rambler

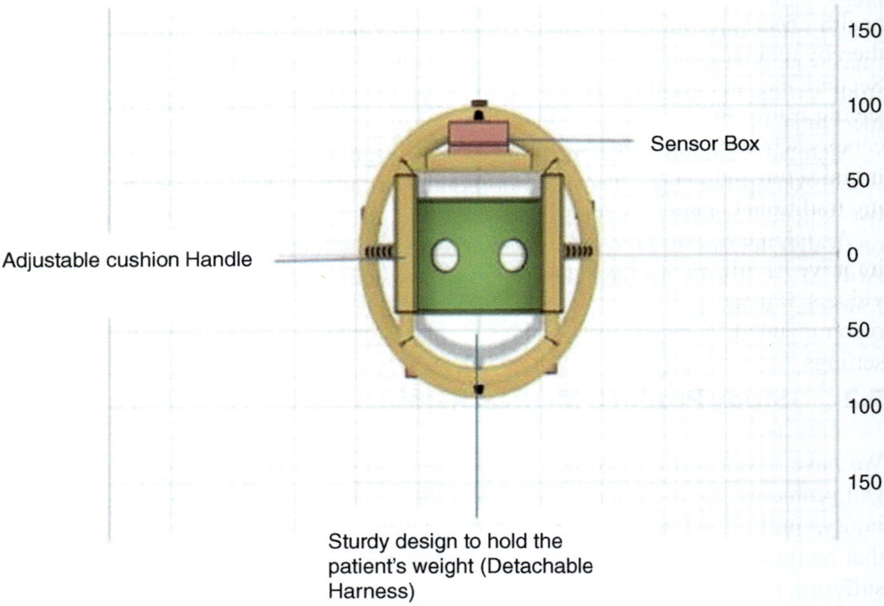


**Fig. 7.2** Top view of the developed Rambler

compact. The sensors are fitted in such a way that they do not interrupt the user when interacting with the rambler. Our rambler is specifically designed in such a way that paraplegic patients can get in and out of the device very easily and without assistance. Our product is very cheap, can be mass manufactured, and made widely available.

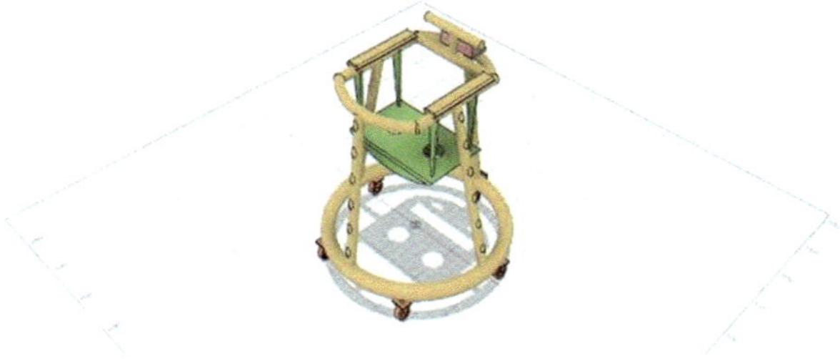

**Fig. 7.3** Complete view of developed medical rambler

A clinical trial is being run at our own institute (PGIMER, Chandigarh) to attest to its efficacy. The front, top, and complete views of our medical rambler are shown in Figs. 7.1, 7.2, and 7.3.

## 7.3 Conclusion

Although the past few decades have seen great advancement in diagnostic and therapeutic services, the same cannot be said for rehabilitation. Accordingly, most people with gait problems remain confined to wheelchair. Even the few medical devices which help in assisted walking, suffer from disadvantages such as high cost and limited availability. Our newly innovated user-friendly and cost-effective medical rambler might play a vital part in helping disabled people to gain more mobility, allowing us to meet the long-term demands of patients with gait problems and paraplegia.

## References


1. Nutt JG, Marsden CD, Thompson PD. Human walking and higher-level gait disorders, particularly in the elderly. Neurology. 1993;43:268–79.
2. Studenski S, Perera S, Patel K, et al. Gait speed and survival in older adults. JAMA J Am Med Assoc. 2011;305(1):50–8.
3. Gait disorders and abnormalities. Downloaded from: https://my.clevelandclinic.org/health/diseases/21092-gait-disorders.
4. Divyalasya TV, Kumar AK, Sahana S, Bhat NR, et al. Quality of life after surviving a spinal cord injury: an observational study in south India. Neurol India. 2021;69(4):861–6.
5. Mathur N, Jain S, Kumar N, et al. Spinal cord injury: scenario in an Indian state. Spinal Cord. 2015;53(5):349–52.
6. Özdemir F. Rehabilitation for patients with paraplegia. J Turk Spinal Surg. 2016;27:185–94.
7. Cubo E, Masdeu JC. Paraparesis and paraplegia. In: Encyclopedia of the neurological sciences. Elsevier Inc.; 2014. p. 790–1.
8. Wheelchair services—World Health Organization (WHO). Downloaded from: https://www.who.int/teams/health-product-policy-and-standards/assistive-and-medical-technology/assistive-technology/wheelchair-services#.
9. Britto P, Rekha V, Sivarasu S. Conceptual design of a paraplegic walker. IET Conference Publications. 2012, p. 1–5. https://doi.org/10.1049/cp.2012.1490.

10. Farmer IR, Poiner R, Rose GK, Patrick JH. The adult ORLAU swivel walker-ambulation for paraplegic and tetraplegic patients. Paraplegia. 1982;20(4):248–54.
11. Stallard J, Major RE. A review of reciprocal walking systems for paraplegic patients: factors affecting choice and economic justification. Prosthetics Orthot Int. 1998;22(3):240–7.
12. Bulea TC, Triolo RJ. Design and experimental evaluation of a vertical lift walker for sit-to-stand transition assistance. J Med Device. 2012;6(1):14504.

# Portable and Rechargeable Digital Automatic AMBU-Bag System for Emergency Mechanical Ventilation

8

Babita Ghai, Varinder Garg, Ravinder Kr. Duvedi, Mandeep Singh, Vikramajit Sharma, Surinder Rana, Sujata Saini, and Shane Dhiman

*Fresh approach to something is what can be used to describe revolutionary changes in thinking, organizations, services, or procedures. It is customary to distinguish between invention and successful application of innovation—a concept made real.*

Dr Varinder Garg

## 8.1 Introduction

The world faced the COVID-19 pandemic with millions of deaths and lots of burden on the healthcare sector. The world was not prepared for it as reflected by the shortage of medical equipment. Although the pandemic has ended, there are many other respiratory illnesses (e.g., severe acute respiratory syndrome [SARS], chronic obstructive pulmonary disease [COPD], asthma, occupational lung diseases, pulmonary hypertension) which need mechanical ventilation. In addition, many other illnesses necessitate the use of ventilatory support to sustain life. Currently available ventilators require trained manpower and are used primarily in intensive care units

B. Ghai
Department of Anesthesia, PGIMER, Chandigarh, India

V. Garg (✉)
ICMR-Centre for Innovation and Bio-Design (CIBioD), Postgraduate Institute of Medical Education and Research (PGIMER), Chandigarh, Chandigarh, India

S. Saini · S. Dhiman
ICMR Center for Innovation and Bio-Design, PGIMER, Chandigarh, India

R. K. Duvedi · M. Singh · V. Sharma
Department of Electrical and Instrumentation Engineering, Thapar University, Patiala, India

S. Rana
Department of Gastroenterology, PGIMER, Chandigarh, India



V. Garg et al. (eds.), *Innovations in Healthcare Technologies in India*,
https://doi.org/10.1007/978-981-97-0244-2_8

or in well-equipped ambulances which is quite expensive. Accordingly, while shifting patients from primary to secondary healthcare centres, AMBU bags are used to provide respiratory support.

Even in secondary or tertiary care centres, many patients in need of ventilatory support are kept waiting due to the unavailability of intensive care unit (ICU) beds or ventilators. During this waiting period, patients can be immensely helped if a less complex ventilator (which can be used easily at the bedside without loss of efficacy) can be provided. In this regard, our indigenous and portable 'digital automatic "AMBU-bag" system' can be used as a substitute to sophisticated ventilators. In absence of any high-skilled computational approach, it can be managed by untrained medical staff or even by attendants of the patient. Accordingly, it can help the patient survive a short period while waiting in a triage room for an ICU bed with ventilatory support.

At present, the number of existing ventilators around the globe is not sufficient during a pandemic or otherwise. This is well exemplified in our own institute (Postgraduate Institute of Medical Education and Research [PGIMER], Chandigarh] where more than 250 seriously ill patients are registered in emergency daily, with 30–40% of them requiring ventilatory support. Emergency wards of PGIMER, Chandigarh, do not have enough ventilators and trained manpower to cater to such a large number of patients.

Therefore, the need for a simple, low cost and easy-to-use ventilatory machine with reasonable efficacy cannot be overemphasized. The AMBU-bag device developed at the Center for Innovation and Bio-Design (CIBioD), PGIMER, Chandigarh, has the potential to meet many of these demands and bridge the gap between the need and the actual availability of ventilatory support machines.

## 8.2 Brief Review of Literature of Portable Emergency Ventilatory Devices

Fahey DG [1] reviewed the history of ventilatory devices. As per the author, based on Vesalius's animal experiments in the sixteenth century, the Royal Humane Society recommended fireside bellows to resuscitate victims of drowning. However, it was in 1957 that the 'AMBU Bag' created by the Danish anaesthetist Dr Henning Ruben appeared and became popular. A similar product was soon developed by Åsmund Laerdal of Norway, in collaboration with the American anaesthesiologists Dr Elam and Dr Safar. Though this self-inflating bag was a simple device, it was extremely effective and enabled medical professionals to support life in virtually any environment, simply by squeezing a bag.

Fogarty et al. [2] proposed to replace traditional bag-valve mask (BVM) with an electric blower ventilator during cardiopulmonary resuscitation. They developed a handheld feedback-controlled device which compensated for mask leaks and allowed delivery of computer-controlled respiratory rates and tidal volumes.

Al Husseini et al. [3] developed a low-cost (prototyping cost = $420; bulk-manufacturing price ≤ $200) portable mechanical ventilator for use in resource-poor settings. It delivered breaths by compressing a conventional bag-valve mask (BVM) with a pivoting cam arm, eliminating the need for a human operator. It was made of acrylic, weighed 9 lbs, was driven by 14.8 VDC (volts of direct current) battery and could adjust the tidal volume (maximum = 750 mL) and respiratory rate via user-friendly input knobs. It also had an assist-control mode and an alarm to indicate over-pressurization of the system.

Jurb et al. [4] created a cheap and small-sized ventilator consisting of a full-face mask, a ventilation blower and integrated sensors without any need for respiration tubes or other external devices. Due to its compact structure, it can be stockpiled and transported easily, thus making it useful during a mass disaster and a pandemic. It was tested and verified in a pneumatical testing environment.

Moundekar et al. [5] reviewed the availability of automatic AMBU-bag ventilatory devices for low-cost ventilation and stressed on inventions made by several researchers. One of these was a low-cost portable ventilator developed by SH Sazal, an M.Sc. Engg student from the Department of Mechanical Engineering, KUET (Khulna University of Engineering and Technology), Khulna. His device delivered breaths by compressing a conventional AMBU bag with a pivoting motor drive mechanism, eliminating the need for a human operator. It supported a tidal volume of 500–600 mL with an adjustable respiratory rate. Another one developed by Rajeev Chauhan and colleagues connected a device (based on the principle of an electric linear actuator which converts the rotary motion into a linear motion) with a mechanism to rhythmically compress a regular adult AMBU. It was provided with a direct current (DC) motor (12–24 V) with a speed regulator which can be used to adjust respiratory rate. Another emergency ventilator called GlasVent was designed by Christou et al. It is an automated version of AMBU bag. It used 3D-printed mechanical parts, widely available materials and off-the-shelf electronic and sensing devices which can be fast assembled. Based on their reviews, Moundekar et al. concluded that existing ventilators are very efficient but have certain drawbacks due to which they are not very helpful. They stressed on the need for future work to achieve low-cost AMBU bag–based automated ventilatory devices by developing policies, updating regulations and securing funding mechanisms for the development and testing of open-source ventilators for everyday use in low-resource settings.

Based on the above review of literature, the need to develop low-cost, efficacious and automated ventilatory device based on existing AMBU-bag technology cannot be overemphasized. We developed one such device at our centre which is being presented. The methodology for developing this device is given below:

## 8.3 Methodology

The whole plan was divided into three steps:

**Phase I**

*Study objective and preparation of prototype:* Our objective was to develop a prototype of low-cost and easy-to-use AMBU bag–based automatic ventilatory device. We proposed a robust and compact mechanism for holding the AMBU bag and subjecting it to successive compression/relaxation while imparting equal clamping thrust from either side. We were able to prepare the ready-to-use final product and obtain a patent granted in its name (376249-001).

**Phase II**

(A) *Clinical Validation and Trials:* The next step is to test and validate our device in real-world settings. This will be performed in the emergency wards of PGIMER, Chandigarh. The study will be subject to approval by the Institutional Ethics Committee and written informed consent will be obtained from all the study participants before their inclusion in the study. The study group will include patients with either primary respiratory (e.g. pneumonia, aspiration pneumonitis, adult respiratory distress syndrome) or non-respiratory illnesses (such as myasthenia gravis, drug overdose) who received ventilatory support with the device in question. The results will be compared with patients who were treated with a conventional AMBU bag system.

The various outcomes are as follows:

(a) Clinical recovery and/or improvement from baseline state.
(b) Success of ventilation: defined as a clinically meaningful rise in chest with auscultable air entry and transcutaneous oxygen saturation above 95%.

Furthermore, we will invite healthcare providers as well as patient attendants to rate the new device on a scale using various parameters with scores ranging from 1 to 5.

(B) *Commercialization:* If results are found in favour of the new device, we will invoke our industrial partners for further processing and marketing.

## 8.4 Results

So far, we have succeeded in preparing our final product and a patent has been granted in its name (376249-001). The technical specifications of the device are as follows:

### 8.4.1 Technical Specifications

**Features**

The main features include:

1. The user can change the inspiration: expiration (I: E) ratio which is fixed in almost all such devices used previously.
2. The user can change breaths per minute (BPM) and select stroke volumes according to the patient's lung capacity.
3. The user can take this anywhere as it is portable and fits easily in a car or an ambulance vehicle.

4. The device can operate on a 12-V charger socket available in modern automobiles/ambulances as well as can charge a dedicated internally integrated 12-V lithium-ion battery power pack simultaneously. The system can switch to battery power supply in case of non-availability of external power.
5. The device uses industrial grade electric drive coupled with a mechanically stable ball screw drive unit for accurately adjusting the digitally controlled reciprocating mechanism for pressing and unpressing of the AMBU bag as per the desired mechanical ventilation control parameters: BPM, I/E ratio and the tidal volume.
6. The device can be switched on using a single toggle switch. All other control settings can be managed from touchscreen-enabled graphical user interface in three easy steps.
7. The presence of two air vents and an exhaust fan for controlling the temperature allows continuous use of the device.
8. The four-rubber based anti-skid mounting pads enable the device a firm positioning on hard surfaces.
9. It has two nylon handles with vertical upright location making the device easy to lift and locate for emergency use.
10. This ventilatory device can accommodate the gold standard AMBU bags of different designs from various standard companies without any internal adjustments.
11. The device can be easily sanitized using ultraviolet light chamber or alcohol-based sanitizers.

Our device is an emergency AMBU bag–based mechanical ventilator. It has a touch-sensitive OLED screen with three different modes which can be selected by the user. The modes include breath per minute (BPM)—10, 12, 14; I/E Ratio: 1, 1.5, 2, 2.5, 3; Displacement: 30 mm, 40 mm and 50 mm. The front and inner views of device as well its internal structure and mode of functioning are illustrated in Figs. 8.1, 8.2, 8.3, 8.4, 8.5 and 8.6.

To conclude, our design is an electromechanical actuating device accepting commands from a microcontroller-based OLED touchscreen panel. It works on a lithium-ion battery with a capacity of 44,000 mAh. It can be charged via a USB type C charger used in mobile phones. Our device can run on battery for at least 8 hours. Our machine can be carried easily with minimal effort.

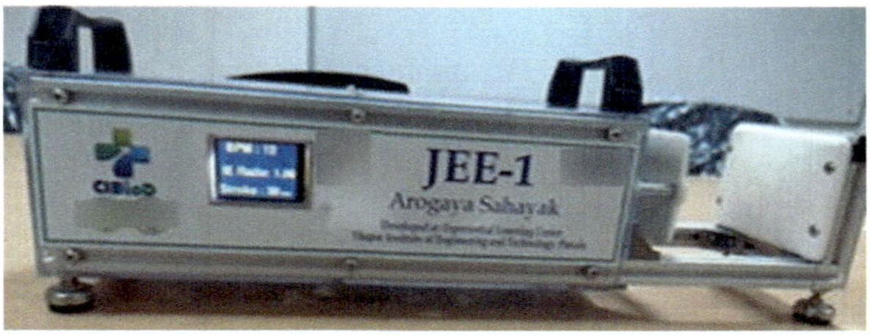


**Fig. 8.1** Front view

**Fig. 8.2** Inner view

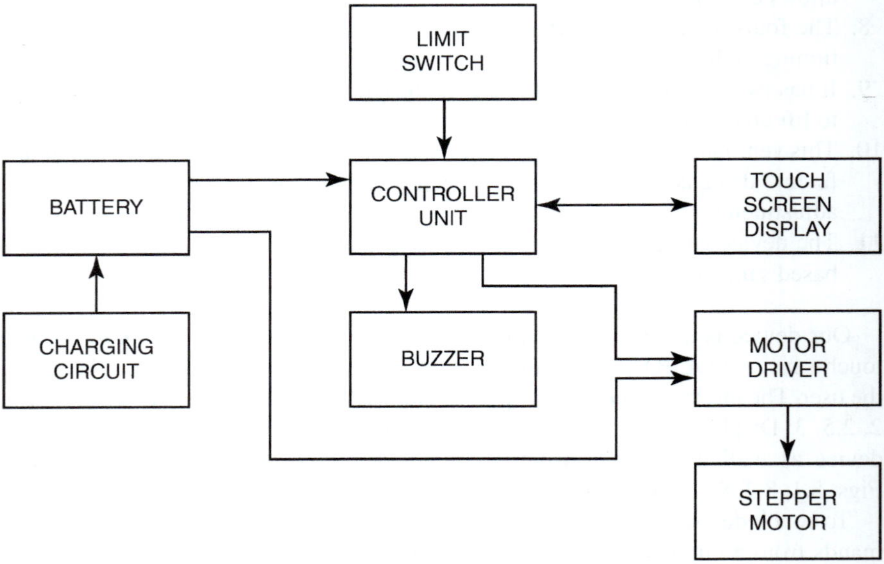


**Fig. 8.3** Electronic block diagram of JEE-1 (automatic AMBU-bag system)

## 8.4.2 Algorithm Used by JEE-1

*JEE-1 uses the following algorithm for its functioning:*

1. *Initialize Device Parameters:* The parameters include *breath rate per minute* ($B_P$), *inhalation/exhalation ratio* ($I$:$E$) and *ram displacement* ($D$) in mM.
2. *C Compute: Cycle time* ($T_C$), *inhalation time* ($T_I$) and *exhalation time* ($T_E$) in seconds are given by the following equations:

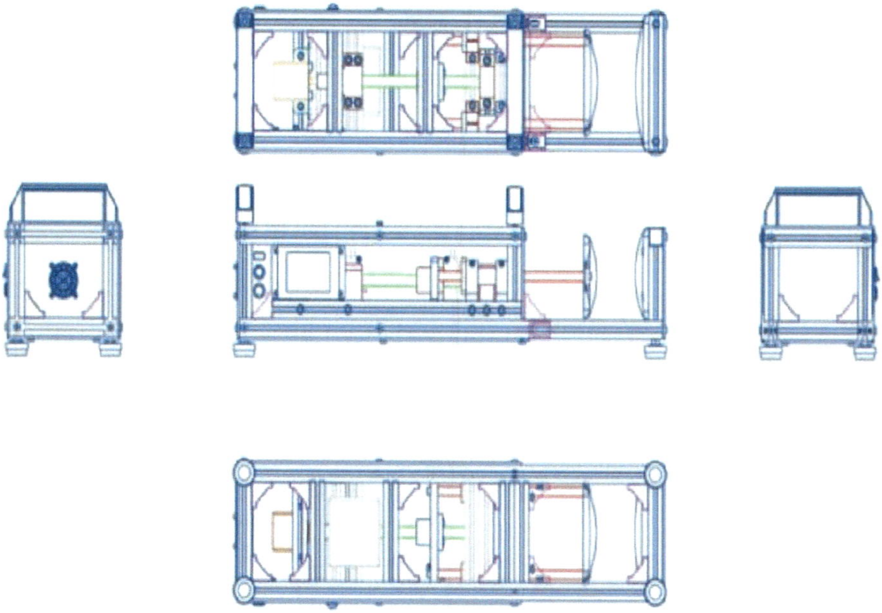

**Fig. 8.4** JEE-1 (automatic AMBU-bag system) from different views

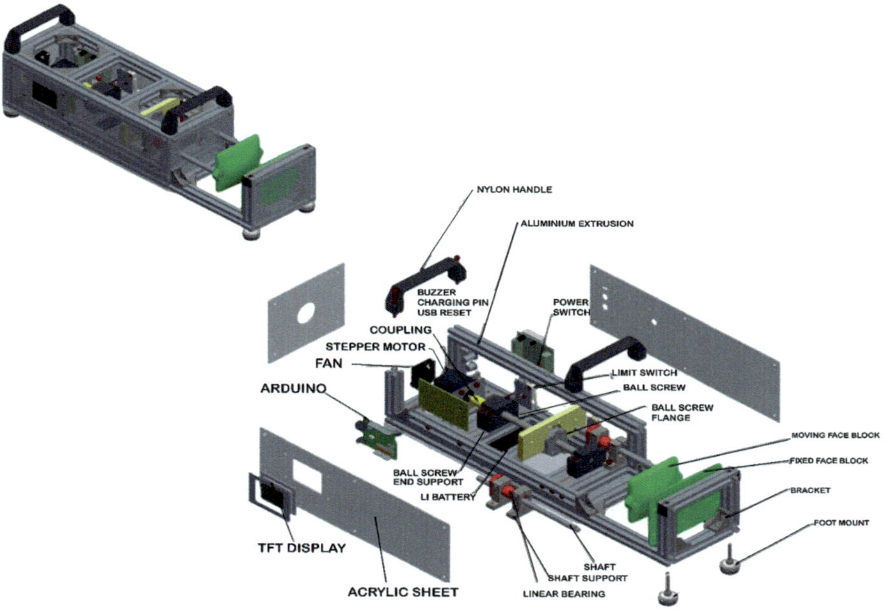


**Fig. 8.5** CAD drawings showing the inner structure of JEE-1 (automatic AMBU-bag system)

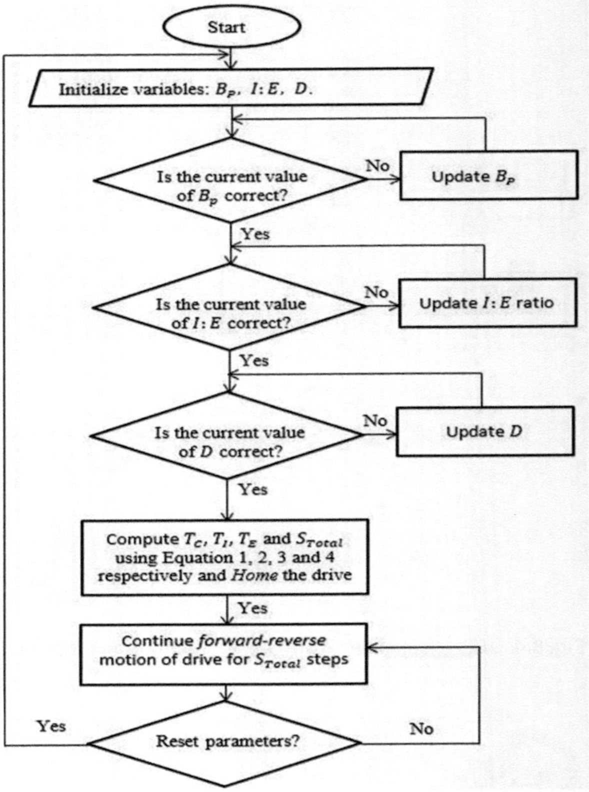


**Fig. 8.6** Flowchart showing the inner working of JEE-1 (automatic AMBU-bag system)

$$T_C = \frac{60}{B_P} \tag{8.1}$$

$$T_I = T_C \times (1/1 + E) \tag{8.2}$$

$$T_E = T_C \times \left(\frac{E}{1+E}\right) \tag{8.3}$$

3. *Computation: Total number of commands* ($S_{Total}$). It is required to execute the *ram displacement* ($D$) during forward-stroke (for inhalation) and reverse-stroke (for exhalation). $S_{Total}$ can be determined in terms of *lead* of *ball screw assembly* ($L$) *in Mm* and the *angular displacement per command* ($\theta_C$) *in degrees* for electric actuator as given by the following equation:

$$S_{Total} = \frac{D \times 360^{\circ}}{L \times \theta_C} \tag{8.4}$$

4. For forward-stroke (during inhalation step), execute $S_{Total}$ steps in forward motor direction within the time period $T_I$.
5. For reverse-stroke (during exhalation step), execute $S_{Total}$ steps in reverse motor direction within time period $T_E$.
6. Execute the device operation.

## References

1. Fahey DG. The self-inflating resuscitator-evolution of an idea. Anaesth Intensive Care. 2010;38(1):10–5.
2. Fogarty M, Orr J, Westenskow D, et al. Electric blower based portable emergency ventilator. 2018. Downloaded from https://api.semanticscholar.org/CorpusID:55227533.
3. Al Husseini AM, Lee HJ, Negrete J, et al. Design and prototyping of a low-cost portable mechanical ventilator. J Med Device. 2010;4(2):027514.
4. Jürß H, Degner M, Ewald H. A new compact and low-cost respirator concept for one way usage. IFAC-PapersOnLine. 2018;51(27):367–72.
5. Moundekar J, Choudhari P, Sahare K, et al. A review on automatic Ambu bag operating device for low-cost ventilator. JETIR. 2021;8:d600–4.

# Antimicrobial Metallo-Detergents as Disinfectants: Smart Materials for Fighting Community-Acquired Infections

9

Gurpreet Kaur, Rakesh Sehgal, Ganga Ram Chaudhary, Harshita Sharma, Varinder Garg, Sujata Saini, and Shane Dhiman

*Since pandemic-like scenarios could arise again, effective cleaning and hygienic measures are still necessary.*

-Dr. Varinder Garg

## 9.1 Introduction

In the aftermath of the COVID-19 pandemic, the need to develop antimicrobial agents with the capability to overcome antibiotic-resistance cannot be overemphasized. This can be achieved by either developing novel drugs or functionalizing the antimicrobial agents that are already available commercially. The development of new antibiotics needs a very long period (10–15 years) and is quite expensive. Thus, we chose the second approach and functionalized the cheaper and easily available surfactants by embedding metal ions in their molecular structures. These functionalized surfactants are termed metallosurfactants (MT) and function through the integration of properties of both organic and inorganic components. More specifically, the integration of metal ions into conventional surfactants affects their solvation, interfacial behavior, adsorption, surfactant geometry, and aggregation characteristics.

G. Kaur · G. R. Chaudhary
Department of Chemistry, Panjab University, Chandigarh, India

R. Sehgal · H. Sharma
Department of Medical Parasitology, PGIMER, Chandigarh, India

V. Garg (✉)
ICMR-Centre for Innovation and Bio-Design (CIBioD), Postgraduate Institute of Medical Education and Research (PGIMER), Chandigarh, Chandigarh, India

S. Saini · S. Dhiman
ICMR Center for Innovation and Bio-Design, PGIMER, Chandigarh, India

 
V. Garg et al. (eds.), *Innovations in Healthcare Technologies in India*,
https://doi.org/10.1007/978-981-97-0244-2_9

Metallosurfactants have several potential advantages over conventional surfactants including better wetting, emulsification, surface tension reduction, and detergency functions. But perhaps their most important advantage lies in possessing a broad spectrum of antimicrobial and antifungal activity. More importantly, metallosurfactants work through multiple mechanisms at the same time to kill microbes which includes the destruction of cell membranes, generation of reactive oxygen species by metal ions, and degradation of internal cellular components such as DNA, RNA, or enzymes. As metallosurfactants exert their antimicrobial effects through multiple mechanisms, to show resistance against these, microbes need multiple simultaneous gene mutations which are unlikely to happen. Thus, it seems prudent to state that metallosurfactants provide a novel way of avoiding microbial infections and can work as disinfectants in food, textile, agricultural, cosmetic, medical, and pharmaceutical industries [1–9]. So, at the Center for Innovation and Bio-Design (CIBioD), we developed metallosurfactants and tested their antimicrobial efficacy with the aim to develop novel disinfectants which are both better in efficacy and resistant to microbial efforts to overcome their efficacy.

## 9.2 Methodology

### 9.2.1 Preparation of Metallosurfactants

We added iron and copper ions, respectively, to CTAC (cetrimonium chloride) and CPC (cetyl pyridinium chloride) surfactants to prepare four different types of single-chain and four different types of double-chain metallosurfactants as follows:

FeCTAC I: Drug 1
FeCTAC II: Drug 2
CuCTAC I: Drug 3
CuCTAC II: Drug 4
FeCPC I: Drug 5
FeCPC II: Drug 6
CuCPC I: Drug 7
CuCPC II: Drug 8

Surfactant metal complexes were synthesized by ligand insertion method [10] using respective metal chlorides as complexing agents and dodecyl amine as ligand. All the reactions were performed by dissolving 1:2 (metal/ligand) molar ratios in dimethylformamide (DMF) and heating the contents at 338 K with continuous stirring for 2 h. Stirring is done to avoid adsorption of unreacted metal salt on the metallosurfactant molecule. The temperature was controlled carefully as exceeding the temperature beyond 338 K resulted in a degraded black product. The addition of ligand to metal ion solution resulted in instantaneous color shift. Crystals obtained after the completion of reaction were filtered and dried under vacuum. Recrystallization was done in a mixture of absolute alcohol and hexane (4:1). Traces of solvent were removed by using a vacuum pump and the crystals obtained were stored in desiccators. Synthesized metallosurfactants were fairly soluble in organic solvents like chloroform and higher alcohols.

After preparing these metallosurfactants, we tested their antibacterial and antifungal activity.

## 9.2.2 Testing for Efficacy for Drugs

### 9.2.2.1 Well Diffusion Assay (To Check Efficacy of Drugs)

**Procedure**

Add nutrient broth (NB) in test tubes. Inoculate different bacterial strains [*Staphylococcus aureus*, methicillin-resistant *Staphylococcus aureus* (MRSA), *Pseudomonas maltophilia*, *Pseudomonas aeruginosa*, *Escherichia coli*, and *Acinetobacter baumannii*] by a loop into nutrient broth and incubate at 37 °C for 24 h. Take 100 mL flasks and add 20 mL of NB in each flask and store at 4 °C. Once turbidity appears in test tubes, add 100 μL of growth into each flask and centrifuge at 3200 rpm for 15 min. Now dilute the bacterial pellet in 300 μL PBS (phosphate buffer solution) and spread 100 μL of this solution on MH (Meuller Hinton) agar plates. Streak plates with bacteria with the help of an L-shaped loop and then puncture the wells under aseptic conditions. Take 50 μL aqueous solution of different metallosurfactants of concentrations ranging from 0.05 to 100 mg/mL and incubate overnight at 37 °C.

**MTT (Dimethyl Thiazole Diphenyl Tetrazonium) Assay**

(a) *Antifungal Assay*
   1. A plate of *C. albicans* was streaked to acquire a 24-h growth so that we can use a single colony for the assay.
   2. The next day, 1 mL saline was prepared in 2 mL MCT (microcentrifuge tube). A single colony of *Candida albicans* was inoculated to MCT.
   3. RPMI (Roswell Park Memorial Institute) 1640 media with MOPS (morpholinopropane-1-sulfonic acid) buffer was prepared.
   4. OD (Optical density) of 0.13 was taken at the wavelength of 540 nm to get $10^8$ cells.
   5. Cells were diluted to $10^6$ cells per well by adding 950 μL of media and 50 μL cells from MCT.
   6. About 50 μL this mixture was added to each well of the plate with 96 wells.

(b) *Antibacterial Assay*
   1. A loop of each bacterium was inoculated to the nutrient broth and left overnight.
   2. Then, 200 μL of growth in 20 mL of MHB was added and left in a shaker at 37 °C for 4 h to obtain the mid-log phase.
   3. The 0.5 Mac Farland was set at 600 nm wavelength to get $10^8$ cells and 100 μL of it was added to their respective metallosurfactants plates and incubated for 24 h.

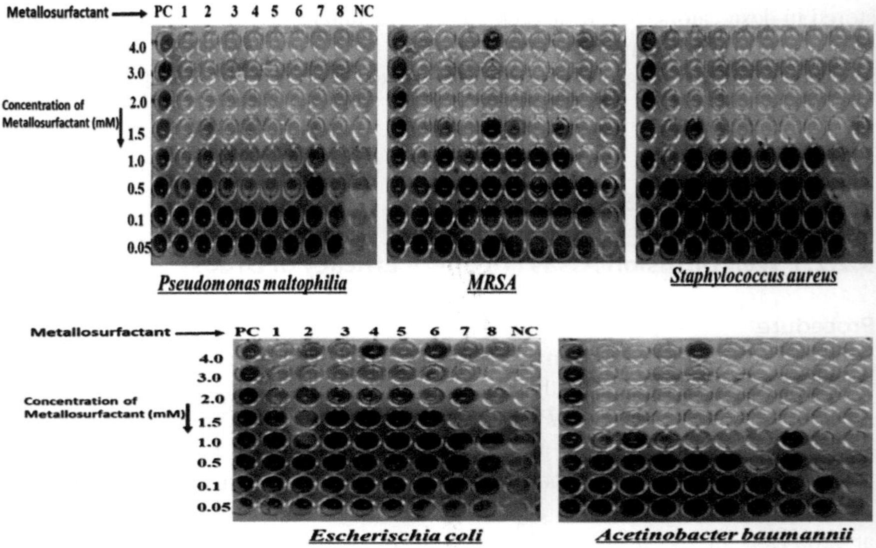


**Fig. 9.1** The image shows four sets of microtiter plates testing the effect of varying concentrations of metallosurfactant on different bacteria: Pseudomonas maltophilia, MRSA, Staphylococcus aureus, Escherichia coli, and Acinetobacter baumannii. Each set includes wells with concentrations ranging from 0.05 to 4.0 mM. The plates display color changes indicating bacterial growth or inhibition, with darker colors suggesting higher bacterial presence. Controls are labeled as PC (positive control) and NC (negative control)

4. MTT assay was performed by adding 10 μL of 5 mg/mL MTT dye and incubated for 4 h.

(c) *Plating of Metallosurfactants*

1. Prepare serial dilutions of 6 μm, 3 μm, 1.5 μm, 0.75 μm, and so on till 46 nm.
2. Now add 50 μL of this to the first well of 6 μm.
3. Add 100 μm of metallosurfactants to 3 μm and add 100 μm RPMI media to each well.
4. Serially dilute it from 3 μm by adding 100 μm to all wells further and dispense 100 μm from the last well.
5. Now add 100 μL of 3 μm of *Candida* and then add 10 μL of MTT dye and incubate for 2 h.
6. Later, 200 μL of absolute ethanol was added and OD was taken at 660 nm. The plates of antibacterial assay are shown in Fig. 9.1.

(d) *Flow Cytometry*

It was performed by ANNEXIN kit purchased from Sigma Aldrich.

## 9.3 Results

For gram-negative bacteria: *E. coli* and *Acinetobacter baumannii*

- $IC_{100}$ = 3 mM for double-chain metallosurfactant.
- Metallosurfactants exhibit more activity toward *E. coli* compared to *Acinetobacter baumannii.*
- Double-chain metallosurfactants (FeCTAC II, CuCTAC II, FeCPC II, CuCPC II) possessed higher inhibition efficiency than single chain metallosurfactants (FeCTAC I, CuCTAC I, FeCPC I, CuCPC I).
- MTT assay showed 100% killing efficacy against all tested bacteria with a 3 mM concentration of metallosurfactants.
- Copper-based metallosurfactants exhibit higher antibacterial efficacy than iron-based metallosurfactants as confirmed by flow cytometry data.
- Flow cytometry displayed approx. 70–80% inhibiting efficiency with single-chain metallosurfactants (FeCTAC I, CuCTAC I, FeCPC I, CuCPC I) and 100% inhibiting efficiency with double-chain metallosurfactants (FeCTAC II, CuCTAC II, FeCPC II, CuCPC II) at 3 mM.
- For *S. aureus, MRSA, Pseudomonas maltophilia*, and *Pseudomonas aeruginosa*:
- The zone of inhibition with metallosurfactants was observed at a very low concentration (1.0 mM), whereas the maximum zone of inhibition was observed at 3.0 mM, $IC_{100}$ = 3 mM.
- Maximum antibacterial activity was noted against *MRSA*.
- Double-chain metallosurfactants (FeCTAC II, CuCTAC II, FeCPC II, CuCPC II) displayed higher inhibition efficiency than single-chain metallosurfactants (FeCTAC I, CuCTAC I, FeCPC I, CuCPC I).
- *Pseudomonas aeruginosa* was found to be resistant to all metallosurfactants.
- MTT assay showed 100% killing efficacy against all tested bacteria with a 3 mM concentration of metallosurfactants.
- Flow cytometry displayed approx. 70–80% inhibiting efficiency by single-chain metallosurfactants and 100% inhibiting efficiency by double-chain metallosurfactants.
- The plates of antibacterial assay are shown in Fig. 9.2.

### 9.3.1 Comparison

- The parent surfactants, i.e., CTAC and CPC, exhibited bacterial inhibition at high concentrations (~50 mg/mL), whereas their metallosurfactants CTAC were effective even at 2 mg/mL (functionalized metallosurfactants) and metallosurfactants CPC was effective at 3 mg/mL concentration. So, our metallosurfactants exhibited high antibacterial activity at lower concentrations compared to parent surfactants.
- Most of the reported metallosurfactants in literature are water-insoluble, while metallosurfactants prepared at CIBioD are highly water-soluble and thus suitable

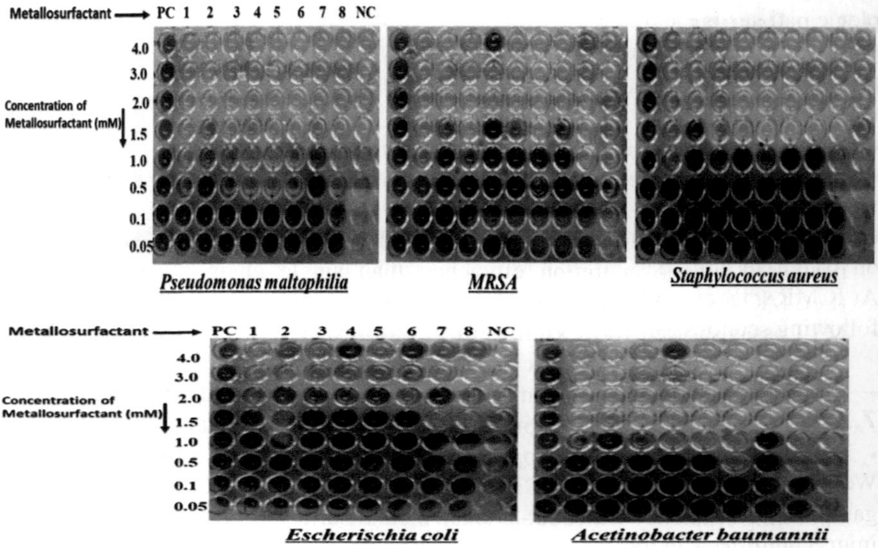


**Fig. 9.2** The image shows four microtiter plates testing the effect of varying concentrations of a metallosurfactant on different bacteria: Pseudomonas maltophilia, MRSA, Staphylococcus aureus, Escherichia coli, and Acinetobacter baumannii. Each plate has wells labeled PC (positive control), 1 to 8, and NC (negative control), with concentrations ranging from 0.05 to 4.0 mM. Color changes in the wells indicate bacterial growth inhibition, with darker wells suggesting higher inhibition

for antimicrobial activity in water samples. Thus, these are environmentally friendly as well.

- In comparison to previous surfactants, these metallosurfactants are cheaper and highly stable.

## 9.3.2 Brief Note and Potential Advantages

- The world has witnessed several incidents of epidemics and pandemics since as far as humans can remember. The gruesome effects of microbial threats pose considerable repercussions on healthcare systems. The continuously evolving nature of viruses due to mutation or re-assortment may make existing medicines and vaccines ineffective. During these times, antimicrobial surfactants help to prevent the rapid spread of infectious diseases by deactivation of microorganisms.
- In the modern world, we need antimicrobial agents which have a broad spectrum of antimicrobial and antifungal activity, and which can overcome antibiotic resistance among microbes. As mentioned earlier, metallosurfactants kill microbes through multiple mechanisms which makes it difficult for microbes to develop resistance to these chemicals.

- Metallosurfactants prepared by CIBioD are cheaper and highly stable and show antimicrobial activity against a wide range of gram-positive and gram-negative bacteria as well as fungi. These can be manufactured easily in large amounts without the need for a new industry or set up. These surfactants are water soluble and biodegradable with very low toxicity and are thus environmental-friendly. They form micelles at lower concentration and thus serve as better cleansing agents than conventional surfactants.
- These metallosurfactants have been synthesized from the already available materials in the market. This combination of surfactants and metal salts in a desirable ratio results in the enhanced activity both in terms of cleansing and antimicrobial action.
- Metallosurfactants developed by CIBioD are alcohol-free. Microbes have already developed resistance against alcohol-based formulations and are banned by the WHO before COVID-19 pandemic.

## 9.4 Conclusion

All the eight metallosurfactants (four single-chain and four double-chain) prepared at CIBioD showed high antimicrobial and antifungal activity. Their detergent-like properties (being amphiphilic in nature) enable them to be used in future as cleansing agents. Their solid formulations can be prepared in convenient sachets and used by just dissolving them in water. Metallosurfactants developed at CIBioD can be used as disinfectants in food, textile, agriculture, cosmetic, medical, and pharmaceutical industries.

## References

1. Mancin F, Scrimin P, Tecilla P, Tonellato U. Amphiphilic metalloaggregates: catalysis, transport, and sensing. Coord Chem Rev. 2009;253:2150–65.
2. Er H, Ohkawa S, Iida M. Aggregation behavior of alkylethylenediamine palladium (II) complexes in water and in water/organic solvent mixtures. Colloids Surf A Physicochem Eng Asp. 2007;301(1–3):189–98.
3. Bowers J, Amos KE, Bruce DW, Webster JRP. Surface and aggregation behavior of aqueous solutions of Ru (II) metallosurfactants. 3. Effect of chain number and orientation on the structure of adsorbed films of [Ru(bipy)2(bipy')]Cl2 complexes. Langmuir. 2005;21(4):1346–53.
4. Fallis IA, Griffiths PC, Hibbs DE, et al. Solid state and solution behaviour of novel transition metal containing surfactants. Chem Commun. 1998;6:665–6.
5. Kriste AG, Vizitiu D, Thatcher GRJ. A metallomicelle enzyme model for phospholipase C catalysis and inhibition. Chem Commun. 1996;8:913–4.
6. Amos KE, Brooks NJ, King NC, et al. A systematic study of the formation of mesostructured silica using surfactant ruthenium complexes in high- and low-concentration regimes. J Mater Chem. 2008;18:5282–92.
7. Behm CA, Creaser KDB, Geue RJ, et al. Novel cationic surfactants derived from metal ion cage complexes: potential anthelmintic agents. J Chem Soc Chem Commun. 1993;24:1844–6.

8. Behm CA, Boreham PFL, Creaser KDB, et al. Novel cationic surfactants derived from metal ion cage complexes: potential antiparasitic agents. Aust J Chem. 1995;48:1009–30.
9. Kumar RS, Arunachalam S. Synthesis, micellar properties, DNA binding and antimicrobial studies of some surfactant-cobalt (III) complexes. Biophys Chem. 2008;136(2–3):136–44.
10. Akanni MS, Okoh EK, Burrows HD, Ellis HA. The thermal behaviour of divalent and higher valent metal soaps: a review. Thermochim Acta. 1992;208:1–41.

# Design and Prototype of an Economical and Reusable Air-Purifying Respirator: Snorkel Mask

10

Ramandeep Virk, Babita Ghai, Varinder Garg, Harish Kumar, Siddhant Mukherjee, Ramandeep Bansal, Sujata Saini, and Anupriya Bhardwaj

## 10.1 Introduction

The coronavirus disease 2019 (COVID-19) first emerged in December 2019 in Wuhan, China, and was declared a pandemic on March 11, 2020 [1]. The most common mode of spread of COVID-19 is through droplet transmission. The enormous load of patients suffering from this life-threatening respiratory illness created extreme pressure on healthcare services resulting in a shortage of both equipment and manpower. Furthermore, numerous healthcare workers (HCWs) also contracted the disease during aerosol-generating procedures further depleting an already overstretched healthcare system [2]. The same pattern was observed during other pandemics as well. During the 2002–2003 severe acute respiratory syndrome (SARS) epidemic, 20% of all patients were HCWs, and about 10% of those infected lost their lives [2]. Considering the fact that the primary mode of transmission of respiratory illnesses is via inhalation of respiratory droplets and aerosols produced during coughing, sneezing, talking, singing, or

R. Virk
Department of ENT (Otolaryngology), PGIMER, Chandigarh, India

B. Ghai
Department of Anesthesia, PGIMER, Chandigarh, India

V. Garg (✉)
ICMR-Centre for Innovation and Bio-Design (CIBioD), Postgraduate Institute of Medical Education and Research (PGIMER), Chandigarh, Chandigarh, India

S. Mukherjee · S. Saini · A. Bhardwaj
ICMR Center for Innovation and Bio-Design, PGIMER, Chandigarh, India

H. Kumar
Department of Computer Science and Engineering, University Institute of Engineering and Technology (UIET) Panjab University, Chandigarh, Punjab, India

R. Bansal
Department of Obstetrics and Gynecology, PGIMER, Chandigarh, India



V. Garg et al. (eds.), *Innovations in Healthcare Technologies in India*,
https://doi.org/10.1007/978-981-97-0244-2_10

breathing, personal equipment to protect HCWs from airborne microbes during aerosol-generating procedures is of paramount importance. The main problems faced with conventional masks/respirators are that these are not washable, sterilizable, sanitizable, or reusable, and these interfere significantly with hearing and communication (as these lack wireless communication systems) during procedures. Moreover, the available respirators are not fully leak-proof exposing HCWs to a risk of inhalation of aerosols. Therefore, the need for an aerosol-tight, anti-microbial, leak-proof, wireless respiratory apparatus which allows for communication during patient care is justifiable.

Some of the available means of protection from airborne microbes include:

### 10.1.1 Respiratory Protective Devices

These include face masks, particulate filtering facepiece respirators (FFR), elastomeric half facepiece or mask respirators, and powered air-purifying respirators (PAPRs). Face masks are simple barriers that can be worn over the mouth and nose to prevent the dispersion and inhalation of respiratory droplets. FFRs are disposable, cover the nose and mouth, and filter out particles such as dust, mist, and fumes. Depending on the filtration capacity, the FFRs can be of N, R, and P series with 95%, 99%, and 100% efficiency levels, respectively—e.g., N95 respirators can filter out 95% of airborne particles, including viruses and bacteria. However, FFRs do not ensure protection against gases and vapors.

PAPRs provide better protection by filtering out the air's harmful particles while simultaneously providing a constant flow of clean air. However, healthcare workers (HCWs) were not able to use PAPR during patient care due to limitations such as:

- The visual field of the HCWs may be disturbed as PAPR allows only a limited vertically downward field of view.
- The HCW's ability to hear may be reduced because of the noise of the blower and the noise induced by the movement of loose head covering.
- The HCW's ability to use a stethoscope is limited.
- PAPR batteries need to be recharged or replaced.
- PAPRs require a significant amount of storage space.
- The facility must train HCWs and other staff to properly disinfect, clean, and maintain the PAPR.

### 10.1.2 Improving Ventilation

Improved ventilation can reduce the concentration of airborne microbes. This can be achieved by increasing the air exchange rate, introducing outdoor air, and installing air filtration systems.

### 10.1.3 Social Distancing

Maintaining a distance of at least 6 feet from others reduces the risk of transmission.

### 10.1.4 Hand Hygiene

Frequent hand washing with soap and water or using alcohol-based hand sanitizers can reduce the risk of acquiring respiratory infections.

### 10.1.5 Avoiding Crowded Spaces

Avoiding crowded places and gatherings helps in reducing the risk of acquiring respiratory infections.

The COVID-19 pandemic has highlighted the risk of spreading of the infection to frontline healthcare workers [3, 4]. Among HCWs, otolaryngologists are one of the most exposed specialists due to the high viral load in the upper respiratory tract of COVID-19 patients [5]. Also, it should be kept in mind that treating doctors and other HCWs are at risk of many infectious diseases other than COVID-19, and, thus, adequate PPE is needed not only during pandemics but also at other times. Though N95 respirators, which correspond to the European respirator standards FFP2/3, and goggles have been recommended to protect the surgeons, there is evidence that higher-level PPE in the form of PAPRs may be more effective in preventing spread of infection to the surgeon, especially during aerosol-producing, high-risk procedures [6, 7].

To account for all those deficiencies, we, at ICMR Center for Innovation and Bio-Design (CIBioD), PGIMER, Chandigarh, developed an economical and reusable air-purifying respirator (design patent application No. 343871-001) which is discussed further in the following sections:

## 10.2 Methodology

### 10.2.1 Device Design

We developed a full-face respirator (at CIBioD) to provide complete isolation to the user while maintaining proper circulation of filtered air and allowing smooth communication with other people. Our respirator comprises high efficiency particulate air (HEPA) filtration assembly with >99.99% filtration efficiency and a heat and moisture-exchanging bacterial and viral (HME BV) filter. We used a polyurethane tube (thickness = 2 mm; inner diameter = 12 mm) to connect the HME filtration assembly with the ventilation assembly. We used a ventilation port to bridge a respirator with an adapter for breathing.

In our mask, an adhesive material is used to attach the tubes with the ventilation assembly and to seal the polyurethane tubes. An adhesive is also used to completely seal the remaining space thereby making the mask fully leak-proof. The mask has adjustable straps for comfort fit and easy wearing. For smooth communication while using the mask, we used a waterproof communication module assembly. Our communication module comprises a wireless miniature FM (frequency modulation) transmitter mic placed in the mouth region inside the respirator. It can be connected wirelessly with an external wireless speaker via FM communication within 10–30 m depending on the length and size of the antenna. The mic and the speaker are subitizable and removable. The voice of the person can be heard clearly within the range of wireless sound transmission. Another attractive feature of our device is the inbuilt anti-fogging mechanism for better visibility. The design of our respirator is inspired by the snorkel mask used for underwater swimmers.

### 10.2.2 Working of the Snorkel Mask

The snorkel mask respirator comes with straps that can be adjusted according to the size of face and head of the wearer (Figs. 10.1 and 10.2). The long polyurethane tubes on top of the mask are connected to the inside of the mask via a hole. These provide a continuous flow of filtered air. The anti-fogging feature of the respirator is associated with nasal mask. It prevents deposition of moisture allowing the person to see clearly through the respirator. The material used for the outer layer of the mask is made of plastic. The tightness of the mask is ensured by a rubber lining which fits firmly with the face of the user.

HME BV filters are connected to the polyurethane tubes to filter out viruses or bacteria. This provides protection from COVID-19 virus and related pathogens. The filters can be easily replaced with new filters after each use.

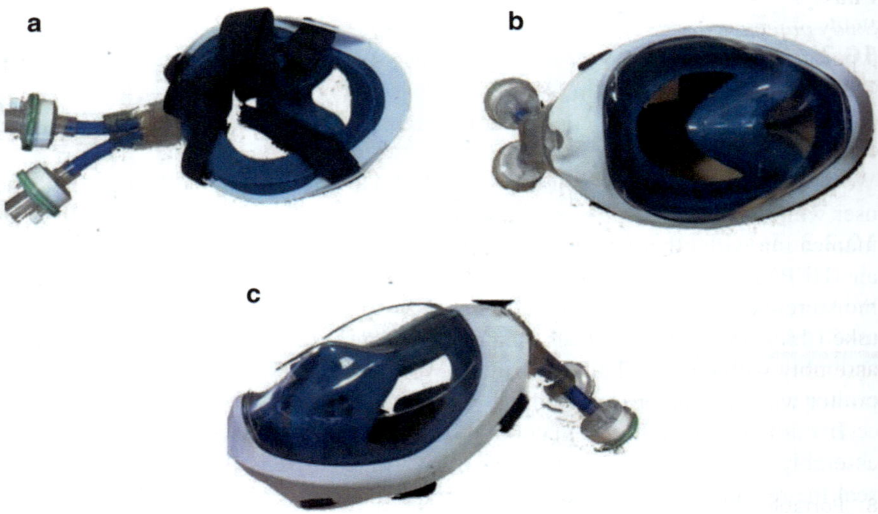


**Fig. 10.1** (**a**) Back, (**b**) top, and (**c**) front views of the developed mask

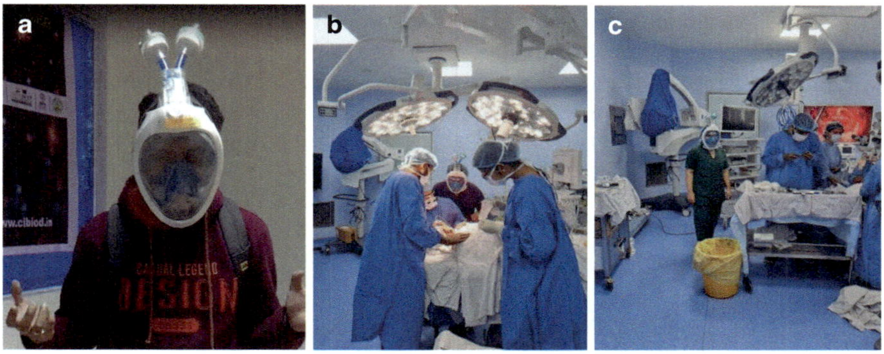


**Fig. 10.2** Respirator worn by a volunteer (**a**) and doctors in operation theatre (**b**, **c**)

Our mask has an FM transmitter with a microphone incorporated into it. This is done as the tightness of the mask dampens amplitude of user's voice which then is not heard properly by others. This FM transmitter is locked at a particular frequency which can be easily accessed via an FM receiver or FM radio within the range of 10–30 m. Our mask is powered via a 3.7 V lithium battery (capable of running for 3–5 h) and is fitted with a battery-charging module, making it rechargeable.

The limitations of a PARP respirator can be efficiently surpassed using this mask. It does not interfere with the field of vision as it does not limit the field of view in any direction. The incoming air does not produce any sound due to the attached filtration units. Also, as the respirator mask is tightly fixed to the face, there is no noise resulting from the movement of loose head coverings. The HCWs can use a stethoscope, as the mask does not cover the ears.

The respirator does not require large storage space and can be placed on a table or in the cabinet. It can be easily cleaned or disinfected as all the components are detachable and can be easily sanitized. All in all, it ensures safety while maintaining comfort for HCWs working in risky environments.

### 10.2.3 Testing the Mask in Actual Clinical Practice

We then proceeded to check how our mask fairs during the actual use. For this, we asked the doctors to assess the masks with respect to their safety, comfort, vision, and communication during surgical and endoscopic procedures. The safety was evaluated in terms of donning complexity, air seal, filter specification, and intraprocedural smell test. The comfort was assessed by the identification of pain and discomfort during prolonged wearing of the mask. The range of movement while wearing the mask was also assessed. The extent of fogging and the visual acuity were evaluated by the ability of the surgeon to distinguish the details as procedural distances. The communication of the surgeon with other team members was assessed. The decontamination methods were investigated. The advantages and disadvantages of modified snorkel masks as PPE were evaluated. The modifications suggested by users to improve mask were noted down in detail. A score of 1–10 (where 1 was the worst and 10 was the best scope) was assigned to each domain.

## 10.3 Results

The assessment of snorkel masks was done in operation theatres of the department of otorhinolaryngology (ENT), where different doctors and nursing staff used the masks and gave their feedback on a questionnaire with comments. The results of the survey are given in Tables 10.1 and 10.2.

## 10.4 Discussion and Conclusion

The above results are comparable to those obtained after the use of conventional masks and thus our mask offers an alternative when commercial full-face respirator is unavailable.

The advantages of our snorkel mask are:

1. It covers the face fully thereby protecting the eyes.
2. It provides high-quality air filtration to protect against viruses and bacteria, thereby achieving zero transmission of communicable diseases.
3. It allows for effective communication during the surgery.
4. There is no problem in breathing as it has in-built air filters.
5. Its shield is protective against splashes which may occur during operation.
6. It is leakage proof which negates any chances of accidental spread of communicable diseases.
7. The dead space inside the mask is minimal preventing rebreathing of $CO_2$.
8. Its major limitation is that it cannot be autoclaved though it can be sterilized with 70% alcohol, isopropanol, and ultraviolet rays.

**Table 10.1** Remarks made by different experts on the questionnaire

| Name, age, and designation | | Duration in hours before you started feeling discomfort | It is easy to see through the facial mask [Agree/ Strongly agree/No | How easy is it to breathe while using the mask? [Easy/Not easy] | Degree of fogging experienced while using the mask? [Partial/ No/Yes] | Ease of communication while using the mask [Easy/Not easy] | Any technical issues/ trouble faced while using mask [No/Yes] | Ease of sterilization of mask [Easy/Not easy] | How many times have you reused the mask in a day? [Frequently/ Rarely] |
|---|---|---|---|---|---|---|---|---|---|
| Dr. Reshma Raj, 27 years, Senior Resident | No | 1–2 | Agree | Not easy | No | Easy | No | Not easy | Frequently |
| Dr. Kiruba Karan, 31 years, Senior Resident | Neither | 3–5 | Strongly agree | Easy | No | Easy | No | Not easy | Not frequently (3–4 times) |
| Dr. Prerna, 28 years, Senior Resident | Strongly Agree | 1–2 | Strongly agree | Neither r | No | Easy | No | Neither | Not frequently (3–4 times) |

(continued)

**Table 10.1** (continued)

| Name, age, and designation | | Duration in hours before you started feeling discomfort | It is easy to see through the facial mask [Agree/ Strongly agree/No | How easy is it to breathe while using the mask? [Easy/Not easy] | Degree of fogging experienced while using the mask? [Partial/ No/Yes] | Ease of communication while using the mask [Easy/Not easy] | Any technical issues/ trouble faced while using mask [No/Yes] | Ease of sterilization of mask [Easy/Not easy] | How many times have you reused the mask in a day? [Frequently/ Rarely] |
|---|---|---|---|---|---|---|---|---|---|
| Dr. Mukul Gajmoti, 25 years, Senior Resident | Agree | 1–2 | Strongly agree | Easy | No | Very easy | No | Very easy | Frequently (7–8) |
| Dr. Krishna, 29 years, Junior Resident | No | 1–2 | Agree | Easy | Yes | No | No | Easy | Frequently |
| Dr. Adhip Neupane, 27 years, Junior Resident | Neither | 3–5 | Strongly agree | Easy | No | Easy | No | Not Easy | Not frequently (3–4) |
| Dr. Shivam, 27 years, Junior Resident | Strongly agree | 1–2 | Agree | Easy | Partial | Easy | Partial | Not easy | Rarely (0–2) |

| Name, age, and designation | | Duration in hours before you started feeling discomfort | It is easy to see through the facial mask [Agree/ Strongly agree/No | How easy is it to breathe while using the mask? [Easy/Not easy] | Degree of fogging experienced while using the mask? [Partial/ No/Yes] | Ease of communication while using the mask [Easy/Not easy] | Any technical issues/ trouble faced while using mask [No/Yes] | Ease of sterilization of mask [Easy/Not easy] | How many times have you reused the mask in a day? [Frequently/ Rarely] |
|---|---|---|---|---|---|---|---|---|---|
| Dr. Priyanka Bhatia, 30 years, Junior Resident | Agree | 1–2 | Agree | Easy | Partial | Easy | No | Easy | Normal (5–6) |
| Dr. Hari, 25 years, Junior Resident | Strongly agree | 1–2 | No | Easy | Partial | Easy | No | No | Rarely |
| Sahi ram, 43, Nursing Officer | Agree | 1–2 | Agree | Easy | Partial | Easy | No | No | Frequently |
| Priyanka Sharma 25 years, Nursing officer | Strongly agree | 1–2 | Strongly agree | Easy | No | Easy | No | No | Frequently |
| Ms. Raman, 25 years, Nursing Officer | Agree | 1–2 | Strongly agree | Neither r | Partial | Easy | Partial | Neither | Not frequently (3–4) |

**Table 10.2** Comments provided by specialists on the overall use of snorkel mask

| | |
|---|---|
| Dr. Reshma Raj | Felt a little bit suffocated, but visibility is clear |
| Dr. Kiruba Karan | Heavyweight and fogging |
| Dr. Prerna | Weight can be reduced; it can become more comfortable after that |
| Dr. Mukul Gajmoti | It is good; It can protect face; You can wear and sanitize it easily; You can also avoid touching your face and eyes while working; It is a good product; I appreciate it |
| Dr. Krishna | Heavy, Fogging, and not able to communicate properly |
| Dr. Adhip Neupane | Heavy; I cannot wear it; It might be difficult for prolonged procedure |
| Dr. Shivam | Different fit sizes for all and fogging problem |
| Dr. Priyanka Bhatia | The mask felt heavy with a little fogging problem too |
| Dr. Hari | It is easy to communicate while wearing it |
| Sahi Ram | One can communicate appropriately while wearing the mask |
| Priyanka Sharma | A bit heavy and tight-fitting |
| Ms. Raman | Heavyweight and fogging |

## References

1. WHO Director-General's Opening Remarks at the Media Briefing on COVID-19. 11 March 2020. The World Health Organization. https://www.who.int/dg/speeches/detail/whodirector-general-s-opening-remarks-at-the-media-briefing-oncovid-19-11-march-2020. Published 2020. Accessed 1 Aug 2020.
2. Verbeek JH, Rajamaki B, Ijaz S, et al. Personal protective equipment for preventing highly infectious diseases due to exposure to contaminated body fluids in healthcare staff. Cochrane Database Syst Rev. 2019;2019(7):23.
3. Tikka G. Covid-19: doctors still at "considerable risk" from lack of PPE, BMA warns. BMJ. 2020;1316:m1316.
4. Patel ZM, Fernandez-Miranda J, Hwang PH, et al. Letter: precautions for endoscopic trans nasal skull base surgery during the COVID-19 pandemic. Neurosurgery. 2020;87(1):E66–7.
5. Zou L, Ruan F, Huang M, et al. SARS-CoV-2 viral load in upper respiratory specimens of infected patients. N Engl J Med. 2020;382(12):1177–9.
6. Roberts V. To PAPR or not to PAPR? Can J Respir Ther. 2014;50(3):87–90.
7. Givi B, Schiff BA, Chinn SB, et al. Safety recommendations for evaluation and surgery of the head and neck during the COVID-19 pandemic. JAMA Otolaryngol Head Neck Surg. 2020;146(6):579–84.

# 11 Namo Gamcha: Public Message, Efficacy, and Awareness of Behaviour in Relation to Face Masks

Varinder Garg, Surinder Rana, Poonam Agarwal, Monika Singh, Ramandeep Bansal, Sujata Saini, Gunjan, and Deeksha Kumari

## 11.1 Introduction

The use of masks is only one component of a complete set of preventive methods which reduce the spread of COVID-19 and related infections. Masks serve dual purposes: they can be worn by infected individuals to prevent spreading the virus to others (source control), or by healthy individuals to shield themselves from exposure when interacting with someone who is infected. To guarantee that any form of mask is as effective as possible and to lower the danger of transmission, it must be used, stored, cleaned, and disposed of properly.

The demand for face masks surged significantly during epidemics, as more people began using them. This widespread increase among the general public intensified the global shortage of masks, driving up prices considerably. This heightened demand caused significant shortages and led to a sharp rise in prices. This shortage of supply was observed during the COVID-19 pandemic resulting in banning of export of face masks by countries such as Germany and South Korea. In light of the global mask shortage, the World Health Organization (WHO) called for a substantial 40% increase in the manufacturing of protective equipment, including face

V. Garg (✉)
ICMR-Centre for Innovation and Bio-Design (CIBioD), Postgraduate Institute of Medical Education and Research (PGIMER), Chandigarh, Chandigarh, India

S. Saini · Gunjan · D. Kumari
ICMR Center for Innovation and Bio-Design, PGIMER, Chandigarh, India

S. Rana
Department of Gastroenterology, PGIMER, Chandigarh, India

P. Agarwal · M. Singh
Northern India Institute of Fashion Technology, Mohali, India

R. Bansal
Department of Obstetrics and Gynecology, PGIMER, Chandigarh, India



V. Garg et al. (eds.), *Innovations in Healthcare Technologies in India*,
https://doi.org/10.1007/978-981-97-0244-2_11

**Table 11.1** Recommendations for the use of face masks in community settings

| Organization/ country | Description |
|---|---|
| World Health Organization | If you are in good health, mask-wearing is generally only necessary when you are providing care to someone suspected of having a SARS-CoV-2 infection [1] |
| China | Even those at a moderate risk of infection should use a face covering, which can include non-medical types like fabric masks [2] |
| Hong Kong | Surgical masks help limit the spread of respiratory infections from those who are unwell. Individuals exhibiting symptoms, no matter how mild, should use a suitable mask. Ensuring that the mask is worn correctly is vital, as is practicing thorough hand hygiene before donning and after removing the mask [3] |
| Singapore | If you have respiratory symptoms like a cough or a runny nose, you should wear a mask [4] |
| Japan | Wearing a face mask may offer only limited protection against virus infection. In closed, poorly ventilated spaces, masks can reduce the chance of inhaling droplets from others. However, their effectiveness is notably reduced in open, well-ventilated environments [5] |
| United States of America | The Centers for Disease Control and Prevention suggests that people use face masks to safeguard themselves against respiratory infections, including COVID-19 [6] |
| United Kingdom | In environments like hospitals, face masks are essential [7] |
| Germany | There is inadequate proof to show that wearing a surgical mask substantially decreases the likelihood of infection for someone who is healthy [8] |

masks. Furthermore, the WHO recommended that health authorities enhance their distribution strategies to prioritize mask allocation for those on the frontlines of healthcare and for high-risk groups, such as the elderly and those with chronic health conditions.

In the event of pandemics characterized by aerosol spread, it is essential to consider widespread mask usage, provided there is a sufficient supply. Nonetheless, due to frequent shortages, this approach is often unfeasible. During the COVID-19 crisis, the World Health Organization (WHO) advised that masks should be worn by individuals displaying respiratory symptoms or those attending to symptomatic patients. Simultaneously, the WHO emphasized the need for research into extending the life of single-use masks and developing reusable mask options. Given the global scarcity of masks, it was predictable that countries would adopt diverse recommendations regarding mask usage throughout the pandemic (Table 11.1).

## 11.2 Scientific Evidence That Wearing a Face Mask Can Protect People from Viruses/Other Respiratory Diseases

### 11.2.1 Spread of the SARS-CoV-2 Virus

COVID-19 is fundamentally a respiratory illness that can range from being asymptomatic to causing severe respiratory distress, potentially leading to death. Evidence suggests that SARS-CoV-2 is predominantly transmitted via close contact between individuals. The likelihood of transmission is affected by several factors, including the viral load an infected individual carries, the nature and duration of contact with others, the environment where the interaction occurs, and the effectiveness of any protective actions taken.

### 11.2.2 Mask Usage in Healthcare Settings

A systematic review of observational studies focused on beta-coronaviruses, including those responsible for SARS, MERS, and COVID-19, reveals that wearing respirators, medical masks, and even cloth masks is linked to a lower risk of infection among healthcare professionals [9]. Additionally, cloth masks, despite offering a lesser degree of protection, can still aid in preventing the transmission of COVID-19 and other respiratory illnesses if they consist of at least three layers of washable woven and non-woven fabrics. Being inexpensive and reusable, these masks can be easily made at home, making them a viable option for public use despite their limited protective capabilities [10].

## 11.3 Novelty of the Developed Cloth Mask: Gamcha

Gamcha is a rectangular piece of cotton cloth worn as headdress or on one side of the shoulder by men in India, Pakistan, Bangladesh, and other parts of South and Southeast Asia. Over time, it has become an essential item of clothing for farmers and laborers to wipe sweat and protect the head from the sun. It is also worn as loin cloth by poorer sections of society. During the COVID-19 pandemic, Gamcha was used as an alternative cloth face mask in rural India where people simply wore it on their face. Its importance as face mask increased further when Prime Minister of India made a television speech wearing Gamcha. During the COVID-19 pandemic, many countries including India faced severe shortage of face masks [11]. To meet this shortage, we planned this innovative product (Namo Gamcha) by introducing a cloth-based mask within the structure of Gamcha itself (Fig. 11.1).

### 11.3.1 Design

The Namo Gamcha, crafted from soft linen fabric, embodies a timeless elegance and comfort. We have incorporated a three-layered mask within the design of Namo Gamcha. The three-layered design comprises of an inner layer, a middle filtration layer, and an outer layer. The inner layer is made of a soft and comfortable material (cotton) that comes into contact with the skin. It aims to absorb water from the wearer's breath, provides comfort, and prevents irritation. The middle filtration layer is the most crucial part and is responsible for filtration. It traps and blocks airborne particles and droplets including bacteria and viruses. It is made of

**Fig. 11.1** Namo Gamcha (Note the triple-layered mask in its central part)

polypropylene. The outer layer is made of durable hydrophobic material (linen) that provides structure to the mask and helps to repel moisture. This layer provides an additional barrier to liquids, preventing droplets containing pathogens from penetrating into the mask. The remaining portion of the Namo Gamcha consists of a single layer throughout. This single layer serves to maintain the fabric's lightweight and breathable qualities, ensuring comfort and versatility in various uses. While the mask portion boasts three layers for enhanced filtration, the rest of the Gamcha maintains simplicity and ease of wear with its single-layer construction. A patent has already been granted in the name of our innovation the "Namo Gamcha" (Application Number: 331445-001).

### 11.3.2 Perceived Benefits of Namo Gamcha

The benefits of the Namo Gamcha mask include:

- *Prevention of the spread of respiratory illnesses.*
- *Ease of use:* Cloth masks offer greater comfort compared to surgical or medical masks, making them particularly suitable for elderly individuals and those with underlying conditions such as cardiovascular issues, high blood sugar, persistent respiratory disorders, malignancies, and cerebrovascular events.
- *Feasibility:* Gamcha is a routine dress for most of the poor people in the Indian subcontinent, and thus the incorporation of mask within the design of Gamcha without any added cost will help in increasing the use of mask in this especially vulnerable section of the society.
- Using masks, such as the Namo Gamcha, could be crucial in educating people about preventing respiratory diseases like tuberculosis and influenza. Consistent mask-wearing may also help in curbing the spread of these conditions.
- *Additional Advantages*: Integrating a washable and reusable mask into the Namo Gamcha can enhance public awareness about respiratory diseases. This approach is likely to promote greater adherence to additional preventive practices, including maintaining physical distance and regular hand hygiene, over time.

## 11.4 Conclusion

Our innovative solution, "Namo Gamcha," has the potential to address scarcity of masks in India. It will not only help in reducing the spread of the COVID-19 virus but also in spreading awareness about the prevention of respiratory illnesses at no additional cost.

## References

1. WHO Coronavirus disease (COVID-19) advice for the public: when and how to use masks. 2020. Downloaded from: https://www.who.int/emergencies/diseases/novel-coronavirus-2019/advice-for-public/when-and-how-to- use-masks.
2. State Council, China Guidelines for the selection and use of different types of masks for preventing new coronavirus infection in different populations 2020 (in Chinese) Feb 5, 2020. Downloaded from: http://www.gov.cn/xinwen/2020- 02/05/content_5474774.htm.
3. The Department of Health, Hong Kong guidelines on prevention of coronavirus disease 2019 (COVID-19) for the general public. Mar 13, 2020. Downloaded from: https://www.chp.gov.hk/files/pdf/nid_guideline_general_public_en.pdf.
4. Ministry of Health, Singapore updates on COVID-19 (coronavirus disease 2019) local situation. Downloaded from: https://www.moh.gov.sg/covid-19.
5. Ministry of Health. Labour and Welfare, Japan Q & A on coronavirus 2019 (COVID-19): When should I wear a facemask? 2020. Downloaded from: https://www.mhlw.go.jp/stf/seisakunitsuite/bunya/kenkou_iryou/dengue_fever_qa_00014.html/
6. CDC Coronavirus Disease 2019 (COVID-19): Steps to prevent illness. Downloaded from: https://www.cdc.gov/coronavirus/2019- ncov/about/prevention-treatment.html.

7. National Health Service: Are face masks useful for preventing coronavirus? 2020. Downloaded from: https://www.nhs.uk/conditions/coronavirus-covid-19/common-questions/.
8. Federal Ministry of Health, Germany daily updates on the coronavirus: Is wearing a surgical mask, as protection against acute respiratory infections, useful for members of the general public? 2020. Downloaded from: https://www.bundesgesundheitsministerium.de/en/press/2020/coronavirus.html.
9. Chu DK, Akl EA, Duda S, et al. COVID-19 Systematic Urgent Review Group Effort (SURGE) study authors. Physical distancing, face masks, and eye protection to prevent person-to-person transmission of SARS-CoV-2 and COVID-19: a systematic review and meta-analysis. Lancet. 2020;395(10242):1973–87.
10. Safe work Australia. Comparison of mask types for COVID-19. Downloaded from: https://covid19.swa.gov.au/comparison-mask-types-covid-19.
11. Gamcha. Downloaded from: https://en.wikipedia.org/wiki/Gamcha.

# Telemedicine: Capabilities, Features, and Applications

12

Varinder Garg, Shankar Prinja, Ramandeep Bansal, Sujata Saini, and Saana Chaudhary

## 12.1 Telemedicine and Medical Care

The availability of advanced technology and high-quality networks has improved the delivery of healthcare, making it accessible to more people. Telemedicine aids in providing healthcare to people who face financial/geographical barriers to receiving adequate healthcare. Several studies have attested to the utility of telemedicine in providing preventive and therapeutic health services. Telemedicine is found to be useful in decreasing the risk of death and hospitalizations and improving the quality of life, particularly in patients with cardiac illnesses [1]. It is a good treatment option for mental health disorders as it removes some of the barriers that hinder patients from opening up in front of a doctor in crowded places [2].

A major advantage of telemedicine is that it allows patients to get medical treatment at a convenient time (for both the caregiver and the care receiver), while remaining safe. Going to a hospital requires sitting in close quarters with other people which may result in acquiring new infections. This is especially dangerous for people with chronic medical conditions or a compromised immune system. The inherent nature of telemedicine which allows for advice without physical contact reduces the risk of catching an infection at the doctor's office [3]. In addition,

V. Garg (✉)
ICMR-Centre for Innovation and Bio-Design (CIBioD), Postgraduate Institute of Medical Education and Research (PGIMER), Chandigarh, Chandigarh, India

S. Saini · S. Chaudhary
ICMR Center for Innovation and Bio-Design, PGIMER, Chandigarh, India

S. Prinja
Department of Community Medicine and School of Public Health, PGIMER, Chandigarh, India

R. Bansal
Department of Obstetrics and Gynecology, PGIMER, Chandigarh, India



V. Garg et al. (eds.), *Innovations in Healthcare Technologies in India*,
https://doi.org/10.1007/978-981-97-0244-2_12

telemedicine provides medical consultation to patients without the need to take time off work or arrange for care of children.

Telemedicine reduces overhead charges for service providers as well. For clinicians, telemedicine may supplement their revenue by allowing them to care for additional patients. Carers who view patients online are not exposed to any diseases that the patient may bring. The major advantages for patients include that they do not have to travel to the office, wait for treatment, or become infected while in the hospital [3].

The next generation of telemedicine may revolutionize healthcare. With advances in internet, the data collected by the healthcare equipment can be sent to an Internet of Things (IoT) cloud platform and subsequently to the IoT systems used by healthcare practitioners to manage patients [4]. The most recent breakthrough in telemedicine is the use of artificial intelligence (AI) to assist physicians in doing their duties more successfully. AI uses wearables, remote patient tracking tools, and even robots to provide specialized care to hitherto untapped locations [3, 5, 6].

Telemedicine can be used to provide healthcare to patients residing in areas with sparse or inaccessible healthcare services. Even in areas with good healthcare services, some clinics provide virtual medical appointments via internet video conferencing. These appointments allow individuals to continue getting treatment from their regular doctor when in-person visits are not required [3]. Other examples of interactive appointments include web-based appointments with a doctor or nurse practitioner and nursing call centers which are staffed by nurses who use question-and-answer style to provide guidance for at-home therapy [3]. Telemedicine technologies help people in innumerable ways some of which include reminders to take blood pressure medication, refilling prescriptions, and remembering appointments. Patients can contact doctors through virtual platforms to obtain consultation, perform self-tests, and participate in step-by-step training programs suited to their unique ailment [3]. Telemedicine helps in improving communication between doctor and distant patient resulting in better utilization of healthcare resources. The use of telemedicine in healthcare helps patients in strictly following their prescription schedules resulting in fewer hospital readmissions [3]. It offers chronic health management, remote services, and care for all in critical instances. Doctors may use telemedicine to create support networks to share their knowledge and deliver better healthcare services [3].

A major advantage of telemedicine is its cost-effectiveness. Telemedicine costs less, resulting in cost savings especially for people residing in rural communities. The cost reductions are likely to become more evident with further advances in technology. When compared to traditional care, telemedicine can save money for both the patient and the practitioner.

Finally, telemedicine can be used to provide a wide range of treatments including primary care consultations, psychotherapy, physical therapy, and many more via video conferencing or via email or phone calls. The various services and advantages offered by telemedicine are illustrated in Fig. 12.1.

Various aspects of telemedicine and its advantages are summarized in Table 12.1.

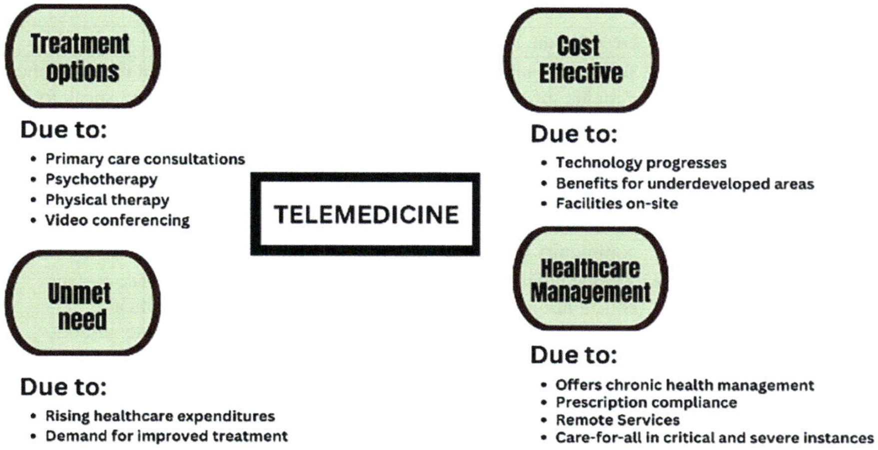


**Fig. 12.1** Various services and advantages offered by telemedicine

**Table 12.1** Telemedicine: applications and advantages

| Sr. no. | Advantage | Description |
|---|---|---|
| 1. | Assistance to patients with disability | Telemedicine makes it easier for patients with functional impairments to obtain health services. It also makes it easier for elderly, the culturally isolated, and the disabled people, to gain access to medical services |
| 2. | Medical services for people living in remote areas | Medical consultation, provided virtually to people living in remote regions, is proved as an effective method of providing healthcare. Through telemedicine, patients living in remote regions can obtain virtual consultation from various specialists without travelling large distances |
| 3. | Patients can travel as little as possible | Telemedicine has the potential to drastically reduce the amount of time consumed for healthcare. In the simplest form of telemedicine-related services, patients can book an appointment online and then use the app to obtain consultation. They no longer need to waste their time commuting to or waiting in a hospital. Through a more advanced version of telemedicine, patients can consult a doctor from the comfort of their own home even when they require immediate medical assistance |
| 4. | Cost-effective | When compared to traditional methods, telemedicine is a more cost-effective method of providing healthcare. This is true since patients do not need to travel every time they seek medical consultation. Online video consultations are not only less expensive than in-person consultations, but they also allow patients to avoid spending money on travel |

(continued)

**Table 12.1** (continued)

| Sr. no. | Advantage | Description |
|---|---|---|
| 5. | Protection from infectious diseases | Telemedicine contributes to a more secure environment for everyone. Patients suffering from the flu or a cold, for example, can speak to their doctor through virtual platforms instead of bringing germs into the workplace. Providers are adequately protected from infectious pathogens when offering counselling and tracking patient success through virtual platforms. During the recently concluded COVID-19 pandemic, telemedicine played an important role in decreasing its community spread through health-related travel |
| 6. | Reduce crowd | Telemedicine has many practical uses. It can provide face-to-face consultation through virtual platforms. It enables healthcare practitioners to monitor several patients at the same time without leaving the hospital. Telemedicine appointments and monitoring assist in decreasing overcrowding in emergency departments. Through telemedicine, hospitals may provide care to needy patients more swiftly than traditional methods |

## 12.2 Conclusion

To conclude, one can say that the time has come for hospital systems, medical groups, suppliers, and other medical service providers to include telemedicine in their medical services. Furthermore, organizations may find it better to work with a telemedicine provider to streamline the process and implementation. Telemedicine is carried out using a telemedicine device, which consists of a computer and portable medical equipment. We have developed such an innovative solution (Telemaster) described in detail in Chap. 6, which is being used currently for providing telemedicine-related healthcare to remote and underserved areas of Himachal Pradesh with great success.

## References

1. Knoll K, Rosner S, Gross S, et al. Combined telemonitoring and telecoaching for heart failure improves outcome. npj Digit Med. 2023;6:193.
2. Link K, Christians S, Hoffmann W, et al. Telemedicine treatment of patients with mental disorders during and after the first COVID-19 pandemic lockdown in Germany—an observational study on feasibility and patient satisfaction. BMC Psychiatry. 2023;23:654.
3. Haleem A, Javaid M, Singh RP, Suman R. Telemedicine for healthcare: capabilities, features, barriers, and applications. Sens Int. 2021;2:100117.
4. Mohammad A, Walaa H. Telemedicine: an IoT based remote healthcare system. Inter J Online Biomed Eng. 2020;16:72.
5. Kuziemsky C, Maeder AJ, John O, et al. Role of artificial intelligence within the telehealth domain. Yearb Med Inform. 2019;28(1):35–40.
6. Sharma S, Rawal R, Shah D. Addressing the challenges of AI-based telemedicine: best practices and lessons learned. J Educ Health Promot. 2023;12:338.

# Transformation of India's Med-tech Ecosystem for Surpassing the Valleys of Death for Societal Impact: A Need for a Multi-sectoral Approach

13

Suchita Markan, Meeta Mukherjee Verma, and Varinder Garg

## 13.1 Initiatives Taken by the Government of India to Transform India's Med-tech Systems

The global medical device and diagnostic business is a multi-trillion-dollar industry, with India now valued at USD (United States dollar) 11 billion [1]. The medical technology industry has been designated as a 'sunrise industry of India' under the Government of India's Make in India programme, and it has seen extraordinary double-digit growth for 3 years in a row. The Indian government has launched several efforts to help this thriving ecosystem reach its full potential. Some recent initiatives by the Government of India to foster value-driven indigenous technology development and to promote public-private partnerships include the 'Production Linked Incentives Scheme' for the medical device sector, which provides financial incentives worth $400 million to boost domestic production, as well as the development of medical device parks across the country, including Himachal Pradesh, Uttar Pradesh, Madhya Pradesh and Tamil Nadu [2]. The Government of India's forward-thinking policy actions for this industry are critical to strengthen this sector and achieve self-sufficiency. Some of these include the National Medical Devices Policy, National Policy on R&D (research and development) and the scheme for Promotion of Research and Innovation in the Pharma-Med Tech Sector (PRIP), ICMR/DHR Policy on Biomedical Innovation & Entrepreneurship for medical professionals, scientists and technologists at medical, dental and para-medical institutes/colleges. Many are involved in this initiative, namely the Department of Biotechnology (DBT) and Department of Science and Technology (DST), the Ministry of Science and

S. Markan · M. M. Verma
Indian Council of Medical Research, New Delhi, India

V. Garg (✉)
ICMR-Centre for Innovation and Bio-Design (CIBioD), Postgraduate Institute of Medical Education and Research (PGIMER), Chandigarh, Chandigarh, India



V. Garg et al. (eds.), *Innovations in Healthcare Technologies in India*,
https://doi.org/10.1007/978-981-97-0244-2_13

Technology, the Department of Pharmaceuticals under the Ministry of Chemicals and Fertilizers, the Indian Council of Medical Research (ICMR) under the Ministry of Health and Family Welfare, Invest India under the Ministry of Commerce and Industry, Ministry of Micro, Small and Medium Enterprises (MSME) and others. Wellcome Trust, Indo-US Science and Technology Forum, Grant Challenges, Canada, and private investors such as Indian Angel Network, India Innovation Fund, India Science Venture Fund, Bharat Innovation Fund and others are also involved. This has resulted in the development of a pipeline of novel medical devices and diagnostic technologies that require a multi-sectoral strategy to assist innovators in overcoming valleys of death for greater public health impact.

To provide holistic support across the medical device development and commercialization cycle including R&D, regulatory compliance, technology evaluation and validation, scale-up and market access and help innovators to accelerate the med-tech innovative product development, ICMR has set up 'Medical Device and Diagnostic Mission Secretariat (MDMS)'. With the mandate to support and catalyze research, development and indigenous manufacturing of cost-effective medical devices to strengthen healthcare sector in India and reduce import dependency, MDMS is adopting a mission mode consortia approach with all key stakeholders in the med-tech ecosystem as its partners including the national regulator- Central Drugs Standard Control Organization (CDSCO), National Health Authority (NHA), Ministry of Health & Family Welfare, National Health Program Coordinators (as potential buyers for public access), Department of Health Research (Health technology assessment conducting body for conducting cost-effectiveness analysis) and the National Standards Making Bodies [such as Bureau of Indian Standards (BIS)] and National Accreditation Bodies [such as National Accreditation Board for Certification Bodies (NABCB)].

The MDMS adopts comprehensive approaches including the bottom-up and top-down methods and a multi-sectoral approach for nurturing the med-tech ecosystem. The bottom-up approach is adopted to support product development and commercialization. This approach includes identifying promising technologies/products contributing significantly to import substitution and supporting technology developers (industry) with demonstrated experience and expertise for product development and commercialization for public use. The top-down approach is used for supporting the creation of a pipeline of innovative medical device(s) by initiating bio-design programmes at medical and engineering institutes to train the next generation of med-tech innovators to develop a pipeline of innovative medical device(s) and diagnostic technologies as per the unmet needs of the country.

Given that the med-tech development journey is a complex cycle (Fig. 13.1), the innovator faces numerous challenges in moving their innovation from concept to regulatory approvals following the pre-clinical/clinical studies confirming the safety and effectiveness of the devices/diagnostic technologies.

Under ICMR-MDMS, multiple schemes (Fig. 13.2) have been initiated for catering to the needs of different stages of med-tech innovation life cycle and for providing strategic handholding support to the innovators for catalyzing technology development to commercialization.

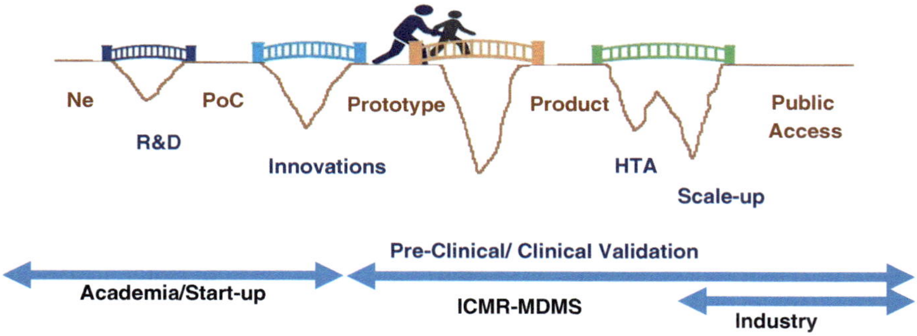


**Fig. 13.1** Life cycle of med-tech innovations: surpassing the valleys of death

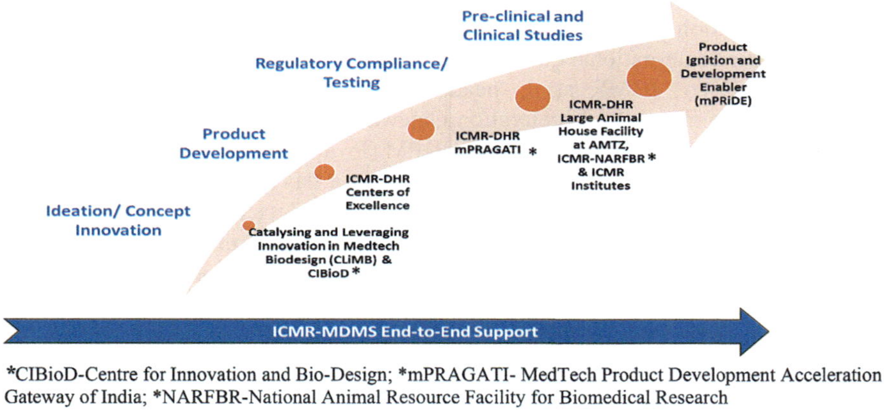


**Fig. 13.2** Different schemes under the ICMR-MDMS for med-tech product development**CIBioD* Center for Innovation and Bio-Design, **mPRAGATI* Med-Tech Product Development Acceleration Gateway of India, **NARFBR* National Animal Resource Facility for Biomedical Research

One of the flagship programmes under ICMR-MDMS is the ICMR-DHR (Department of Health Research)-CoE. For this programme, the ICMR-DHR has established the Centre of Excellences (CoE) at six IITs (Indian Institutes of Technology) (IIT Bombay, IIT Chennai, IIT Kanpur, IIT Hyderabad, IIT Kharagpur and IIT Guwahati) in partnership with premier medical institutes like All India Institute of Medical Sciences (AIIMS), New Delhi, Niloufer Hospital, Telangana, King George's Medical University (KGMU), Lucknow, and Guwahati Medical College and Hospital, Guwahati, for strategic Make in India product development and their commercialization in the medical device and diagnostic technologies sector. The thematic areas under the CoE have been strategically designed to ensure that the products/technologies developed by CoEs are aligned with the requirements of the National Health Mission (NHM), Ayushman Bharat and public health programmes of the Government of India for their potential deployment. The setting up of the ICMR-DHR-CoEs at IITs is to bridge the demand and supply gap by the indigenous technology development through a collaborative approach, wherein clinicians and engineers come together to develop affordable and accessible—unmet—healthcare needs driven by technology development, particularly for middle- and lower-income segments. Some examples of NHM-oriented products developed by the ICMR-DHR-CoEs are given in Fig. 13.3.

The medical device industry in India is dominated by imported devices, which account for around 80% of the total sales, while domestic firms are primarily involved in the production of low-cost goods for both domestic and foreign markets. Furthermore, there are several medical device discoveries that have the potential to transfer into effective healthcare solutions, but providing infrastructure and resources to scale up separately may be impractical.

With the rise in globalization trend, the need for the state-of-the-art facility was strongly felt to support Indian industry for testing and International Organization for Standardization (ISO)-certified pilot batch manufacturing while complying with the national and international quality standards. Considering this urgent need of the med-tech industry, ICMR at its headquarter initiated mPRAGATI (Med-tech Product Development and Acceleration Gateway of India) (Fig. 13.4) programme [under the prestigious government scheme PM (Prime Minister), Ayushman Bharat Health Infrastructure Mission (PM-ABHIM)], as a flagship programme for infrastructure development and to strengthen the medical device and diagnostic sector for epidemiological diseases. The facility was established to foster innovation and product development in the area of medical device and diagnostics and create a common platform for medical device and diagnostic product development, alteration, testing, fabrication, certification and translating medical devices from TRL (technology readiness level) 4 to TRL 7 at IIT Delhi. mPRAGATI, a premier

**Fig. 13.3** Examples of NHM-oriented products supported under ICMR-DHR-CoE by ICMR-MDMS

**Fig. 13.4** ICMR-DHR-mPRAGATI, a state-of-the-art facility at IIT Delhi (*in process)

med-tech translation facility, bridges the gap between innovative medical devices and their journey into clinical trials. The centre has a state-of-the-art ISO13485 certified* pilot batch manufacturing facility and an ISO 17025, NABL-accredited* (*in process) certified testing facility.

## 13.2 Pre-clinical and Clinical Testing

The bench-top testing provides the initial proof-of-concept regarding the device's suitability for the intended use and indicates the extent to which the device design meets the target specifications; however, in the case of novel devices or devices with no precedent, pre-clinical studies are required to ensure the safety and performance of the device(s) before it is used in first-in-human studies. The ICMR-MDMS has established the ICMR-DHR-LAHF (large animal house facility) at Andhra Pradesh MedTech Zone (AMTZ), Vizag (Fig. 13.5), a state-of-the-art facility for making India self-reliant to validate innovative medical devices through large animal studies, as this is a critical requirement prior to bringing medical devices to the stage of clinical evaluation.

The ICMR headquarters, New Delhi, being an apex body in India for the formulation, coordination and promotion of biomedical research, felt the need of a consortia approach at pan-India level for conducting independent, large-scale, multi-centric clinical studies to ensure the intended use and effectiveness of the device(s)/diagnostic technologies to be used for the diagnosis/treatment of diseases and health issues of national and/or regional importance. Considering this vital need, the ICMR has launched a multi-institutional network widely known as INTENT (Indian Clinical Trial and Education Network) to provide support for

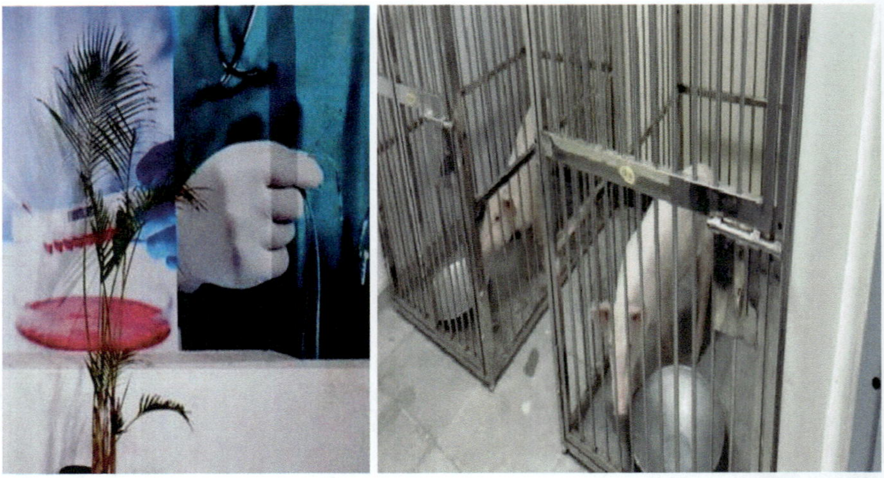

**Fig. 13.5** ICMR-DHR-LAHF facility at AMTZ for pre-clinical studies on animals

conducting clinical studies and delivering evidence-based, cost-effective, scientifically sound, and culturally appropriate solutions to diseases and health issues of national and/or regional importance. The network consists of 47 premier institutes across the country with proven excellence in clinical studies [3]. These institutes have appropriate infrastructure and domain-specific expertise. These are closely associated with community health centres (CHC) or primary health centres (PHC) for conducting usability studies, validating its intended purpose and evaluating whether the proposed medical devices/diagnostic technologies meet the quality standards and are safe and reliable for public use.

## 13.3 Health Technology Assessment (HTA)

The Government of India has taken many initiatives to extend healthcare services to its 1.42 billion population as a part of India's universal health coverage (UHC) agenda and to reduce import dependency in the healthcare sector. Accordingly, public spending has been increased in healthcare services from the existing 1.15% to 2.5% of GDP for the development of indigenous technology, which will significantly reduce the out-of-pocket expenditure of the overall healthcare spending. Also, it is essential for the government to ensure optimal utilization of existing resources to ensure that the greatest amount of health benefit is generated for every rupee spent. To bridge the gap between the world of research and the world of decision-making and to facilitate the process of transparent and evidence-informed decision-making in the field of health, the Government of India has created an institutional arrangement called the Health Technology Assessment in India (HTAIn) [4] under the Department of Health Research (DHR) for Health Technology Assessment

(HTA), evaluating clinical effectiveness, cost-effectiveness, social and ethical issues related to the available and new health technologies in the country in a systematic, transparent, unbiased and robust manner.

Under HTAIn, there is a network of premier institutes at pan-India level with domain experts for evaluation of technologies with respect to their technical and cost-effectiveness supported with significant data, to facilitate the process of transparent and evidence-based decision making in the field of healthcare.

## 13.4 The Way Forward

With the mandate of encouraging technology development in the medical device(s)/diagnostic technologies sector, the ICMR-MDMS drafted a National Policy entitled 'ICMR/DHR Policy on Biomedical Innovation and Entrepreneurship' which was formally launched by the Hon'ble Minister and Secretary DHR and DG (Director General) ICMR on 24 February 2022 for medical professionals, scientists and technologists to promote biomedical innovation in 605 medical institutes/colleges to spur the culture of innovation and entrepreneurship in the country for a wider societal impact [5]. MDMS has also launched *ICMR-Technology Transfer and Revenue Sharing Guidelines* for standardization of key principles during the strategic collaboration for royalty determination in various cases, viz. validation by ICMR, material transfer, grant-in-aid extramural funding and licensing.

The MDMS, through its various schemes, has supported more than 50 technologies aligned with National Health Priorities, conducted more than 20 capacity-building initiatives with more than 600 people trained from start-ups/innovators/academicians in technology development, regulatory strategy, importance of preclinical/clinical studies, HTA and public access. Through its centres of excellence (CoEs), more than 50 people with different capacities (project scientists/consultants/domain-specific manpower/technicians) have been recruited in the premier institutions. Out of 50 technologies supported under MDMS, 10 technologies which have received necessary regulatory approvals, have been recommended to HTAIn, DHR for health technology assessment for evaluating their cost and technical effectiveness, facilitating deployment of technologies to national programs.

With the recent launch of National Medical Policy, 2023, the Government has put comprehensive efforts in place to facilitate an orderly growth in medical device(s)/diagnostic technologies sector to meet the public health objectives of accessibility, affordability, quality and innovation, by building an enabling ecosystem for promoting R&D and innovations, creating a robust and streamlined regulatory framework, providing support in training and capacity building programmes, promoting higher education to foster talent and skilled resources for production of medical devices and complementing Government's 'Atmanirbhar Bharat' and 'Make in India' initiatives. The policy talks about creating a 'Single Window Clearance System' for licensing of medical devices co-opting all the stakeholder departments/organizations such as the Atomic Energy Regulatory Board (AERB), Ministry of Electronics and Information Technology (MeitY), Department of

Animal Husbandry and Dairying (DAHD) and ICMR, for prioritization of devices for developing Bureau of Indian Standards (BIS) for the medical devices and diagnostic technologies in a mission mode for ensuring the quality of the Make in India devices/diagnostic technologies at par with the global standards. The policy is expected to provide essential support and directions to strengthen the med-tech ecosystem into a competitive, self-reliant, resilient and innovative industry that accommodates to both national and global healthcare needs.

## 13.5 Conclusions

The medical device(s)/diagnostic technologies sector is a critical component of the healthcare delivery system. Following the pandemic, the government's initiatives to make India self-sufficient in the healthcare sector have highlighted the urgent need for an efficient and resilient ecosystem, enabling the development of affordable and accessible innovative 'Make in India' 'medical device/diagnostic technologies' with broader societal impact, and thereby reducing India's huge reliance on medical device imports to meet healthcare needs. Med-tech development is investment oriented and involves multiple stakeholders for bringing high-quality healthcare solutions for underserved community, catering to the last mile. It is the need of the hour to empower the med-tech ecosystem and different stakeholders of the healthcare ecosystem, i.e. policymakers, clinicians, academicians, biomedical engineers and legal experts so that they work hand in hand with med-tech industries for bringing policy reforms, capacity enhancement and creating a pipeline of innovative *Make in India* technologies, which are also globally relevant considering that world is a global village.

Similarly, it is critical to identify constraints to medical device quality and find creative solutions to overcome such restrictions to provide patients with access to high-quality medical equipment. To ensure the development of indigenous, high-quality and cost-effective med-tech innovations that strengthen the healthcare ecosystem, ICMR has established pan-India institutional networks that include key stakeholders for mentoring and strategic handholding support for the development of products/technologies aligned with national health priorities.

## References

1. Investment Opportunities in India's Health Sector. https://www.niti.gov.in/sites/defaul/files/202103/InvestmentOpportunities_HealthcareSector_0.pdf.
2. INVEST INDIA. https://www.investindia.gov.in/sector/medical-devices#:~:text=The%20size%20of%20the%20Indian,over%20the%20last%203%20years.
3. ICMR-INTENT. https://www.icmr.gov.in/pdf/covid/techdoc/Notification_INTENT_Result.pdf
4. DHR-HTAIn. https://dhr.gov.in/health-technology-assessment-india-htain
5. https://main.icmr.nic.in/sites/default/files/upload_documents/ICMR_DHR_Policy_on_Biomedical_Innovation_and_Entrepreneurship_final.pdf

# Future Commercial Potential of Various ICMR-CIBioD Devices

# 14

Varinder Garg, Suchita Markan, Harish Kumar, and Anupriya Bhardwaj

The Indian Council of Medical Research (ICMR's) Center of Innovation and Bio-Design (CIBioD) is a platform at Post-Graduate Institute of Medical Education and Research (PGIMER), Chandigarh, founded under the aegis of ICMR, New Delhi. The primary aim of this center is to promote frugal and disruptive innovation (through promotion of quality research) and indigenous technologies to fabricate robust, sustainable, and affordable healthcare ideas into viable products by creating a conducive ecosystem with the involvement of multiple premier technology institutes in collaboration with PGIMER, Chandigarh. Our mission is to create innovative solutions to overcome the existing bottlenecks in "affordable healthcare" by bringing together the best Indian medical and technical experts so that they work jointly on cutting-edge technologies.

## 14.1 Aims and Objectives of ICMR-CIBioD

The ICMR-CIBioD was established with the following objectives:

- To emerge as a world-class innovation center for designing and developing indigenous technologies, instruments, and devices for affordable healthcare. The center acts as a pivotal platform and provides necessary infrastructure and funds for small-

V. Garg (✉)
ICMR-Centre for Innovation and Bio-Design (CIBioD), Postgraduate Institute of Medical Education and Research (PGIMER), Chandigarh, Chandigarh, India

S. Markan · A. Bhardwaj
ICMR Center for Innovation and Bio-Design, PGIMER, Chandigarh, India

H. Kumar
Department of Computer Science and Engineering, University Institute of Engineering and Technology (UIET) Panjab University, Chandigarh, Punjab, India

 
V. Garg et al. (eds.), *Innovations in Healthcare Technologies in India*,
https://doi.org/10.1007/978-981-97-0244-2_14

scale start-ups aimed toward prototyping of selected ideas. The center also facilitates larger projects by sending their ideas to ICMR and other funding agencies.

- To promote and foster cooperation among premiere medical institutes, research institutes, and well-known industry partners, thereby establishing an effective network of engineers, clinicians, and medical technology people for designing processes that focus on technological developments.
- To establish automated solutions and approaches for the prevalent medical problems.
- To provide skill enhancement training for researchers, clinicians, and numerous faculties working in the area of medical sciences. The center organizes seminars, workshops, and symposiums to motivate different stakeholders to work toward the advancement and innovation in the field of medical devices and equipment.

This chapter represents the list of the products developed at ICMR-CIBioD which includes telehealth kiosk, digital e-stethoscope, JEE-1 Arogya Sahayak, surgical snorkel mask, medical rambler, metallosurfactants, and Arogya Prahari app.

## 14.2 Telehealth Kiosks

An easy and affordable access to quality healthcare is a necessity of human beings. Such easy access to quality healthcare also boosts the economic growth of the country. Telehealth kiosk (Fig. 14.1) is a health ATM (automated teller machine) with a

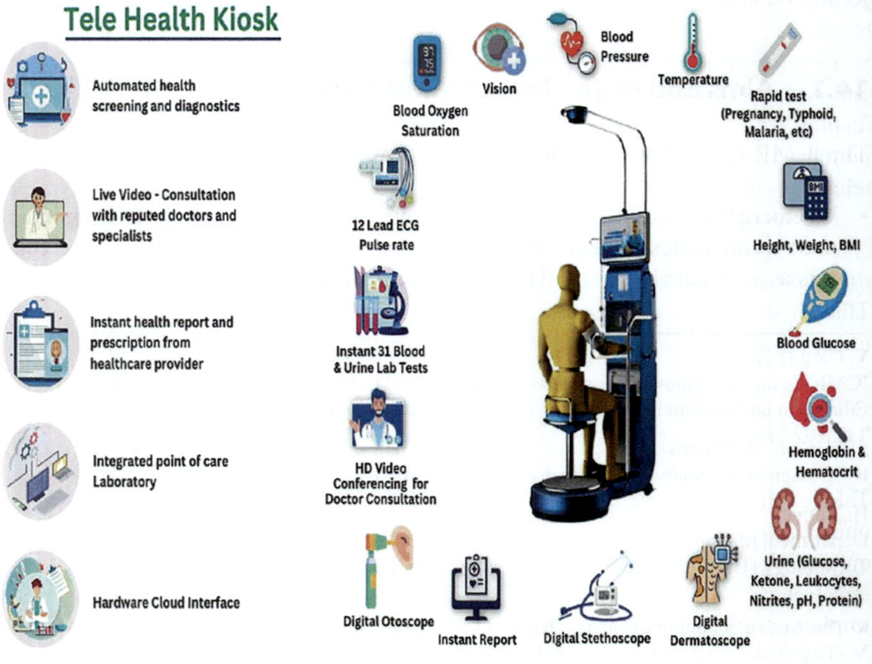


**Fig. 14.1** ICMR-CIBioD telehealth kiosk

built-in, integrated diagnostic lab and a hardware-cloud interface. These kiosks are developed to provide point-of-care diagnostic and tele-consultation services to the rural and marginal population at their first point of contact. This easy-to-install and operate telemedicine clinic—which is an all-in-one diagnostic lab and specialists consultation hub, with artificial intelligence (AI)-enabled real-time data management platform—has the potential to bridge this gap in the service delivery among the underserved areas, to bring community closure to the services and ensure uninterrupted service delivery even during the epidemics.

Telehealth kiosk allows quick and easy screening of the health status of an individual. It connects the patients in remote areas and the healthcare professionals. It is equipped with medical devices and communication tools to enable virtual consultations and remote monitoring. The ICMR-CIBioD, PGIMER Chandigarh, has its incubated start-up to upgrade the primary healthcare system with telehealth kiosks. At CIBioD, we have devised two kiosk models, i.e., Tele-Master 201 (TM 201) (telehealth kiosk with integrated biochemistry lab) and Tele-Master 101 (telehealth kiosk without integrated biochemistry lab). Tele-Master 101 can be integrated with TM 201 in a hub and spoke manner.

### 14.2.1 Tele-Master 201 (TM 201)

TM 201 is a health ATM having a built-in, integrated diagnostic lab with a hardware-cloud interface. The kiosk has been developed to provide a point-of-care diagnosis and tele-consultation services to the rural and marginal population at their first point of contact. It can automatically measure ten noninvasive body parameters and has facilities to conduct 65+ biochemistry tests/parameters. It also has a 12-channel ECG and a digital spirometer. From the vital acquisition to the laboratory tests, the entire process is automated, and data is stored in cloud storage. It has a 19" LED display with a touch screen and user-friendly module. All these facilities make it a human error-free virtual platform that can provide point-of-care diagnostics and tele-consultation services anywhere.

*Our telehealth kiosk is a one-stop-shop for multiple screening tests and ensures end-to-end referral with the aim to decongest the tertiary care centers and strengthen the primary healthcare system, warranting higher penetration and compliance.* This kiosk bridges the gap in service delivery and provides communities with uninterrupted service delivery even during situations like epidemics.

### 14.2.2 Advantages

Telehealth kiosks offer several benefits such as improved access to healthcare in underserved areas, reduced healthcare cost, increased convenience for patients, enhanced efficiency for healthcare providers and promotion of timely diagnosis, and treatment of communicable and noncommunicable diseases. It helps in the implementation of various national programs to achieve the Sustainable Development

Goal 3 (SDG3) goals in future. It also helps to improve the treatment adherence rate of rural and remote patients and synchronize all the health data of various programs and schemes under the National Digital Health Mission. It helps to build the capacity of primary healthcare teams to deliver essential health services with the support from technology and integration of National Programme for Prevention and Control of Cancer, Diabetes, Cardiovascular diseases and Stroke (NPCDCS). It explores the opportunities for integrating the model with multisectorial partnerships, promotes social stability by reducing travel expenditure, time, and out-of-pocket expenses, and reduces carbon footprint due to health-related travel of the patients and their attendants.

## 14.3 Digital Stethoscope

Practically, every doctor learns to use a stethoscope as a method to listen to heart sounds. However, its use was limited during the COVID-19 pandemic owing to heavily fortified PPE (personal protection equipment) kits. At CIBioD, we have developed electronic wireless digital stethoscope which can play and show the PCG (phonocardiogram) data on the android application via Bluetooth and save it on cloud for future reference. The data can be easily retrieved even by a nonmedical technician. The e-stethoscope (electronic stethoscope) can be used safely in patients with contagious diseases. The potential advantages of our e-stethoscope include wireless connectivity, better sound amplification, reduced ambient noise, adjustable sound frequencies, a system for audio recording and playback, the ability to visualize sound waves, cost-effectiveness, easy handling, and its ability to serve as an educational tool.

### 14.3.1 Commercial Potential of Digital or Electronic Stethoscope

The future of digital stethoscope or electronic stethoscope looks promising given the need for more accurate and efficient diagnostic tools and growing adoption of telemedicine. The integration of e-stethoscope with telemedicine platforms/mobile applications enables healthcare professionals to auscultate patients' heart and lung sounds in real time while sitting at a distance, making it an extremely effective tool for virtual consultations and remote patient monitoring. Integration of artificial intelligence (AI) algorithms with e-stethoscopes further enhances their diagnostic capabilities. AI-powered algorithms can analyze auscultation sounds, compare them with extensive databases of known patterns, and provide automated diagnoses, thereby helping clinicians in decision-making. Furthermore, e-stethoscopes can be customized and optimized for different medical specialties, such as cardiology, pulmonology, and pediatrics. By catering to specific clinical needs, digital stethoscopes can target niche markets and expand their commercial potential. Digital stethoscopes help in medical education and research. They enable instructors to capture and share auscultation sounds with students, facilitating learning and skill

**Table 14.1** E-stethoscope in Indian market

| E-stethoscope manufacturers | Battery life | Cost |
|---|---|---|
| AYU-SYNK [4] | It is connected to a Bluetooth device; so, it requires both Bluetooth device and the mobile phone to be full on battery for continuous use | INR 18,000 |
| Thinkable One [5] | 100–125 patients/4 h | INR 53,125 |
| C-DAC MOHALI digital stethoscope [6] | Provides 100 h of continuous power operation | INR 8000 |
| *ICMR-CIBioD e-stethoscope* | *4–5 h* | *INR 10,000* |

development. Researchers can utilize digital stethoscopes to collect data for studies, clinical trials, and large-scale health monitoring initiatives. Seamless integration with electronic health record (EHR) systems allows for efficient documentation and storage of patient's auscultatory data. This integration streamlines clinical workflows, improves data accessibility, and enhances continuity of care.

In 2020, traditional acoustic stethoscope dominated the market with a revenue share of 72.79%, as it is comparatively inexpensive, simple to use, and widely available for use by paramedics and nurses. The global stethoscope market size was valued at USD 569.61 million in 2021 and is expected to expand at a compound annual growth rate (CAGR) of 5.9% from 2022 to 2030 [1, 2]. With a number of doctors estimated to be 6.5 lakhs in India [3], this product holds a great promise.

To maximize the commercial potential of digital stethoscopes, it is important for manufacturers to focus on factors such as usability, affordability, durability, battery life, and interoperability with healthcare systems. Additionally, engaging healthcare professionals, obtaining endorsements, and establishing partnerships with telemedicine providers and healthcare institutions can further drive the adoption and commercial success of digital stethoscopes. Some of the future innovations which will help to increase the use of e-stethoscope includes enhanced sound amplification, noise reduction algorithms, wireless connectivity, integration with artificial intelligence (AI) for automated analysis, and the incorporation of additional sensors for comprehensive patient monitoring. Table 14.1 shows the comparison of e-stethoscope developed at CIBioD with other e-stethoscopes available in India.

## 14.4 JEE-1 Arogya Sahayak

A ventilator is a breathing apparatus used to provide mechanically assisted ventilation to a patient who cannot breathe sufficiently of his/her own. Currently, the available ventilators are expensive and require trained manpower, thereby limiting their use to intensive care units and specially equipped ambulances with adequately trained manpower. This limits their use for the transportation of patients when ventilation is needed for a short period of time and during pandemics when mainstream ventilators fall out of supply or cannot be used due to lack of trained manpower. During these times, AMBU bags are used to provide ventilatory support to critically ill patients. Most of the time, AMBU bags are used by attendants of patients resulting in inadequate and improper ventilatory support to patients along with psychological trauma for attendants providing end-of-life care to loved ones.

At ICMR-CIBioD, we have prepared an automatic AMBU bag operating device with a simple mechanism. JEE-1 is a cost-effective lifesaving machine with a new outlook. Its functions are detailed in Chap. 8. Ours is an automatic, portable, cheap, and compact device with mechanisms to adjust I:E (inspiration:expiration) ratio, breaths per minute (BPM), and stroke volume. It can be used to provide emergency ventilation to patients during transportation to emergency department and in areas where conventional ventilators cannot be used due to either shortage of ventilators or lack of trained manpower.

### 14.4.1 Future Commercial Potential of AMBU Bag

At present, the commercial potential of automatic AMBU bag device seems promising, although it is yet to be evaluated in clinical settings. It can be used for training healthcare professionals, allowing them to practice emergency ventilation techniques and improve their skills in a controlled environment.

Although already cheap (estimated cost per device is INR 25,000), its cost is expected to decrease further as manufacturing processes become more streamlined. Another advantage is its user-friendly nature wherein even minimally trained staff can use them. The affordability and user-friendly nature will make it accessible to a wider range of healthcare settings, including resource-limited areas and developing countries, increasing its market penetration and commercial potential. The demand for automatic AMBU bags in home healthcare settings is expected to rise. With the increasing aging population and the growing preference for home-based care, these devices can provide effective respiratory support in emergencies, enabling patients to receive immediate assistance until professional help arrives. Automatic AMBU bags offer several advantages over manual bag valve masks, including consistent and controlled ventilation, reduced user fatigue, and the ability to deliver precise tidal volumes and respiratory rates. AMBU bags are particularly relevant in emergency medical services (EMS), including ambulances, emergency rooms, and intensive care units. These devices can help EMS personnel deliver consistent and reliable ventilatory support to patients during critical moments, improving the chances of survival and minimizing potential complications.

The global mechanical ventilator AMBU-bag market size was valued at USD 2.90 billion in 2022 and is expected to expand at a compound annual growth rate (CAGR) of 4.8% from 2023 to 2030. Compliance with safety regulations and quality standards and obtaining necessary certifications will be crucial for manufacturers to ensure the commercial success of automatic AMBU bags. Adhering to regulatory requirements and obtaining necessary approvals will inspire confidence among healthcare providers and facilitate market entry. The future automatic AMBU bags may see advancements in technology, such as improved automation capabilities, integrated monitoring features, enhanced user interfaces, and connectivity options for seamless integration with other healthcare systems [7, 8].

## 14.5 Surgical Snorkel Mask

Currently, the available equipment for personal protection [i.e., personal protection equipment (PPE)] are not good enough to provide adequate protection during high-risk aerosol-generating procedures, especially during the pandemics. We modified and prepared a full-face snorkel mask (Fig. 14.2) and used it as PPE. Our modified mask provided a good seal, comfort, vision, and protection and seemed to be a good alternative to standard PPE (refer Chap. 10 for details).

The global surgical mask market size was valued at USD 3.60 billion in 2021 and is expected to expand at a compound annual growth rate (CAGR) of 5.1% from 2022 to 2030. The growth of the market can be attributed to improved healthcare expenditure as well as the increasing significance of respiratory protection in the healthcare industry, particularly during the COVID-19 pandemic. According to a study by Shane Neilson, it is clear that "face masks are not designed or certified to protect the wearer from exposure to respiratory hazards," such as COVID-19. Therefore, to overcome such problems, we at CIBioD, developed surgical snorkel masks which can be used by doctors during routine patient care and surgical procedures and in intensive care units [9, 10].

Some potential advantages of our mask are given ahead. It is available in three sizes: small, medium, and large. It has a sanitizable communication module assembly. It is completely leak-proof and is equipped with a ventilation system that filters bacteria and viruses. It has a microphone for smooth communication and can be

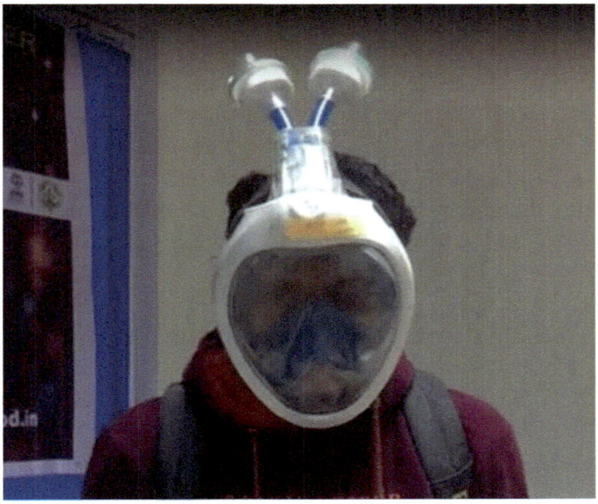

**Fig. 14.2** Surgical snorkel mask

sanitized easily. It has built-in antifogging and antiglare mechanisms. It is low cost, reusable, easy to wear, and can be autoclaved. All these facts make it a reliable and easy-to-use device. However, there is still a scope for improvement in this device (discussed in Chap. 10) which we are working on. We are still in the process of finalizing the design and are coordinating with our industry partner to get the final product.

## 14.6 Medical Rambler

Approximately 60–80 million people worldwide are confined to wheelchairs. Although several devices including ramblers have been developed over time to help these people in walking, these suffer from disadvantages such as high cost, limited availability, and—above all—most are not user-friendly. We, at ICMR Center for Innovation and Bio-Design, PGIMER, Chandigarh, have developed a cheap, user-friendly medical rambler to assist patients with gait problems and paraplegia during walking (refer Chap. 7 for details).

The number of elderly people living in India in 2022 is approximately 149 million. In addition to suffering from gait problems related to advancing age, elderly people also suffer from diseases such as Parkinson disease, dementia, and stroke. Also, many young people suffer from gait problems related to spinal cord damage such as multiple sclerosis, trauma, and tumors. Nearly 5.4 million Indian people live with paralysis [11].

### 14.6.1 Advantages

We have developed a cost-effective and user-friendly assisted rambler for people suffering from paraplegia and gait problems due to various illnesses including (though not limited to) spinal cord injury, multiple sclerosis, and Parkinson disease. Its design is developed in a way that facilitates an elderly individual, with lower hip and knee pain. It is equipped with infrared sensors and built-in sensors to alert the user with impaired vision about upcoming obstacles. Our device can withstand 150 kg of weight. It has an automated braking system to help the paraplegic patients to avoid falls. Its sensor bag is sleek and compact. The sensors are fitted not to interrupt the user in interacting with the rambler. In our rambler, paraplegic patients can get in and out of the device without assistance (see Fig. 14.3).

### 14.6.2 Future Commercial Potential of Medical Rambler

A medical rambler, designed specifically for elderly people or disabled people, particularly suffering from paraplegia due to spinal cord injury, multiple sclerosis, Parkinson's disease, and coordination problems, and who need additional support to maintain balance, has a great future commercial potential. A medical rambler can

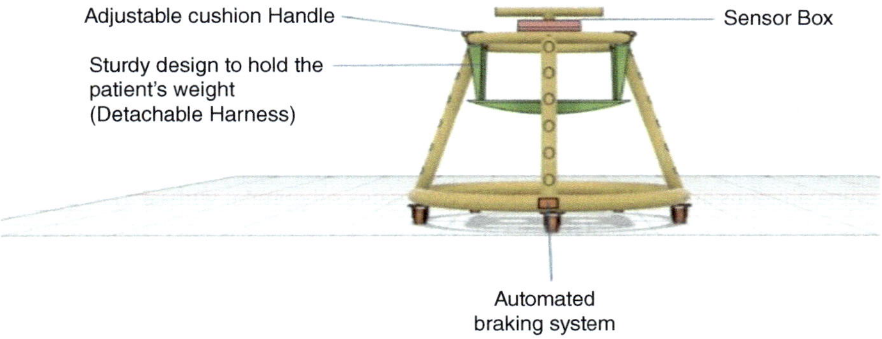


**Fig. 14.3** Overview of assisted medical rambler developed at CIBioD

provide paraplegic patients with increased mobility and independence. By incorporating advanced technologies such as motorized assistance and intuitive controls, the rambler can enable users to navigate various terrains, both indoor and outdoor. Future medical ramblers can be designed with customizable features, allowing individuals to personalize their devices such as adjustable seat heights, backrest angles, armrest positions, and control mechanisms to enhance comfort and accommodate individual requirements. Medical ramblers can prioritize safety features to ensure stability and prevent accidents. This includes anti-tipping mechanisms, automatic braking systems, obstacle detection sensors, and adaptive suspension to provide a smooth and secure ride. The integration of smart technologies (wireless connectivity to smartphones or wearable devices for remote controlling of rambler, navigation assistance, facilities for monitoring of health data, and connection with healthcare professionals for remote consultations) can improve the capabilities of the device further. Medical ramblers can also be used as a tool for rehabilitation and physical therapy. Incorporating features such as adjustable resistance levels, gait analysis, and biofeedback mechanisms can assist users in improving their strength, balance, and overall motor skills over time.

At present, the cost of our rambler is estimated to be about INR 4000 per unit. With an estimated 5.6 million people living with paralysis and 149 million elderly people in our country, the estimate of the total sales amount to INR 60 crore, assuming that only 1% of needy people use our rambler. However, we are still in the process of finalizing the design and are coordinating with our industry partner to get the final product.

## 14.7 Antimicrobial Metallosurfactants

### 14.7.1 Metallosurfactants and Hand Hygiene: Global Scenario and Future Commercial Potential

As per the World Health Organization (WHO), compliance with hand hygiene recommendations during healthcare delivery remains suboptimal with an average compliance level of 59.6% in intensive care units during 2018. Also, there is a substantial difference with regard to hand hygiene compliance among high- and low-income countries (64.5% vs 9.1%). Out of every 100 patients receiving acute care in hospitals, seven patients in high-income countries (HICs) and 15 patients in low- and middle-income countries (LMICs) will acquire at least one healthcare-associated infection during their hospital stay [2]. As per the 76th Round Report 2019 of the National Sample Survey (NSS), 25.3% of households in rural India and 56% in urban India wash hands with soap or detergent before a meal while 2.7% of households in India wash hands with ash, mud, and sand before meals. In rural areas, 70% of people wash hands with water without soap or detergent before a meal and in urban areas, 42% of people follow this practice. About 26% of people in India do not wash their hands with soap or detergent after defecation. About 13.4% of households (15.2% rural and 9.8% urban) wash hands only with water after defecation. Two-thirds of toilets in India have water and soap/detergent available in or around the toilets [12]. Concluding all these data, it is evident that we need to deploy low-cost metallosurfactants in the Indian market so that the basic necessity of cleanliness is fulfilled for every individual.

Metallosurfactants developed at CIBioD (refer Chap. 9 for details) have a broad spectrum of antimicrobial and antifungal activity. They exert their effects through multiple mechanisms which include destruction of cell membrane, generation of reactive oxygen species (ROS) by metal ions, and through interaction with and degradation of internal cellular components such as DNA, RNA, and enzymes. Our metallosurfactants are affordable, biodegradable, environmental-friendly, and are compatible even with hard water. We are still in the process of finalizing the design and are coordinating with our industry partner to get the final product.

## 14.8 Arogya Prahari App

The National Health Policy (NHP), 2017, seeks to reach everyone in a comprehensive way to move toward wellness. It aims at achieving universal health coverage and delivering quality healthcare services at affordable cost. The policy advocates extensive deployment of digital tools for improving the efficiency and outcome of the healthcare system and proposes the establishment of National Digital Health Authority (NDHA) to regulate, develop, and deploy digital health across the continuum of care. Arogya Prahari app is a system to track patients and provide multi-disease platform with support for COVID-19, HIV (human immunodeficiency virus), hepatitis B, and tuberculosis (TB). It is a self-help application available in the public domain. This app is a one-stop alert app which offers various questionnaires related to COVID-19, HIV, hepatitis B, and TB in adults, children, and parents.

Our app is the only app which is based on user sign in and thus fully maintains the privacy of users. It is the only offline app based on progressive web apps (PWA) technology that tracks patients (multi-disease platform with the support for COVID-19, HIV, hepatitis B, and TB) and catches and retrieves updated content from the server to render latest data.

## References


1. Stethoscope market size, share & trends analysis report by technology, by sales channel, by end-use and segment forecasts, 2022–2030. Report linker 2022. Downloaded from https://finance.yahoo.com/news/u-stethoscope-market-size-share-090800161.html?guccounter=1.
2. Stethoscope market size, share & trends analysis report by technology type (Electronic/digital stethoscope, smart stethoscope), by sales channel, by end-use, by region, and segment forecasts, 2024–2030. Downloaded from: https://www.grandviewresearch.com/industry-analysis/stethoscopes-market.
3. Jankharia B. We don't even know how many doctors currently practice in India. Downloaded from: https://timesofindia.indiatimes.com/blogs/voices/we-dont-even-know-how-many-doctors-currently-practice-in-India.
4. AyuSynk 2+. Wireless digital stethoscope. Downloaded from: https://www.ayusynk.ai/products/ayusynk-2/.
5. Stethoscope. Thinklabs one. https://www.thinklabs.com/stethoscopes.
6. C-DAC Mohali designed digital stethoscope to reduce price significantly. Downloaded from: https://www.electronicsb2b.com/industry-buzz/c-dac-mohali-designed-digital-stethoscope-to-reduce-price- significantly/.
7. Mechanical ventilator market size, share & trends analysis report by product (Critical care, neonatal, transport & portable), by ventilation mode (Invasive, non-invasive), by end-use, by region, and segment forecasts, 2024–2030. Downloaded from: https://www.grandviewresearch.com/industry-analysis/mechanical-ventilators-market.
8. 24/7 Emergency ambulance care with Medulance. Downloaded from: https://medulance.com/.
9. Surgical masks market size, share & trends analysis report by product (Basic, anti-fog foam, fluid/splash resistant, others), by distribution channel (online, offline), by region, and segment forecasts, 2023–2030. Downloaded from: https://www.grandviewresearch.com/industry-analysis/surgical-masks-market.
10. The surgical mask is a bad fit for risk reduction. Medicine and society. CMAJ. 2016;188(8):606–7.
11. Dhamija RK, Garg D. World Brain Day 2020—challenges and opportunities in India. Ann Indian Acad Neurol. 2021;24(1):1–2.
12. SATO Tap, an award-winning handwashing solution, primed to improve hygiene practices in the country, is now accessible to all. Downloaded from: https://www.thehindubusinessline.com/news/only-358-households-in-india-wash-hands-with-soap-before-a-meal-says-nss-report/article31171079.ece.

# Global Paramedical Employment Trends in India's E-health Industry

# 15

Varinder Garg

## 15.1 Global Medical Device Market and India

At present, the Indian medical device market constitutes 1.6% of the global health market [1]. It is the fourth largest in Asia, behind Japan, China, and South Korea [2]. Approximately 65% of Indian manufacturers are domestic firms that primarily produce consumables for domestic consumption with minimal exports [3]. In India's medical device industry, which includes more than 800 manufacturers, the majority—65%—generate annual sales under INR 10 crores (around \$1.5 million). A quarter of these companies have yearly revenues ranging from INR 10 to 50 crores (about \$1.5–\$6 million), while just 2%, generally large multinational firms, surpass INR 500 crores in turnover (approximately \$73 million). Understandably, the medical device business in India is dominated by large multinational corporations.

Indian medical device market continues to battle with challenges such as import regulations and supply chain distributions. The top five nations from which India imports medical equipment include the United States (21%), Germany (14%), Singapore (11%), China (10%), and the Netherlands (7%) [4]. The import bill of India has risen to more than INR 46,000 crore. The main reason for this rise is because more than 20 devices are exempt from import duties.

India does not have enough equal playing fields for competing economies when it comes to the manufacture of medical devices. Challenges such as inadequate infrastructure, limited domestic logistics, and high financing costs have rendered about 12–15% of the medical device manufacturing sector inactive. Additionally,

Disclosures: This chapter was written on December 2022 and all the data given below was up till December 2022.

V. Garg (✉)
ICMR-Centre for Innovation and Bio-Design (CIBioD), Postgraduate Institute of Medical Education and Research (PGIMER), Chandigarh, Chandigarh, India



V. Garg et al. (eds.), *Innovations in Healthcare Technologies in India*,
https://doi.org/10.1007/978-981-97-0244-2_15

issues like unreliable power supply, insufficient design capabilities, and a lack of focus on research and development, along with minimal emphasis on skill enhancement, contribute to the sector's difficulties. To address these issues and stimulate investment in the production of essential medical devices, the government introduced a 5-year incentive program in May 2020. This initiative offers funding of up to US dollars (USD) 4.9 billion, but only to those manufacturers who commit to establishing facilities for the production of crucial medical equipment [1]. To increase exports, businesses can focus on diversifying their product range and expanding into new international markets.

Only 3.9% of GDP (Gross domestic product) is spent on healthcare in India, compared to 8.9% in Brazil, 6.2% in Russia, and 5.2% in China. Only 25% of the population has insurance; hence, 61% of costs are out-of-pocket expenses [5]. The Central Drugs Standard Control Organization (CDSCO) and the Indian Ministry of Health and Family Welfare (MOHFW) have established the following steps to enhance the export of medical devices which include:

(a) Review and implementation of "Schedule MIII" Preliminary Guidelines on Production Standards and Infrastructure Requirements
(b) Development of a framework for export labeling
(c) Explanation of clinical assessment and incident documentation
(d) State licensing authority to increase the validity of free sales certificates from 2 to 5 years in order to permit exports
(e) Compilation of a list of export-licensed manufacturers for regulatory bodies around the world for easy access
(f) The "Medical Devices Virtual Expo" to display Indian products and allow Indian providers and buyers/importers from participating nations to communicate directly [1]

Due to its capacity to enable precise illness identification, the diagnostic imaging segment is regarded as the largest. Up until 2022, it held a market share of roughly 30.41% [6].

## 15.2 What Shall India Do to Increase Local Production?

The global medical device business has traditionally been controlled by nations like the United States, China, Germany, and Ireland, among others. However, original equipment manufacturers (OEMs) are now looking at other countries for contract manufacturing. The factors driving this segment include growing geopolitical and economic issues like:

(a) High overall costs that include labor and raw material costs
(b) Heightened intricacies in supply chains arising from a reduced number of providers managing various service aspects
(c) Adverse trade regulations

(d) Rising expenses associated with importing devices, which subsequently drive growth within the local industry
(e) Concerns with intellectual property (IP) protection
(f) The requirement to shorten time-to-market
(g) A rapidly changing technology environment necessitating large capital expenditures [7]

The Indian Medical Devices Industry is anticipating five regulatory amendments to increase local production, namely:

(a) Predictable tariff policy tied to global competitiveness.
(b) Gradual increase in customs duty from present 0–7.5% to 10–15%.
(c) Reduced GST (Goods and services tax) from 18% to 12% because medical devices are not considered luxury items.
(d) The health levy currently imposed on certain medical devices will be extended to include additional medical devices.
(e) Research and development–related tax benefits to encourage indigenous development [8].

The top five medical device manufacturing hubs in our country can then assist in reducing our country's forced 80–85% import dependence and annual import cost of more than INR 46,000 crores.

## 15.3 Increasing Status of India as a Manufacturing Hub in the Digital Health Sector over the Years

Between April 2000 and December 2021, India attracted a significant $104.18 billion in foreign direct investment (FDI), making it an increasingly attractive destination for global investors. Initiatives such as "Make in India" and "Atmanirbhar Bharat" have significantly boosted local production and assembly capabilities. Consequently, India's position improved remarkably in the World Bank's Ease of Doing Business Rankings, climbing from 142nd place in 2014 to 63rd in 2019. The medical device sector is poised for substantial growth in the near future. Additionally, the current Indian Public Procurement Policy presents further opportunities. Geopolitical dynamics have also intensified foreign investor interest in India.

## 15.4 What Is the Government of India (GOI) Doing to Improve the Medical Device Sector in India?

### 15.4.1 100% FDI (Foreign Direct Investment)

For both existing and new setups within the sector, the expectation is that full foreign direct investments (FDIs) will significantly benefit the industry. Robust FDI inflows reflect the confidence that global companies have in the Indian market for medical devices. The most FDIs have been drawn to industries like implants, consumables, equipment, and instruments. The amount of FDI that entered the market for medical and surgical appliances from April 2000 to September 2020 was USD 2.17 billion. Between April 2000 and December 2021, FDI inflow into the market for medical and surgical appliances totaled USD 2.35 billion. Diagnostic imaging is anticipated to grow by USD 50 billion at a CAGR (compound annual growth rate) of 13.5% between 2020 and 2025. India received USD 600 million between 2015 and 2020 in the form of investments from nations including Singapore, the United States, Europe, and Japan.

### 15.4.2 Government Initiatives

To stimulate the domestic production of medical devices, the Department of Pharmaceuticals has initiated a Production Linked Incentive (PLI) scheme. This program, which spans from 2021 to 2028, offers financial support totaling INR 3420 crore (about USD 468.78 million) to enhance local manufacturing capabilities and draw considerable investments [1]. As part of this initiative, the establishment of eight new manufacturing plants (refer to Table 15.1) is anticipated to secure an investment of INR 260.40 crore and generate approximately 2599 employment opportunities.

The government has also sanctioned nine qualifying project proposals expected to secure commitments from companies including Siemens Healthcare Private Limited, Allengers Medical Systems Limited (AMSL), Allengers OEM Private Limited (AOPL), Wipro GE Healthcare Private Limited, Nipro India Corporation Private Limited, Sahajanand Medical Technologies Private Limited, and Involution Healthcare Private Limited, among others, amounting to a cumulative investment of INR 729.63 crore (approximately USD 100.01 million).

#### 15.4.2.1 Top Domestic Companies That Are Involved in the Med-Tech Industry

Some of the companies involved in med-tech are as follows:

- Allied Medical Limited is a company that develops life-saving tools such as anesthesia machines, ventilators, consumables, infusion pumps, and electrocardiography machines. Its revenue during the financial year (FY) 2020 amounted to INR 60 crore.
- Trivitron Healthcare: Its revenue is INR 700 crores.
- Transasia Bio-Medicals: This company has evolved into an INR 1000 crore unit over the years. It offers goods and services in the fields of biochemistry, hematology, coagulation, erythrocyte sedimentation rate, study of the immune system, analysis of urine, intensive care, managing diabetes, the study of microorganisms, and genetic and molecular testing.
- Paramount Healthcare: Its annual revenue amounts to INR 50 crores.
- Bioline India: Its annual revenue amounts to INR 25 crores

**Table 15.1** Plants, products, and committed investment

| S. no. | Name of the applicant | Name of the product | Committed investment (in crore) |
|---|---|---|---|
| Target segment 1: radiology and imaging medical devices (both ionizing and nonionizing radiation products) and nuclear imaging devices | | | |
| 1 | M/S. Philips Global Business Services LLP (limited liability partnership) | MRI (magnetic resonance imaging) coils | 103.46 |
| Target segment 2: anesthetics, cardio-respiratory medical devices (including cardio-respiratory catheters), and renal care medical devices | | | |
| 1 | M/S. Allied Medical Limited | Anesthesia workstation, unit gas scavengers, kits, masks-anesthesia, unit vaporizers, ventilators, automated external defibrillators (AEDs), oxygen concentrator and other products, bi-phasic defibrillators, infusion pumps—syringe and volumetric, intensive care ventilators, emergency ventilators, high flow oxygen devices, multi-parameter monitor, and suction machine | 22.89 |
| 2 | M/S. Deck Mount Electronics Limited | Anesthesia unit ventilators, dialyzer, and oxygen concentrators | 10 |
| 3 | M/S. Microtek New Technologies Private Limited | Oxygen concentrators | 4.5 |
| Target segment 3: all implants including implantable electronic devices | | | |
| 1 | M/S. Meril Healthcare Pvt. Ltd. | Hip implants, knee implants, and other implants | 30.03 |
| 2 | M/S. Meril Life Sciences Pvt. Ltd. | Heart valves, stents, and PTCA (percutaneous transluminal coronary angioplasty) balloon catheter | 35.06 |
| 3 | M/S. Envision Scientific Pvt. Ltd. | Stents and PTCA balloon catheter | 48.73 |
| 4 | M/S. Bio India Interventional technologies Pvt. Ltd. | Drug-eluting stents and drug-eluting balloon | 5.37 |

### 15.4.3 Med-Tech Rules and Creation of Medical Device Parks

The "Medical Devices Rules 2017" was released by the Central Drugs Standard Control Organization (CDSCO) in 2017 and came into effect in 2018. These included the regulatory frameworks that importers and manufacturers of medical devices were required to obtain in order to be registered and granted a license. Two new amendments were introduced in February 2020. These were:

(i) The first amendment introduced a chapter focused on the mandatory registration of medical devices by manufacturers and importers.
(ii) The second amendment exempted 37 categories of medical devices, which were either already regulated or notified, from the new registration requirements. [1].

In January 2020, the government established the National Medical Devices Promotion Council, aiming to foster the domestic production of advanced medical devices and attract investments into the industry. This council is chaired by the secretary of the Department for Promotion of Industry & Internal Trade (DPIIT). Additionally, the Indian government authorized the development of four medical device parks in Andhra Pradesh, Telangana, Tamil Nadu, and Kerala, with a funding allocation of INR 100 crore (USD 13.5 million). These parks, designed to provide essential infrastructure for businesses to quickly start operations, are expected to reduce production costs [1].

AMTZ (Andhra Pradesh MedTech Zone) has experienced exceptional growth in 2017, with businesses pledging to invest INR 1500 crores and creating approximately 7000 direct jobs. A medical devices park is anticipated to be built in Madhya Pradesh's Pitampura-Dhar-Mhow region, covering 360.06 acres (as suggested by the state), at a cost of INR 222.77 crore, in order to create 1000 jobs. The government stated in July 2021 that it will construct a medical park in Uttar Pradesh, which is anticipated to bring in an estimated INR 500 crores (USD 67.13 million) in revenue and create employment for 2300 people. To generate 20,000 jobs, the Government of India (GOI) sanctioned a proposal in September 2021 to invest INR 5000 crore (USD 674.36 million) for the development of a medical devices park in the industrial township of Nalagarh, located in the Solan district of Himachal Pradesh [40].

In September 2021, the government approved the construction of a medical devices park in Oragadam (Tamil Nadu), which is anticipated to attract an estimated investment of INR 3500 crore (USD 472.05 million) and provide direct and indirect employment to 10,000 people. Punjab's industry and commerce minister, Mr. Sunder Sham Arora, revealed plans for a 210-acre medical device park in Rajpura, Punjab. The project is expected to cost around INR 180 crores (USD 24.67 million), and it will generate 600 jobs.

## 15.5 A Fruit of GOI Efforts: Foreign Med-Tech Companies Investing in India

Thanks to GOI initiatives, various foreign companies are showing interest in investing in the Indian med-tech sector. Omron Healthcare, with its headquarters in Japan and office in India since 2010, has been developing growth strategies for the country that could involve opening a factory and increasing its retail presence. The company aims to expand its footprint in Southern India, expecting this region to account for

40% of its sales in FY 2020. To achieve this, it plans to establish a center in Warangal and open ten retail outlets across India by the end of 2021. The company projects generating INR 220 crore (USD 30 million) in revenue within India during this period. To improve patient monitoring in India, Stasis Health Private Limited and Medtronic India Private Limited teamed together in September 2021. Siemens Healthineers declared in September 2021 that its Gujarat unit, Vadodara, would produce molecular testing kits in India [1]. Due to GOI initiatives, foreign medical device manufacturing nations in China may also receive a wonderful opportunity to operate from India. The list of businesses that can open manufacturing facilities in India is given in Table 15.2.

### 15.5.1 Jobs Which Can Be Created in India by Foreign Med-Tech Companies

About 50,476 people work directly for foreign manufacturing nations in China. This number could be transferred to India provided we are able to attract foreign manufacturing units to work in India. As per the Advanced Medical Technology Association, for every five jobs in the medical technology sector, an additional seven to ten positions are created. Thus, we can expect that the total number of jobs created would be around 1,00,000 if these foreign manufacturing units decide to operate in India. The health sector in India has had a significant increase in employment opportunities during the previous few years. According to a KPMG (Klynveld Peat Marwick Goerdeler) and FICCI (Federation of Indian Chambers of Commerce & Industry) analysis, the healthcare industry of India directly employed 4.7 million people in 2015, making it the fifth largest employer overall. As per NSDC (National Skill Development Corporation), by 2022, the healthcare sector is projected to directly employ approximately 7.5 million individuals, with an estimated annual growth of 500,000 jobs, leading to an increase of about 2.7 million jobs between 2017 and 2022.

## 15.6 Employment Opportunities for Indian Paramedics in Other Nations

The world of healthcare is evolving rapidly, with advances in technology and medical practices revolutionizing patient care. The digital health sector in India is gaining prominence, offering a plethora of employment opportunities. Additionally, paramedical jobs across the globe, including Europe, Japan, the United Kingdom, Australia, and North America, are in high demand. These roles include various healthcare professionals such as registered nurses, physical therapists, medical technologists, and support staff involved in patient care. However, this area is grappling with challenges that span different regions of the world, requiring prompt and diverse solutions.

**Table 15.2** List of businesses that can open manufacturing facilities in India

| S. no. | Countries | Companies | No. of employees | References |
|---|---|---|---|---|
| 1 | United States | Baxter | 450 | |
| | | Abbot | 4000 | [9] |
| | | Medtronic | 2000 | [10] |
| | | Stryker | 300 | [11] |
| | | 3M | 2227 | [12] |
| | | Johnson & Johnson | 8000 | [13] |
| | | General Electric | 20,000 | [14] |
| 2 | Japan | Nipro | 3000 | [15] |
| | | Sysmex | 800 | [16] |
| | | Nihon Kohden | 400 | [17] |
| | | Fukuda | 350 | [18] |
| | | Konica Minolta | 500 | [19] |
| | | Menicon | 1416 | [20] |
| | | Shimadzu | 200 | [21] |
| 3 | South Korea | Osstem Implants | 900 | [22] |
| | | Dentium | 577 | [23] |
| | | Trismed | 400 | [24] |
| | | Sejong Industrial Co. | 146 | [25] |
| 4 | United Kingdom | Intersurgical group | 300 | [26] |
| | | Keeler | 350 | [27] |
| | | Convatec | 1000 | [28] |
| 5 | Europe | Fresenius | 2288 | [29] |
| | | B. Braun Melsungen | 1317 | [30] |
| | | Drager | 700 | [31] |
| | | Hartmann | 255 | [32] |
| | | Karl Storz | 30 | [33] |
| | | Colopast | 500 | [34] |
| | | Getinge | 2400 | [35] |
| 6 | Australia | Cochlear | 1000 | [36] |
| | | LBT | 1000 | [37] |
| | | AusBiotech | 400 | [38] |
| | | Australian Cardiovascular Alliance | 200 | [39] |
| | **Total number of employees** | | **57,406** | |

### 15.6.1 Europe's Paramedical Workforce Shortfall and Cross-Border Solutions

The European Commission, in its staff working document on an action plan for the European Union (EU) health workforce, raises concerns about an impending shortfall of approximately 1 million paramedical workers by 2020. With a population of 447 million inhabitants, the stakes are high. Health workforce shortages have forced some member states to recruit paramedical staff from nations outside the EU. As per a survey of ten member states, nearly 30% of all migrant workers in countries like Austria, Belgium, Denmark, Germany, the Netherlands, and Poland come from nations outside the EU. The situation is even more dire in countries like France, Italy, Ireland, and the United Kingdom, where the figures rise to as high as 80%. India, with its skilled paramedical staff, stands poised to address this shortage through proper language training and the fulfillment of necessary medico-legal certifications [41].

### 15.6.2 Japan's Aging Population and the Need for Healthcare Workers

Japan is facing the challenges of an aging population. The Ministry of Health, Labour, and Welfare estimates a need for around two million healthcare workers by 2025. The shortage of about 8 nurses per 1,00,000 individuals highlights the urgency to address this gap to cater to the rapidly aging population. The nation's "Leave No One behind" policy emphasizes the importance of equal healthcare access. As Japan seeks foreign workers with medical knowledge and Japanese language proficiency, Indian paramedical staff can capitalize on this opportunity by acquiring relevant qualifications, hands-on experience, and language skills [42–44].

### 15.6.3 The United Kingdom's (UK's) NHS (National Health Services) Staffing Crisis and Indian Expertise

The United Kingdom's NHS is grappling with a staffing crisis. With a population set to reach 8–9 crores by 2050 due to increased migration, the demand for trained healthcare professionals is on the rise. Shortages of 39,652 nurses and 8158 doctors have raised alarms. The aging nursing workforce, retirement of experienced professionals, and a shortage of nurse educators contribute to this deficit. Recruitment efforts have turned to overseas professionals, with nurses from outside the United Kingdom frequently working more hours and staying longer in NHS hospitals than their UK counterparts. India, a commonwealth nation with a significant English-speaking population, boasts over 24,000 nursing staff and 40,000 paramedical healthcare assistants serving in NHS hospitals. Further deployment of Indian paramedical staff can address the challenges of an aging population and shortage of paramedic staff in the United Kingdom [45].

### 15.6.4 Australia's Healthcare Struggles and the Potential for Indian Staff

Australia's vast landmass is characterized by desert expanses, with about 75% covered by desert. Despite a population of 2.6 crores, growth projections of 20% in 14 years and 65% in 65 years necessitate enhanced medical facilities and healthcare professionals. The demand for nurses is predicted to outstrip supply, requiring approximately 85,000 nurses by 2025 and 1,23,000 by 2030. Stress on the existing healthcare system and a reluctance among Australians to enter the sector have contributed to this shortage. With a paramedical, nursing, and midwifery workforce of 1.2 lakh from outside Australia, the nation looks to South and Southeast Asia. India, positioned as a significant contributor, could further strengthen its presence through lenient visa allowances and language training [46].

### 15.6.5 North America's Healthcare Workforce Demand and Indian Talent

The North American region, encompassing Canada and USA, is home to a population of approximately 57.9 crores, with a projected growth of 25–30% over the next 12 years. This growth necessitates a robust healthcare workforce. The American Nurses Association (ANA) predicts a need for over 2,75,000 additional nurses between 2020 and 2030, with nursing employment opportunities projected to grow at a rapid 9%. The registered nursing workforce is anticipated to rise to 3.3 million by 2029, up from 3 million in 2019, reflecting an increase of 221,900 nurses. Canada faces a worse scenario, with a demand for 191,100 registered nurses and registered psychiatric nurses between 2019 and 2028. The Canadian government employs immigration as a solution, allowing internationally trained medical professionals to apply for supervised 30-day medical licenses. Similarly, the USA is attracting healthcare workers with visa exemptions and improved pay schemes. India, renowned for its nursing and paramedical staff, particularly in North America, can seize these opportunities by preparing for English language certifications, staying updated on medical advances, and understanding the medico-legal landscape of developed countries [47, 48].

### 15.6.6 India's Healthcare Future and Bridging the Gap

By 2022, India's healthcare sector is set to directly employ about 7.5 million individuals. Between 2017 and 2022, the sector is projected to create roughly 2.7 million new positions, averaging around 500,000 jobs per year. However, the nation grapples with a shortage of qualified nursing and paramedical experts, particularly in rural areas. With a nurse/medical assistant population ratio of 1.7 per 1000 population (falling short of the World Health Organization's [WHO] prescribed ratio of 3 per 1000), there is a huge disparity not only between rural and urban India but also between different states. This predicament underscores the need for targeted investment and improvement in hospital environments to attract and retain skilled paramedical and nursing staff. The path to resolving this shortage involves embracing the latest technological advancements, creating diverse job opportunities, and equipping paramedical staff to ensure efficient and smooth healthcare delivery to rural populations.

In conclusion, the global healthcare landscape presents a range of employment opportunities in the paramedical sector, both within India's burgeoning digital health industry and across various regions facing healthcare workforce challenges. With the right training, language proficiency, and expertise, Indian paramedical staff can bridge these gaps and contribute significantly to healthcare delivery worldwide [1–7].

## 15.7 National Healthcare Scenario: India

The healthcare sector in India faces numerous challenges despite significant government efforts. These include operational inefficiencies, high costs, and inconsistent quality of care. Compared to other low- and middle-income countries, India lags behind in several health metrics. For instance, the country has higher infant and maternal mortality rates and a lower life expectancy of 62 years, which is 3 years below the average for LMICs. Additionally, a 2010 report on the global burden of diseases shows that India lost a substantial number of disability- adjusted life years (DALYs), totaling 518,879,000. The Indian healthcare system is burdened by a massive economic cost estimated at around USD 600 billion. Millions of people across the country are affected by limited access to and high costs of quality healthcare. The situation is further compounded by a shortage of medical professionals and inadequate infrastructure. Currently, there are only 1.65 trained doctors and nurses per 1000 people, falling short of the World Health Organization's recommended 2.5 per 1000. Similarly, hospital bed availability is just 0.9 per 1000 people, significantly below the global average of 3.0 and the WHO's recommended 3.5. India's healthcare expenditure is only 3.9% of its GDP, compared to Brazil's 8.9%, Russia's 6.2%, and China's 5.2%. Additionally, 61% of healthcare costs are borne out-of-pocket, as only 26% of the population has health insurance coverage, and the private sector's share is a mere 3–5%. By 2020, the number of elderly individuals (aged 60 and above) is projected to reach 97 million, up from approximately 64 million in 2010. India is projected to experience a significant increase in diabetes cases, reaching 100 million by 2030 from 60 million in 2011. Noncommunicable diseases (NCD) are also expected to account for 76% of health issues by that year. Although India has over 1.3 million registered doctors, the doctor-to-patient ratio is 1:834, surpassing the WHO's recommended ratio of 1:1000. However, with a population of around 1.38 billion, the country still faces a shortage of medical professionals. The distribution of doctors is uneven, with 80% concentrated in urban areas, where only 27% of the population resides. Many doctors work in the private sector, which can be financially inaccessible for many. Additionally, 75% of India's healthcare infrastructure is located in urban areas. India's rural healthcare facilities often fall short of standards, with only a small percentage meeting the Indian Public Health Standards. Many primary health centers lack essential staff, such as doctors, laboratory technicians, and pharmacists. To meet the World Health Organization's recommended health worker ratio, India needs to hire an additional 1.8 million healthcare professionals.

The country faces a complex health crisis, characterized by a rising prevalence of communicable and noncommunicable diseases. Noncommunicable diseases, including heart disease, lung diseases, and stroke, are the leading causes of death and disability in India, and their economic burden is expected to reach $4.58 trillion by 2030 [49, 50].

Therefore, to curb these problems, our futuristic healthcare delivery ecosystem (based on telemedicine) can revolutionize NCD detection at an early stage and provide appropriate treatment, treatment adherence, and better compliance with reduced carbon footprint and enhanced social stability, without putting any extra burden on state/patient.

## 15.8 Job Opportunities in the Domain of Telemedicine

With changing demographics, increasing consumer spending, and rising lifestyles, diseases drive the need to build better, accessible, and inclusive healthcare infrastructure for all. Telemedicine has developed as a potent, trustworthy, and reasonably priced medical method to achieve the goal of providing affordable and quality health care to all. We have developed a cutting-edge, reliable, thorough, simple-to-install and -operate telemedicine clinic that is an all-in-one diagnostic lab and specialist consultation hub, with artificial intelligence (AI)-enabled real-time data management platform, to deliver telemedicine services. These kiosks will not only assist in attaining SDG3 goals but will also provide employment, which is currently the main challenge faced by a huge population.

Our ICMR-CIBioD telehealth kiosk is dedicated to advance health equity as an outcome which will target cost barriers, distance barriers, and the quality-of-service barriers.

It is estimated that, if one kiosk serves 15,000 rural people, then to target 897,968,854 Indian rural people at present, we require 59,865 kiosks. For the 169,676,507 Indian urban slum population, one kiosk can serve 30,000 people. Therefore, in urban slums, we require around 5655 kiosks. This will generate employment for 151,354 people. For teleconsultation services, we require one comprehensive health officer (CHO) per machine. There are about 6,64,369 villages in India. If we install one machine per village, then on average it will provide employment to around 6,64,369 rural people across the country.

## 15.9 Global Healthcare Scenario

### 15.9.1 Africa

According to estimates, Africa has the second-largest continental population (1,398,312,019). In Africa, there are 45 people per square kilometer. About 56.2% of the population is rural (785,697,541 people), while 43.8% of the population is urban (612,614,478 people). The average doctor-to-population ratio is 0.79, which indicates that there are now 1,104,667 open positions in the medical field. With an estimated 243,514,255 urban slum dwellers, Africa accounts for a total of 39.75% of the world's urban slums. In tropical Africa, there is a significant risk of new infectious illnesses that are transmitted through vectors and by wildlife. In Africa, the rise of noncommunicable diseases (NCDs) is increasingly contributing to both mortality and disability. A significant proportion of the population is impacted by these conditions, with 48% suffering from hypertension, 20% dealing with obesity, and 5.1% diagnosed with diabetes. Despite significant advancement over the past 20 years, the African Region still lags significantly below the global average in terms of HIV, tuberculosis, and malaria. In the African region, the ratio of healthcare workers is notably low, with just 1.5 doctors, nurses, and midwives available per 10,000 individuals [51]. If one kiosk serves 15,000 people, then to target 785,697,541 rural people, we require 52,380 kiosks. For the 243,514,255 urban slum population, assuming that one kiosk can serve 30,000 people, we need 8118 kiosks. This will generate about 139,751 jobs.

### 15.9.2 South America

South America has a population of 437,156,285. The rural population is 109,332,787 and the urban population is 327,823,498. Its population density is 25 per square km. The typical ratio of doctors to patients in the region is 2.3 doctors for every 1000 individuals. The number of people living in urban slums is 68,056,159. Applying the previously mentioned rates (1 kiosk for 15,000 rural people and 30,000 urban slum dwellers), we will need 7289 kiosks for rural areas and 2269 kiosks for urban slums. This will provide employment to 22,081 people [57].

### 15.9.3 Southeast Asia

Over a quarter of the world's population (675,118,4759) lives in Southeast Asian countries, which are made up of 11 nations. This includes 322,301,560 rural and 352,816,915 urban residents. There are 222,274,657 individuals living in urban slums. Southeast Asian nations struggle with an uneven distribution of health professionals, and rural areas frequently lack sufficient staff. According to estimates, there are 5.9 doctors for every 10,000 people in this region. Cambodia, Indonesia, Laos, Myanmar, and Vietnam are among the five nations that fall below the WHO's acute shortage criteria of 228 physicians, nurses, and midwives per 1000 people [52]. Applying previously mentioned rates (1 kiosk for 15,000 rural people and 30,000 urban slum dwellers), we will need 21,487 kiosks for rural people and 7409 kiosks for urban slums. This will provide employment for 66,710 people.

### 15.9.4 SAARC (South Asian Association for Regional Cooperation)

There are roughly 1.7 billion people living in SAARC countries with Maldives having the lowest population (0.54 million) and India having the highest population (1380 million). Most people live in rural areas (1,150,560,000). The population density of this region is 557 people per square kilometer with Maldives having the highest (1802 people per square km) and Bhutan having the lowest population density (20 people per square km).

A mistaken belief is that communicable diseases account for most deaths in SAARC countries. However, this is not true and noncommunicable diseases far outscore communicable diseases in causing deaths in most of SAARC countries. In Maldives (2019), maternal, prenatal, nutrition problems, and communicable diseases accounted for 8.16% of all deaths while noncommunicable diseases resulted in 85.18% of deaths. In Bhutan, the percentage of deaths caused by noncommunicable diseases in 2019 was 72.74%. In Sri Lanka, 9.47% of deaths resulted from communicable illnesses, maternal, perinatal, and nutritional disorders while 82.52% of deaths were caused by noncommunicable diseases. In Nepal, maternal, prenatal, and nutrition-related illnesses account for 24.82% of all deaths, while noncommunicable illnesses caused 66.46% of deaths. In Afghanistan, communicable diseases, maternal, prenatal, and nutrition-related ailments are the leading causes of mortality in 2019. Noncommunicable illnesses accounted for 49.78% of all deaths. In Bangladesh (2019), maternal, perinatal, and nutrition-related disorders accounted for 22.61% of all deaths, while noncommunicable diseases accounted for 70.26% of all deaths. In Pakistan (2019), maternal, perinatal, and nutrition-related disorders accounted for 33.15% of all deaths, while noncommunicable diseases caused 59.86% of deaths.

The average doctor-to-population ratio is 0.93 doctors per 1000 people in India. Applying the previously mentioned rates (1 kiosk for 15,000 rural people and 30,000 urban slum dwellers), we will need 76,704 kiosks. This will generate 177,186 jobs.

The estimated number of kiosks needed and jobs created are given ahead in Tables 15.3 and 15.4.

## 15.10 Conclusion

To conclude, it seems pertinent to state that the entire world is facing a shortage of healthcare workers. The changing global scenario is likely to create numerous employment opportunities for Indian medical and paramedical personnel. To obtain the full benefit of these opportunities, Indian medical and paramedical personnel shall be proficient in different languages (especially English) and aware of medico-legal issues in different countries. The shortage of healthcare professionals could be mitigated through the use of telemedicine. Telemedicine can not only provide easily accessible, quality healthcare at affordable prices, but can also help in the creation of innumerable jobs.

**Table 15.3** Estimated number of telekiosks needed in different regions

| Human resource | India | Africa | Southeast Asia | SAARC | South America |
|---|---|---|---|---|---|
| Kiosk service engineers | 655 | 605 | 289 | 767 | 96 |
| Software experts | 655 | 605 | 289 | 767 | 96 |
| Supporting staff | 2621 | 2420 | 1116 | 3069 | 383 |
| Doctors | 16,380 | 15,125 | 7224 | 19,176 | 2390 |
| Lab technicians | 65,520 | 60,498 | 28,896 | 76,704 | 9558 |
| Attendants/helpers | 65,520 | 60,498 | 28,896 | 76,704 | 9558 |
| **Total kiosks required** | **65,520** | **60,498** | **28,896** | **76,704** | **9558** |
| **Total estimated employment generated** | **1,51,351** | **1,39,751** | **66,710** | **1,77,186** | **22,081** |

**Table 15.4** Estimated staff requirement for telekiosks

| Human resource | Requirement in numbers/100 kiosks |
|---|---|
| Kiosk service engineer | 1 |
| Software experts | 1 |
| Supporting staff | 4 |
| Doctors | 25 |
| Lab technicians | 100 |
| Attendants/helpers | 100 |
| **Total** | **231 per 100 kiosks** |

## References


1. Medical device report, March 2021, Indian brand equity foundation (IBEF). Downloaded from: https://www.ibef.org/industry/medical-devices.
2. Medical device for emerging markets: Potential Indian market, TATA ELXSI. 2019. Downloaded from: https://www.tataelxsi.com/storage/insights/August2021/Tata-Elxsi-Whitepaper-5-Emerging-Markets-for-Medical-Device-Manufacturers.pdf.
3. Medical devices making in India—a leap for Indian healthcare. Deloitte. 2016. Downloaded from: https://www2.deloitte.com/content/dam/Deloitte/in/Documents/life-sciences-health-care/in-lshc-medical-devices-making-in-india-noexp.pdf.
4. Import of medical devices up by record 24%; White Papers; June 2019. Downloaded from: https://www.biospectrumindia.com/reports-white-papers/17/14035/import-of-medical-devices-up-by-record-24.html#:~:text=Imports%20of%20medical%20devices%20are,stated%20a%20visibly%20upset%20Mr.
5. Global spending on health: Weathering the storm; WHO; 2020. Downloaded from: https://www.who.int/publications/i/item/9789240017788.
6. India medical device market outlook to 2023. Downloaded from: https://www.kenresearch.com/industry-reports/india-medical-device-market.
7. Building resilient supply chains, revitalizing American manufacturing, and fostering broad-based growth. Downloaded from: https://www.whitehouse.gov/wp-content/uploads/2021/06/100-day-supply-chain-review-report.pdf.
8. Sarwal R, Prasad U, Madangopal K, et al. Investment opportunities in India's healthcare sector. NITI Aayog. 2021. Downloaded from: https://www.niti.gov.in/sites/default/files/2023-02/InvestmentOpportunities_HealthcareSector.pdf.

9. Abbot expanding manufacturing capacity in China to meet demands of fast growing nutrition market. Downloaded from: https://www.prnewswire.com/news-releases/abbott-expanding-manufacturingcapacity-in-china-to-meet-demands-of-fast-growing-nutrition-market127864158.
10. Medtronic to build Chinese facility for manufacture of advanced diabetes devices. Downloaded from: https://www.fiercebiotech.com/medical-devices/medtronic-to-build-chinese-facility-for-manufacture-advanced-diabetes-devices.
11. Stryker plant expanding, will make surgical instruments in China. Downloaded from: https://www.mlive.com/business/west-michigan/2009/05/stryker_plant_expanding_will_m.html.
12. 3M mask plant in Shanghai in full swing to fulfill US orders. Downloaded from: https://www.globaltimes.cn/page/202004/1185585.shtml.
13. Johnson and Johnson still bullish on China health care industry even as US-China trade war rages on. Downloaded from: https://www.scmp.com/business/china-business/article/2172515/johnson-johnsonstill-bullish-chinese-health-care-industry.
14. Ge.com has been updated to serve our three go forward companies. Downloaded from: https://www.ge.com.
15. Our heritage. Downloaded from: https://www.nipro-group.com/en/our-company/our-heritage.
16. Sysmex news. Downloaded from: https://www.sysmex.co.jp/en/news/2018/index.html.
17. Made in China. Nihon Kohden reagents. Downloaded form: https https://www.made-in-china.com/products-search/hot-china-products/Nihon_Kohden_Reagents.html.
18. Fukuda Denshi. Production systems. Downloaded from: https://fukuda.com/about/production-systems/.
19. Konica Minolta. Downloaded from: https://www.konicaminolta.com/global-cn/corporate/groupglobal.html.
20. Menicon Co., Ltd. Downloaded from: https://www.menicon.com/product/.
21. Shimadzu integrated report 2022. Downloaded from: https://www.shimadzu.com/sites/shimadzu.com/files/ir/pdf/shimadzu_integrated_report_2022p_e.pdf.
22. Osstem implant Co., Ltd. Company profile. Downloaded from: https://www.dnb.com/business-directory/company-profiles.osstem_implant_coltd.cd4a7389b43107bd28c0d73b3bf7dc0b.html.
23. Dentium China Co., Ltd. Information. Downloaded from: https://www.apollo.io/companies/Dentium-China-Co%2D%2DLtd-/56e68fd8f3e5bb023600a212.
24. Professional China Trismed Vitapia 7000k neonate disposable Spo2 sensor. Downloaded from: https://www.med-linket.com/professional-china-trismed-vitapia-7000k-neonate-disposable-spo2-sensor.html.
25. SJG Sejong Co., Ltd. https://www.marklines.com/en/top500/sejong-industrial.
26. Intersurgical China. Downloaded from: http://haitianinter.com/en/2020/06/11/intersurgical-china/.
27. Direct ophthalmoscopes. Downloaded from: https://www.keeler.co.uk/products/handhelds/direct-ophthalmoscopes.html.
28. Convatecgroup.com. Locations. Downloaded from: https://www.convatecgroup.com/about-us/locations/.
29. A market in motion. Fresenius medical care. Downloaded from: https://www.freseniusmedicalcare.com/en/media/insights/patient-stories/a-market-in-motion.
30. B. Braun locations: Asia Pacific. Downloaded from: https://www.bbraun.co.in/en/company/bbraun-asia-pacific/locations.html.
31. Bloomberg. Quick search: company profiles and news. Downloaded from: https://www.bloomberg.com/profile/company/3385986Z:US.
32. PTR Hartmann. Lechang/China. Downloaded from: https://www.ptr-hartmann.com/company/news/news-press-releases/lechang-china/.
33. Karl Storz. Shanghai, China. Downloaded from: https://www.karlstorz.com/in/en/china-shanghai.htm.

34. Report. Boosting the Indian medical device industry. Downloaded from: https://pharmaceuticals.gov.in/sites/default/files/Final%20Boosting%20of%20Medical%20Devices%20 Industry%20-%20Report%20-%202023.pdf.
35. Getinge group acquires 100% of Acare medical sciences ltd. Downloaded from: https://www.clearwaterinternational.com/de/transaktionen/getinge-group-acquires100-of-acare-medical-science-ltd.
36. Cochlear: Winning in Asia. Downloaded from: https://www.winninginasia.com.au/cochlear/.
37. LBT secures capital from Autobio diagnostics. Downloaded from: https://biotechdispatch.com.au/news/lbt-secures-capital-from-autobio-diagnostic.
38. Australian biotechnology sector snapshot 2022. Downloaded from: https://www.ausbiotech.org/documents/item/707.
39. Mesoblast enters into strategic cardiovascular alliance for China with Talsy pharmaceutical group. Downloaded from: https://www.globenewswire.com/news-release/2018/07/17/1538149/0/en/Mesoblast-Enters-Into-Strategic-Cardiovascular-Alliance-for-China-With-Tasly-Pharmaceutical-Group.html.
40. Outlook: Medical device park worth Rs 5000 crore to come up at Nalagarh. Centre clears Himachal proposal. Downloaded from: https://www.outlookindia.com/website/story/india-news-medical-device-park-worth-rs-5000-cr-to-come-up-at-nalagarh-centre-clears-himachal-proposal/395704.
41. "Healthcare personnel statistics – nursing and caring professionals". Eurostat statistics explained. Downloaded from: https://ec.europa.eu/eurostat/statisticsexplained/index.php?title=Healthcare_personnel_statistics_-_nursing_and_caring_professionals.
42. More than 1 in 10 people in Japan are aged 80 or over. Here is how its aging population is reshaping the country. Downloaded from: https://www.weforum.org/agenda/2023/09/elderly-oldest-population-world-japan/.
43. "Japan Health System Review". Health Systems in Transition 2018;8(1):2018. ISBN 978–92-9022–626-0. © World Health Organization 2018. Asia Pacific Observatory on Health Systems and Policies.
44. Nursing in Japan. Downloaded from: https://www.nurse.or.jp/english/assets/nursing/nursing-in-japan-en.pdf.
45. Staffing crisis deepens in NHS England with 110000 posts unfilled. Downloaded from: https://www.theguardian.com/society/2022/mar/03/staffing-crisis-deepens-in-nhs-england-with-110000-posts-unfilled.
46. "Australia's Future Health Workforce – Nurses: Overview Report. Downloaded from: https://www.health.gov.au/sites/default/files/documents/2021/03/nurses-australia-s-future-health-workforce-reports-overview-report.pdf.
47. American Association of Colleges of Nursing: The Voice of Academic Nursing. Fact sheet: Nursing shortage. Downloaded from: https://www.aacnnursing.org/Portals/0/PDFs/Fact-Sheets/Nursing-Shortage-Factsheet.pdf.
48. World Health Organization. National Health Workforce Accounts Data Portal. Downloaded from: https://apps.who.int/nhwaportal/Home/Index.
49. Bhattacharya S, Heidler P, Varshney S. Incorporating neglected non-communicable diseases into the national health program-a review. Front Public Health. 2023;10:1093170.
50. World Health Organization. Global strategy on human resources for health: workforce 2030. Downloaded from: https://www.observatoriorh.org/sites/default/files/webfiles/fulltext/2019/global_strategy_workforce2030_who.pdf.
51. Ahmat A, Okoroafor SC, Kazanga I, et al. The health workforce status in the WHO African Region: findings of a cross-sectional study. BMJ Glob Health. 2022;7(Suppl 1):e008317.
52. The World Bank: Physicians (per 1000 people). Downloaded from: https://data.worldbank.org/indicator/SH.MED.PHYS.ZS.

# 16 Piloting a Futuristic Healthcare Delivery Ecosystem in Rural Parts of Himachal Pradesh

Varinder Garg, Manoj Goyal, Surinder Rana, Basant Kumar, Shankar Prinja, Harish Kumar, Anupriya Bhardwaj, and Sujata Saini

## 16.1 Emergence of Telehealth During the COVID-19 Pandemic

The novel coronavirus (COVID-19) pandemic has brought a revolution into the thinking of healthcare systems and paved the way for the emergence of new and disruptive technologies. For example, during the coronavirus outbreak, telehealth emerged as a lifeline by bridging the communication gap between patients, physicians and symptomatic patients, allowing them to stay at home and still obtain quality healthcare [1].

In April 2020 (during the lockdown), the Center for Innovation and Bio-Design (CIBioD), PGIMER, Chandigarh, in collaboration with the Sri Venkteshwara Indo

V. Garg (✉)
ICMR-Centre for Innovation and Bio-Design (CIBioD), Postgraduate Institute of Medical Education and Research (PGIMER), Chandigarh, Chandigarh, India

A. Bhardwaj · S. Saini
ICMR Center for Innovation and Bio-Design, PGIMER, Chandigarh, India

M. Goyal
Department of Neurology, Postgraduate Institute of Medical Education and Research (PGIMER), Chandigarh, Chandigarh, India

S. Rana
Department of Gastroenterology, PGIMER, Chandigarh, India

B. Kumar
Department of Cardiology, PGIMER, Chandigarh, India

S. Prinja
Department of Community Medicine and School of Public Health, PGIMER, Chandigarh, India

H. Kumar
Department of Computer Science and Engineering, University Institute of Engineering and Technology (UIET) Panjab University, Chandigarh, Punjab, India



V. Garg et al. (eds.), *Innovations in Healthcare Technologies in India*,
https://doi.org/10.1007/978-981-97-0244-2_16

Global Medicare (SVIG), Nirogya Life Line Foundation (NLLF), Menthosa Solutions Private Ltd and Aavishkar Innovation Ventures, launched telemedicine services at PGI satellite centres in Una (Himachal Pradesh) and Sangrur (Punjab). During the lockdown, both centres were equipped with telemedicine and point-of-care testing, allowing patients to receive consultations from doctors.

On April 2021, CIBioD, in collaboration with Tata Communication (Glo Heal), SVIG, NLLF, Menthosa Solutions Private Ltd and Aavishkar Innovation Ventures, launched Telemedicine Services in Thunag (Mandi), Thana Kalan (Una) and Awah Devi (Hamirpur), inaugurated online by the Honorable Chief Minister of Himachal Pradesh Sh. Jai Ram Thakur ji and Information and Broadcasting Minister Sh. Anurag Thakur ji.

The 'ICMR CIBioD' at PGIMER, Chandigarh, encourages innovations in the field of medical devices and instruments by fostering a suitable environment with the participation of many premier technical institutes/industries to attain the ultimate aim of Affordable Healthcare. Through a 'futuristic healthcare delivery ecosystem', CIBioD is promoting telemedicine and artificial intelligence solutions for integrated healthcare in tier II/III towns and rural regions in Himachal Pradesh, Punjab, Haryana, Jammu and Kashmir and Chandigarh.

The Nirogya Life Line Foundation (NLLF) is a non-profit company established with the technical support from CIBioD, PGIMER, Chandigarh. It was set up in 2018 under Section 8 of the Companies Act 2013 with the objective of providing affordable and comprehensive healthcare that meets the international standards for each and every citizen of India. NLLF intends to provide telemedicine services. Its team of experts helps in providing world-class treatment to the patients. NLLF is making constant endeavours to provide healthcare facilities, diagnosis and treatment at an affordable cost to the citizens of India without compromising on the quality of treatment.

## 16.2 India Health Conclave

India Health Conclave was a thought exchange forum which brought together the brightest minds in India's health and medical sectors to discuss the problems and possibilities that lie ahead. The event uncovered and investigated advances in the realm of health. During the conclave, various stakeholders also addressed difficulties in implementing health-related policies.

In terms of income and employment, the Indian healthcare industry has grown to become one of the largest in our country and has seen a major change in the recent decade. The Indian Constitution has given the responsibility to the establishment for raising the level of nutrition, standard of living of the people and public health. However, despite 75 years of independence, medicines and medical devices remain out of bound for most of the country's population due primarily to their high cost. The improvement of infrastructure has happened at a very slow pace; little is added to the research and the talent pool remains limited.

Today, healthcare is undergoing a major transformation, set to reverse the ills of the last several decades. Healthcare is now a priority for the government, and significant efforts are being made to bring it to the people's doors. To meet this goal, the government's policies are focused on disruptive technologies that will influence the entire healthcare ecosystem. This list contains initiatives aimed at achieving universal health coverage. We would like to congratulate the Hon'ble Prime Minister, Shri Narendra Modi, for leading a regime that pushed for schemes like Ayushman Bharat Yojana, Pradhan Mantri Jan Arogya Yojana or PMJAY; National Nutrition Mission or POSHAN Abhiyan; Mission Indradhanush; and AMRIT Pharmacies. Attempts are ongoing to increase health insurance coverage to INR 10 crore per family [2].

In accordance with all these efforts, the Indian Health Conclave was hosted by the Centre for Economic Policy Research and Society for Affordable Healthcare, Hyderabad, on 21 December, 2018, at the Le Meridien, New Delhi.

## 16.3 Objectives

The aim of this Conclave are:

- Collaboration with the health sector, academicians and makers of law and policies
- To establish a think tank to promote indigenous technology
- To device policies for indigenous solutions to complicated health diseases
- To examine the value of technology in improving healthcare provision and efficacy
- To make the health sector more formidable to take on the challenges of the next decade

## 16.4 What Did This Conclave Provide?

The Conclave achieved the following purposes:

- Enhanced awareness on the aspects that go into improving availability of affordable health facilities
- Showcased innovations and best practices in the healthcare sector which will revolve around the theme of supporting quality initiatives in the health sector
- Facilitated a forum to understand 'how innovation is making healthcare delivery more affordable'
- Provided a platform to network with key leaders in health sector

## References

1. Smith AC, Thomas E, Snoswell CL, Haydon H, Mehrotra A, Clemensen J, Caffery LJ. Telehealth for global emergencies: implications for coronavirus disease 2019 (COVID-19). J Telemed Telecare. 2020;26(5):309–13. https://doi.org/10.1177/1357633x20916567.
2. India Health Conclave—CEPR. n.d. https://cepr.in/india-health-conclave-2/.

# The Global Landscape of Med-Tech Industry with Special Reference to the Indian Scenario

17

Varinder Garg

## 17.1 Emergence and Evolution of the Med-Tech Industry

Medical technology (med-tech) has seen a remarkable evolution resulting in changes in healthcare-related practices across the world. This chapter presents an overview of the current global situation of the med-tech business, concentrating on important innovations, problems, and future prospects.

Med-tech has undergone tremendous growth in recent years, owing to improvements in technologies such as artificial intelligence (AI), robotics, telemedicine, and wearable technologies. These have resulted in better patient care, diagnostic accuracy, and treatment outcomes. The occurrence of COVID-19 pandemic has hastened the deployment of telehealth solutions, improving the delivery of and accessibility to healthcare services. The future of medical technology seems bright. Continued AI and machine learning integration into medical devices will improve predictive analytics, medication development, and personalized treatment. Furthermore, the advances in remote monitoring and wearable health technology will enable individuals to take more proactive roles in their health management.

However, "all that glitters is not gold," and accordingly med-tech industry is also facing many problems, chief among which are regulatory hurdles, data privacy concerns, and the requirement for interoperability among multiple healthcare systems. Achieving a balance between innovation and regulatory compliance is a crucial problem for industry stakeholders. Accordingly, global collaboration, ethical considerations, and legal frameworks play a critical role in shaping industry's direction as it evolves. This chapter emphasizes the fluid nature of the med-tech ecosystem and its potential to transform healthcare on a global scale.

V. Garg (✉)
ICMR-Centre for Innovation and Bio-Design (CIBioD), Postgraduate Institute of Medical Education and Research (PGIMER), Chandigarh, Chandigarh, India



V. Garg et al. (eds.), *Innovations in Healthcare Technologies in India*,
https://doi.org/10.1007/978-981-97-0244-2_17

## 17.2 Med-Tech Industry Scenario: International Status

Between 2021 and 2027, the global medical device industry is expected to expand at a compound annual growth rate (CAGR) of 5.2%, building on its estimated value of US$ 455.1 billion in 2021 (Fig. 17.1). The heightened investments in research and development (R&D) by companies within the medical technology sector, alongside more streamlined regulatory approvals, are key drivers of growth in the medical device industry. These factors are expected to significantly boost the market's expansion in the upcoming years.

North America accounted for the greatest revenue share in 2020, and if we go by prediction, it is likely to maintain its supremacy in the years to come (Fig. 17.2). This region has experienced substantial growth due to better healthcare infrastructure and growing interest in living a healthy lifestyle. The major power in North America is the United States. The rapid adoption of innovative medical technologies aimed at enhancing the diagnosis and treatment of severe diseases is expected to be a key driver of market growth in the region.

The Asia-Pacific region has demonstrated the most rapid growth in the medical device market, largely driven by factors such as an aging population, increased income levels, and heightened health awareness. China and India, leading nations in this region, hold the second and fifth positions in global market revenue, respectively. This expansion is expected to be bolstered by significant investments in healthcare infrastructure. The local governments in these countries provide incentives and implement healthcare reforms, which heavily influence the medical device market. In contrast, while North America maintained the highest revenue share throughout the 2020s, its growth rate was slower compared to that of Asia Pacific.

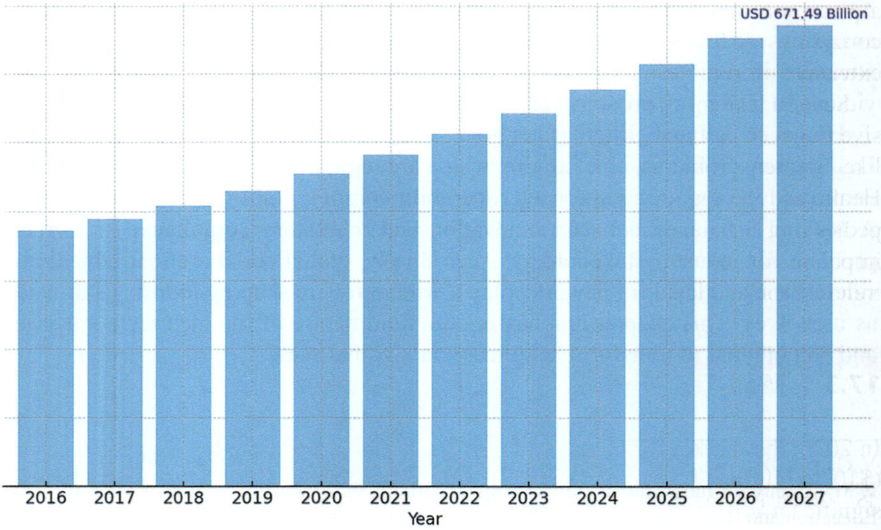


**Fig. 17.1** Medical device market size (2016–2027) [1]

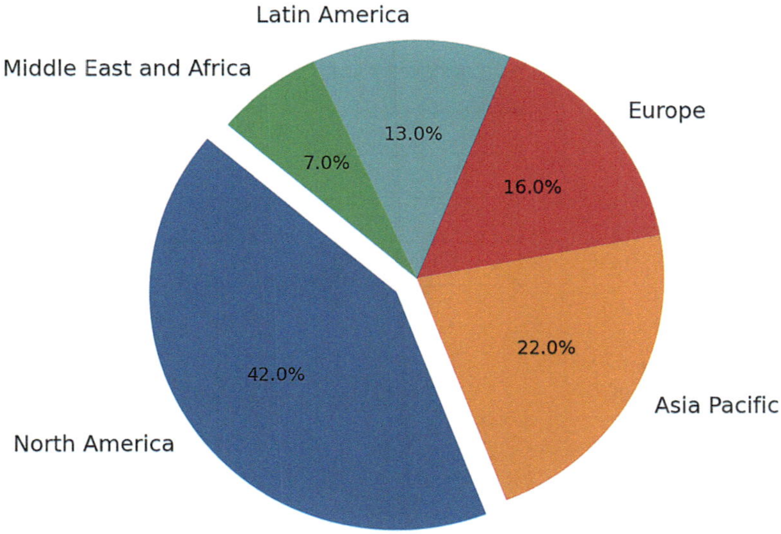


**Fig. 17.2** Medical device market share by region (2020) [1]

### 17.2.1 Key Organizations and Global Market Share Insights

The medical device market is characterized by its fragmentation, with a diverse array of players operating at both global and regional levels. Investment in research and development (R&D) is a prominent focus, driving companies to innovate and enhance their product offerings. Expanding distribution networks worldwide is also a priority for many firms, allowing them to reach broader markets. Among these companies, Medtronic stands out for its substantial market share, attributed to its extensive product portfolio and strong global presence.

Several leading firms dominate the medical device sector, known for their extensive range of products and significant influence in the industry. These organizations like Siemens Healthineers, Medtronics, Dickinson and Company, and Cardinal Health are recognized for their advancements in various medical fields, from orthopedics and cardiovascular solutions to diagnostics and imaging technologies. Their impact is notable in driving innovation, enhancing patient care, and shaping market trends through substantial research and development efforts.

## 17.3 Med-Tech Industry Scenario: National Status

In 2020, the market for medical equipment in India was valued at Rs. 75,611 crore ($10.36 billion). According to Fig. 17.3, India's medical device market is poised for significant growth between 2020 and 2025. The market value is expected to reach approximately US$ 50 billion by 2025, with an estimated annual growth rate of

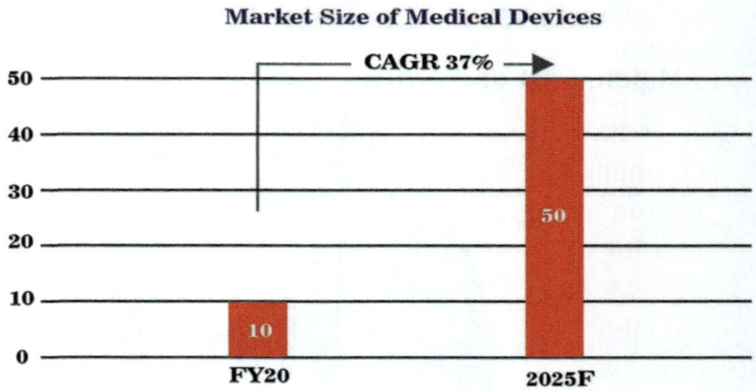


**Fig. 17.3** Medical device market in India (2020–2025)

**Fig. 17.4** Reason and advantages of growth of medical device in India

37%. In 2019, India's medical equipment exports amounted to US$ 2.1 billion. This figure is projected to increase to US$ 10 billion by 2025, driven by a compound annual growth rate of 29.7%. As a result, India's dependence on medical equipment imports is likely to rise, reaching between 75% and 80%. The important nations that import Indian medical devices include the United States, Germany, China, Brazil, and Iran.

## 17.4 Potential of Medical Device Industry to Grow in India

India's medical device production is distributed across states such as Gujarat, Maharashtra, Karnataka, Haryana, Andhra Pradesh, Telangana, and Tamil Nadu. Predictions made during the Bio-Asia 2021 Panel suggest that the country will become self-reliant in medical device manufacturing by 2025–2026. This forecast is supported by the government's proactive measures, which include initiatives to boost domestic high-tech medical device production, implement Production Linked Incentives (PLIs), and establish new medical device manufacturing hub (Fig. 17.4). The reasons for anticipated growth of medical device market in India are discussed as follows:

1. *Increasing Demand*

   The market's need for medical equipment will increase with an increase in the number of medical institutions and government programs, including the creation of medical parks and schemes such as the Production Linked Incentives (PLI) Scheme for Medical Devices 2020.

2. *Opportunities in Export*

   India's reliance on imports from countries like the United States, China, and Germany covers 75–80% of its medical equipment needs. Plans are underway for India and Russia to elevate their bilateral trade to $30 billion by 2025, highlighting the substantial growth potential within India's medical device sector. The Medical Devices Virtual Expo 2021 showed Indian products, offering a valuable platform for direct interactions between Indian suppliers and international buyers. Around 300 global healthcare purchasers participated in this event, further emphasizing the expanding market opportunities.

3. *Policy Support*

   In India, the market for medical equipment is open to 100% foreign direct investment (FDI). The most FDI is drawn to industries like implants, consumables, equipment, and instruments. In February 2021, a Production Linked Incentive (PLI) scheme was launched, featuring a financial allocation of Rs. 3420 crore (US$ 468.78 million) for the fiscal years 2021 through 2028. This initiative aims to boost the domestic development of medical devices by incentivizing local production. Nine further projects, including those from Siemens Healthcare and Wipro GE Healthcare, were approved by the Ministry of Chemicals and Fertilizers.

4. *Increasing Investment*

   Over time, *this* industry has drawn large investments. In the financial year 2020, the medical equipment sector saw a substantial rise in foreign investment, climbing by 98%. The investment amount jumped from Rs. 1108 crore (US$ 151.87 million) to Rs. 2196 crore (US$ 301.01 million).

## 17.5 Categories of Medical Devices

The Indian Ministry of Health has categorized medical devices into four separate groups based on the regulations governing medical devices and in-vitro diagnostics (IVD) as shown in Fig. 17.5.

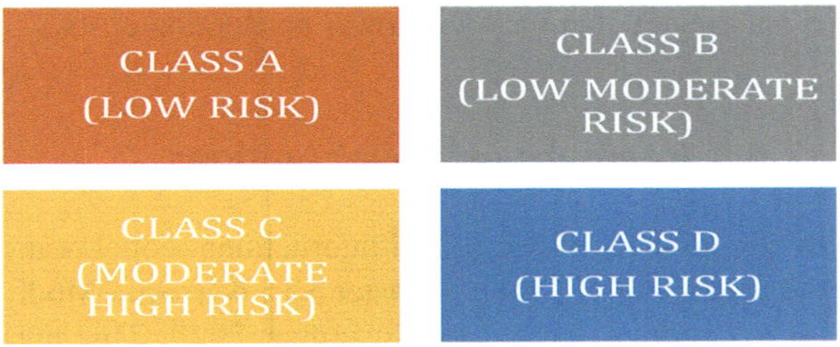


**Fig. 17.5** Categories of medical devices

## 17.6 Government Initiatives for Promoting Growth of Med-Tech Industry in India

To support the medical equipment industry, the government has implemented a system allowing 100% foreign direct investments (FDIs) for both existing (brownfield) and new (greenfield) projects. This robust influx of foreign investment underscores the growing confidence international firms have in India's medical equipment sector. Over the past 5 years (2015–2020), India has attracted approximately US$ 600 million in FDI, with substantial investments coming from countries such as Singapore, the United States, various European nations, and Japan. The most FDIs have been drawn to industries like implants, consumables, and equipment and instruments. The amount of FDI that entered the market for medical and surgical appliances from April 2000 to September 2020 was $2.17 billion.

### 17.6.1 Incentive Schemes

To enhance domestic production of medical devices, the Indian Department of Pharmaceuticals has rolled out a Production Linked Incentive (PLI) scheme. This program, covering the period from FY 2021 to FY 2028, is supported by a substantial budget of Rs. 3420 crore (about US$ 468.78 million). The initiative aims to stimulate local manufacturing and attract substantial investments to the sector. In addition, the government has sanctioned nine projects expected to secure financial commitments totaling Rs. 729.63 crore (approximately US$ 100.01 million) from various firms. Among these are Siemens Healthcare Private Limited, Allengers Medical Systems Limited, Allengers OEM Private Limited, Wipro GE Healthcare Private Limited, Nipro India Corporation Private Limited, Sahajanand Medical Technologies Private Limited, and Involution Healthcare Private Limited.

### 17.6.2 Introduction of Medical Parks

In 2019, the government allocated Rs. 100 crore (US$ 13.5 million) to each of the four states—Andhra Pradesh, Telangana, Tamil Nadu, and Kerala—to support the development of medical device parks. Because the medical device parks will have the required infrastructure and will act as plug-and-play locations for businesses, it is anticipated that they will lower production costs.

### 17.6.3 International Collaborations

In a significant move toward international collaboration, the Union Cabinet, under the leadership of Prime Minister Shri Narendra Modi, endorsed a memorandum of understanding (MOU) in November 2020. This agreement between the Central

Drugs Standard Control Organization (CDSCO) and the UK Medicines and Healthcare Products Regulatory Agency (UKMHRA) aims to foster cooperation in the regulation of medical products.

## 17.7 Ongoing Trends in the Medical Devices Sector

Figure 17.6 illustrates the categorization and developments of medical devices in India, after the COVID-19 pandemic, with additional details.

### 17.7.1 Big Data

In 2019, a collaboration between Medtronic and IBM led to the creation of a mobile personal assistant app that delivers real-time glucose monitoring for individuals with diabetes. This innovation is part of a broader trend where companies are leveraging predictive analytics to gather critical patient data and insights from various devices, enabling informed decisions about patient health. This management method assists patients in selecting their medications by assisting them in understanding the connections between glucose readings, lifestyle choices, and medicine administration.

### 17.7.2 Robotics

Strict observance robots with articulating arms, or SCARAs, can be put on a tabletop and work effectively in cramped areas. Siemens Healthineers unveiled Corindus, a robotic system, in February 2021 to power cardiovascular therapies with robotic support in India. Still later, SS Innovations, a New Delhi-based company founded

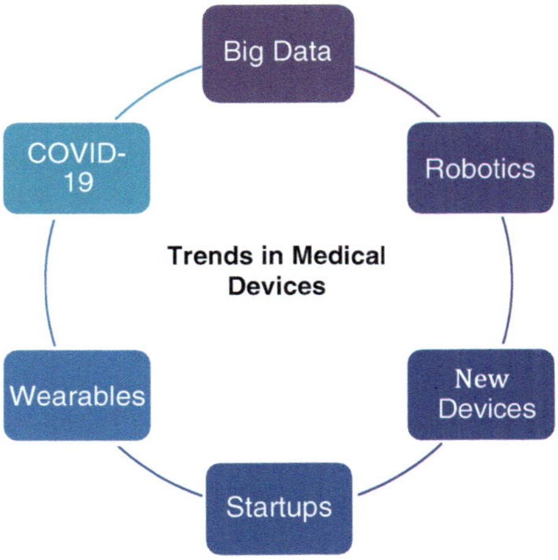


**Fig. 17.6** Trends in medical devices post-COVID-19

by renowned robotic cardiothoracic surgeon Dr. Sudhir P Srivastava, introduced India's first and least expensive multi-arm robotic surgical system called "Mantra" which has completed 100 surgeries in 2023 itself.

### 17.7.3 New Devices

Apollo Hospitals Group and Anatomiz 3D Medtech Pvt. Ltd. began working together in February 2021 to construct 3D-printing facilities in India, beginning with Apollo Health City in Hyderabad. The Competition Commission of India (CCI) approved Siemens Healthineers' request to purchase all the shares of Varian Medical Systems in February 2021 to develop a more creative, dependable, and all-inclusive oncology solution provider. A single-use, absorbent antibacterial envelope called TYRX Envelope was introduced by Medtronic India Pvt. Ltd. in February 2021. It is intended to maintain an implanted neurostimulator or implantable cardiac electronic device (CIED) while dispensing antimicrobial chemicals for at least 7 days.

### 17.7.4 Start-Ups

As a result of ongoing research and innovation that makes medical equipment more accessible and inexpensive, the market for medical devices is growing quickly. Numerous start-ups and small- and medium-sized enterprises (SMEs) from India have entered the medical device sector and are providing cutting-edge solutions. As new businesses enter this industry, the market is seeing new investments.

### 17.7.5 Wearables

Devices such as blood sugar monitors, activity trackers, and mental wellness wearables are gaining traction among Indian consumers due to their user-friendly nature. In December 2020, the Central Drugs Standard Control Organization (CDSCO) granted medical device registration to three wearable products developed by the California-based fitness tech company GOQ. These tools can assess vital signs like blood pressure, and heart rate along with facilities such as electrocardiography (ECG), body temperature measurement, and a pulse oximeter.

### 17.7.6 Impact of COVID-19

Before the onset of the COVID-19 pandemic, just 20 companies in India were manufacturing 6.2 million personal protective equipment (PPE) kits each year, according to the Association of Indian Medical Device Industry (AiMeD). However, within 2–3 months following the pandemic's onset, the number of manufacturers

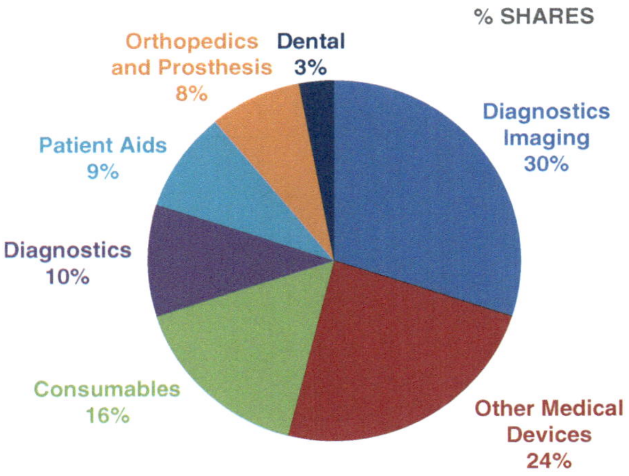


**Fig. 17.7** Segment-wise percentage share of Indian market

registered with AiMeD surged to 140, drastically increasing the annual production capacity to 255.5 million kits. During the COVID-19 pandemic, the production of essential medical supplies in India saw significant growth. Hindustan Syringes and Medical Devices Ltd., the leading producer of auto-disable syringes for vaccinations, ramped up its annual production from 700 million to 1 billion syringes in early 2021, increasing its output rate from 5900 to 8200 syringes per minute to aid COVID-19 immunization efforts. The number of companies manufacturing ventilators grew from 8 to 17, while mask producers surged from 30 to 108. Additionally, five new companies began producing swabs and sanitizer manufacturers increased from 35 to 49. The production of RT PCR kits also commenced, with eight companies entering this space where none existed previously. To address the changing requirements of the Indian healthcare system, especially in the context of COVID-19, the Engineering Exports Promotion Council of India partnered with the National Institute of Design in November 2020. This partnership aimed to enhance and innovate design and technological solutions within the medical devices field to more effectively meet these emerging needs. The segment wise share of various healthcare related facilities is shown in Fig. 17.7.

## 17.8 Import-Export Scenario of Medical Devices in India

India's medical device sector is on a strong growth trajectory, with projections indicating the market could hit $50 billion by 2025. Currently, India ranks among the top 20 global markets for medical devices and stands as the fourth largest in Asia, behind Japan, China, and South Korea. During the COVID-19 pandemic, India emerged as a key supplier, exporting essential items such as ventilators, PPE, diagnostic kits, sanitizers, and surgical gloves. In 2019, the country's exports in this sector totaled Rs. 14,802 crore (about US$ 2.1 billion). This figure is expected to surge, with an anticipated annual growth rate of 29.7%, potentially reaching Rs.

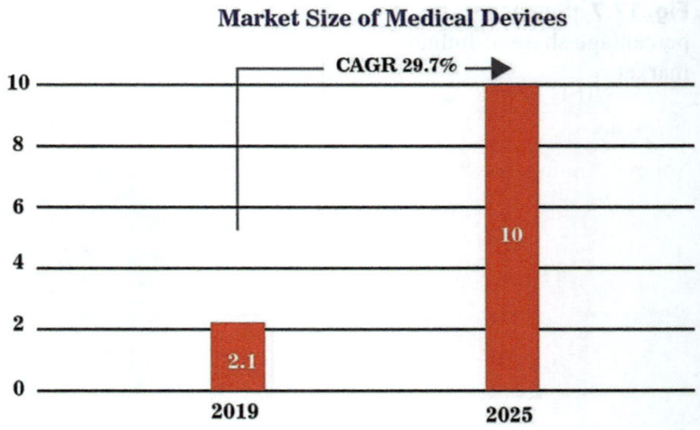


**Fig. 17.8** Medical device export market in India (2019–2025). (Source: IBEF, 2020)

70,490 crore (approximately US$ 10 billion) by 2025, Fig. 17.8 illustrates India's projected exports of medical equipment.

The Indian Ministry of Health and Family Welfare (MOHFW) and the Central Drugs Standard Control Organization (CDSCO) have implemented several initiatives to boost medical device exports. These initiatives include updating and enforcing Schedule MIII, which outlines good manufacturing practices and facility requirements. Additionally, they have created a new export labeling system, clarified procedures for clinical trials and adverse event reporting, and increased the involvement of state licensing authorities.

### 17.8.1 Challenges: Import Scenario

India's medical equipment market, despite facing several challenges, presents a lucrative export opportunity for US manufacturers. Valued at $10 billion, the market is heavily reliant on imports, especially for advanced devices like cancer detection devices, diagnostic imaging, ultrasound examinations, and polymerase chain reaction techniques. This trend is fueled by the growing number of leading healthcare providers, such as renowned healthcare chains like Max, Hinduja Group, Fortis, and Apollo, which are constructing state-of-the-art facilities and promoting health tourism in India. Health tourism now contributes $2 billion to the Indian healthcare sector.

Despite significant economic growth over the past 25 years, India's healthcare sector remains difficult to navigate due to its competitive nature and focus on low- to mid-tech products. The market is often described as a "crossroads," influenced by a multitude of manufacturers and trade routes. Nontariff barriers and price controls pose further challenges, restricting the sector's market potential. Additionally, insufficient intellectual property protection and enforcement have impeded biopharmaceutical exports to India. To combat these issues, the Indian government has introduced a new Production Linked Incentive (PLI) scheme, designed to enhance domestic manufacturing, attract large investments, and reduce dependency on imports.

**Table 17.1** Imports and exports during financial years 2018–2019 and 2019–2020

| Imports | | Exports | |
|---|---|---|---|
| 2018–2019 | 2019–2020 | 2018–2019 | 2019–2020 |
| 5700.44 | 5845.41 | 2138.14 | 2292.87 |

Source: Engineering Export Promotion Council of India [EEPC]

India's medical device industry is comprised of approximately 750–800 domestic medical device manufacturers, each investing between $2.3 and $2.7 million and generating sales from $6.2 to $6.9 million. Major manufacturing centers are located in western, southern, and northern India. While multinational companies lead the advanced technology sector, local businesses account for the majority of the consumables market, primarily serving domestic demand.

Since 2014, when the Indian government labeled the sector as a "sunrise sector," it has seen a notable increase in investment. The sector has garnered $2.1 billion in foreign direct investment (FDI) since April 2000, with most of this influx occurring in the last 5 years. Additionally, the implementation of 100% FDI through an automatic process for both greenfield and brownfield projects has contributed significantly to this rise in investment. India's significant import dependency makes the country's medical equipment supply chain vulnerable to global crises. Medical device exports and imports for the last two fiscal years are given in Table 17.1 and Fig. 17.9.

Over the past 2 years, the medical devices sector in India has seen fluctuations in trade, as shown in Fig. 17.9. Although exports increased by 7.2%, rising from $2138.14 million in 2018–2019 to $2292.6 million in 2019–2020, imports still outpaced this growth, showing a 2.5% increase from $5700.44 million to $5845.41 million during the same period. This persistent reliance on imports resulted in a stable but significant trade deficit of around $3550 million for both fiscal years 2018–2019 and 2019–2020, highlighting the sector's dependency on foreign goods (Fig. 17.10).

India primarily imports medical devices from the United States, Germany, China, Singapore, and the Netherlands. Together, these five countries accounted for nearly 60% of India's total medical device imports in the last two fiscal years, with a cumulative value of approximately $3500 million. Imports from these top five countries have slightly increased over the past two fiscal years, with the United States remaining the leading source, exporting $1190 million in medical devices to India during the 2019–2020 fiscal year (Fig. 17.11).

India's medical device exports to the United States and China have been the highest over the past two fiscal years, followed by significant contributions from Germany, Singapore, and France. Together, these five countries saw a 10.5% increase in exports from India, growing from $862.25 million in the 2018–2019 fiscal year to $953.13 million in 2019–2020. These five countries accounted for approximately 40% of India's total medical device exports during this period.

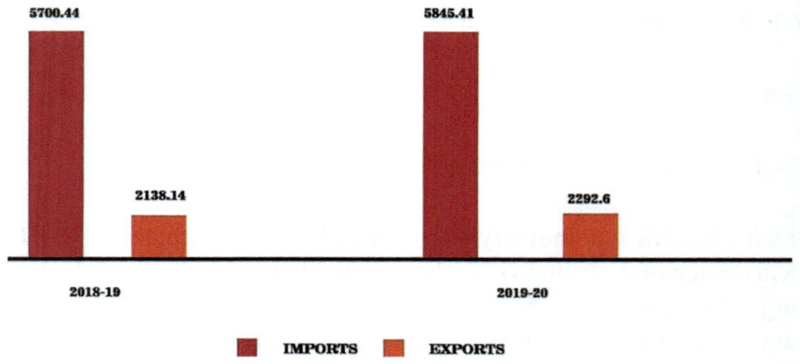


**Fig. 17.9** Medical device trade in India (2018–2020)

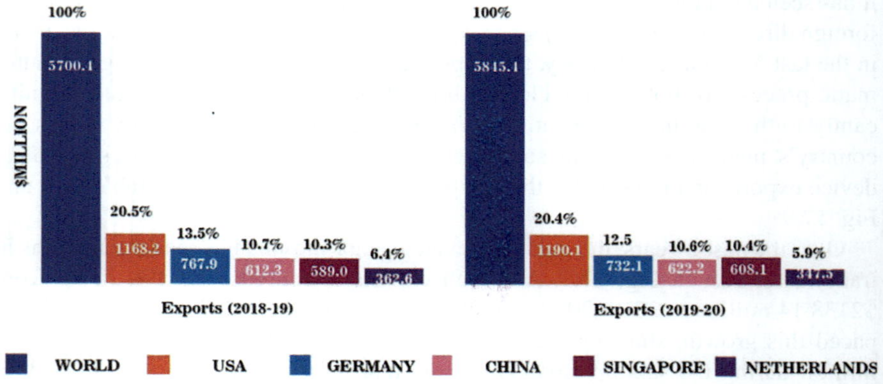


**Fig. 17.10** Major medical device importers to India (2018–2020)

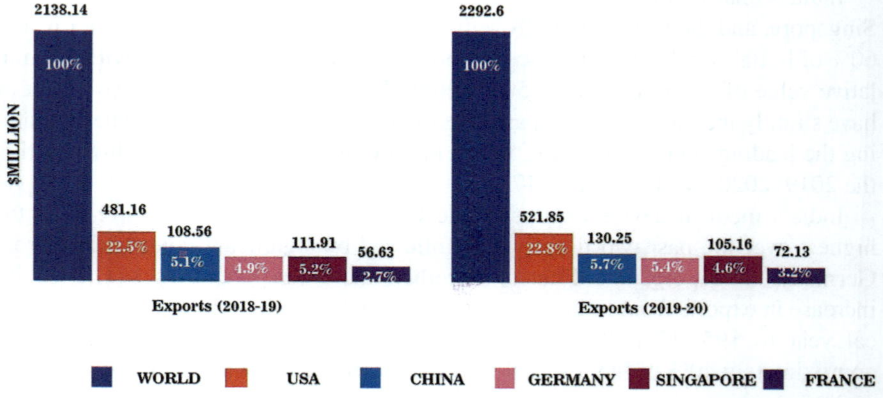


**Fig. 17.11** Major medical device importers from India (2018–2020)

## 17.9 Medical Tourism

Medical tourism involves individuals traveling across borders to seek a wide range of medical treatments, including dentistry, aesthetic surgery, elective procedures, and fertility services. Differentiating between health tourism and medical tourism for trade purposes can be challenging, as not all medical procedures qualify as healthcare. Medical tourism differs from health tourism in terms of the types of procedures, the settings where they take place, and the resources utilized.

### 17.9.1 India as a Medical Value Travel and Wellness Tourism Destination

India has become a sought-after destination for health tourism and wellness tourism, offering exceptional healthcare services and affordable treatments. The country boasts world-class hospitals staffed by highly skilled medical professionals capable of performing complex surgical procedures. This combination of top-tier care and competitive pricing has established India as a leading hub for medical tourism. The southern and western regions of India are home to a robust network of medical value travel (MVT) providers, highlighted by a substantial presence of Joint Commission International (JCI) accredited hospitals. India's prominence as a destination for Yoga and Wellness tourism has been bolstered by its emphasis on traditional therapies such as AYUSH. The influx of international patients seeking these services grew dramatically from 4.3 million in 2016 to 7 million in 2019. By the end of 2019, the market for these services was projected to reach an estimated USD 5–6 billion (Table 17.2).

**Table 17.2** Number of Joint Commission International Accredited hospitals in India

| Place | JCI (Joint Commission International) accredited hospitals |
|---|---|
| Delhi | 9 |
| Mumbai | 6 |
| Bangalore | 3 |
| Chennai | 2 |
| Hyderabad | 2 |
| Ahmedabad | 2 |
| Kolkata | 1 |
| Nagpur | 1 |
| Cochin | 1 |
| Pune | 1 |
| Nasik | 1 |

In 2017, India captured the seventh spot in the global wellness tourism market, attracting 56 million trips and generating USD 16.3 billion in revenue

## 17.10 Medical Device Parks: Need and Why to Invest?

A medical device park is a contiguous tract of land with common infrastructure facilities (CIF) for the exclusive manufacture of medical devices.

To boost the medical devices industry, the Ministry of Chemicals and Fertilizers has proposed the development of dedicated parks for manufacturing medical devices. These parks will offer state-of-the-art testing facilities and foster the establishment of top-tier manufacturing centers. The primary objective is to reduce production costs, making medical devices more affordable and widely available throughout India. This approach is also anticipated to contribute to substantial socioeconomic advancements, improving public health and overall quality of life for the population. India's medical device sector, recognized as one of the largest in Asia and among the top 30 globally, is an industry requiring substantial capital investment with promising opportunities for research and development. Government programs such as "Make in India" and "Atmanirbhar Bharat Abhiyaan" have significantly contributed to the growth of this sector. The layout of a medical device park is depicted in Fig. 17.12. With these med-tech parks, India will take the world lead in health technology and medical gadgets. However, this sector does need ongoing training for all stakeholders, including health practitioners, in order to adapt to new and developing technology.

As illustrated in Fig. 17.13, the provision of common testing and laboratory facilities/centers significantly reduces production costs and establishes a healthy ecosystem for medical device manufacturing.

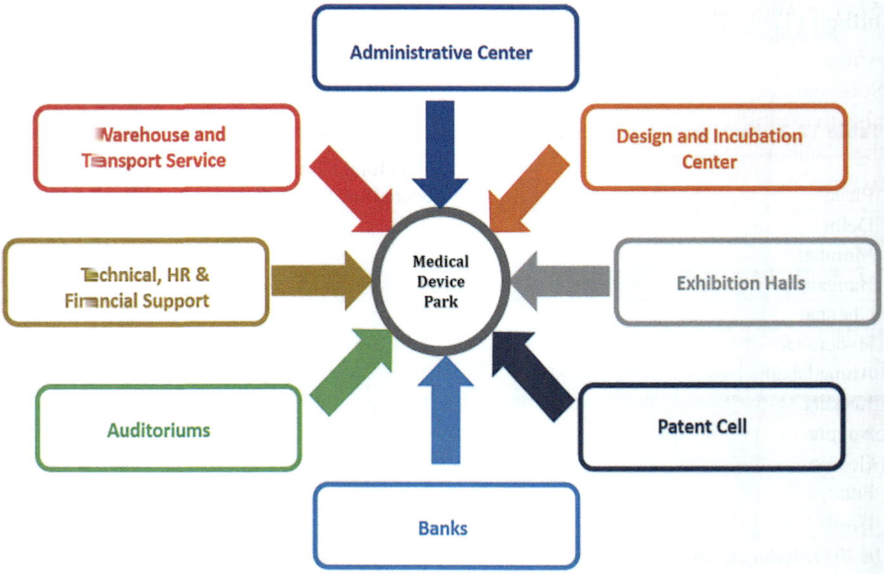


**Fig. 17.12** Feature of medical devices park

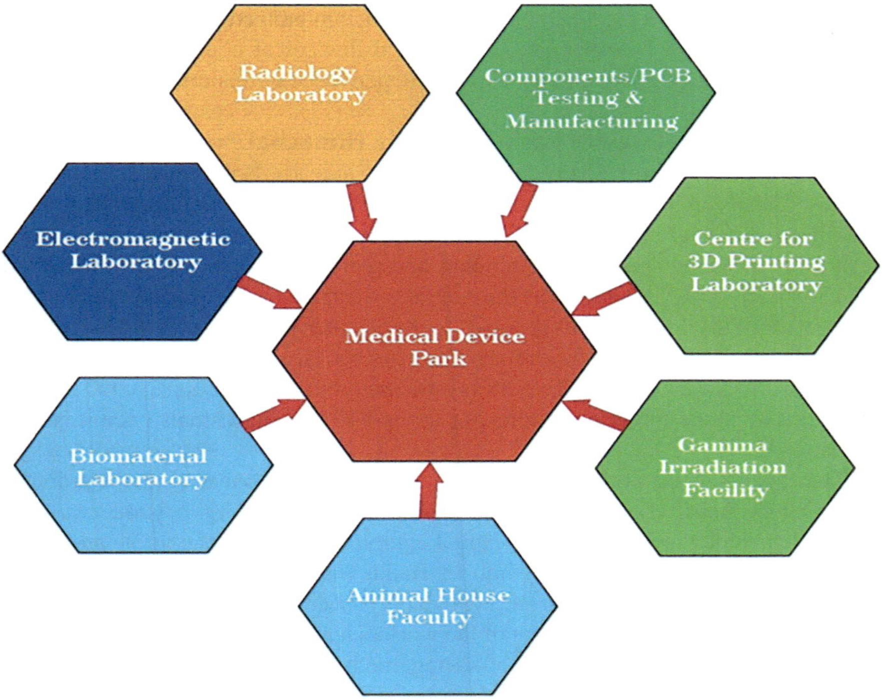


**Fig. 17.13** Feature of medical devices park (testing and manufacturing)

The creation of medical device parks has been sanctioned by the governments in Andhra Pradesh, Telangana, Tamil Nadu, and Kerala, with the majority located in South India. These parks will provide the essential infrastructure needed for companies to establish operations seamlessly. Additionally, they are intended to strengthen the "Make in India" initiative by delivering world-class products at competitive prices.

### 17.10.1 Introduction to Medical Parks

In 2020, the Indian medical device market was valued at Rs. 77,539 crores (equivalent to US$ 11 billion). Projections indicate that this market is poised for substantial growth, with a projected CAGR of 35.4% from 2020 to 2025. This expansion is expected to propel the market's worth to Rs. 352,450 crores (approximately US$ 50 billion) by 2025. It is worth noting that India currently relies on imports for over 86% of its medical devices, while its medical device exports reached Rs. 10,467 crores in 2020. Forecasts suggest that exports are set to increase with a CAGR of 29.7%, potentially reaching Rs. 70,490 crores by 2025. The Government of India is actively promoting the medical device sector, encouraging state governments to compete vigorously in establishing medical device manufacturing hubs. The aim is to ensure that these facilities produce medical devices at competitive prices and contribute to reducing the country's import dependence in this critical sector.

#### 17.10.1.1 Medical Device Park, Nalagarh, Himachal Pradesh

The construction of a medical device park in Nalagarh, Solan district, Himachal Pradesh, has been authorized by the central government with an investment of Rs. 266.95 crore. Covering an area of 265 hectares, this facility is set to become a major center for producing medical equipment and gadgets. The state government will contribute Rs. 160.95 crore, while the central government will provide Rs. 100 crore in grant aid. This development is poised to attract over Rs. 5000 crore in investment to Himachal Pradesh, which already hosts Asia's largest pharmaceutical hub in Baddi-Brotiwala-Nalagarh. The park is anticipated to generate Rs. 20,000 crore in revenue and create job opportunities for around 10,000 individuals once it is fully operational.

The establishment of the first medical device park in Northern India is poised to significantly boost the region's industrial growth, extending beyond consumer goods to include the production of capital equipment such as machinery and industrial plants. The pharmaceutical hub in Baddi-Brotiwala-Nalagarh generates an annual revenue of Rs. 40,000 crore, with exports accounting for at least Rs. 15,000 crore. This region is home to some of the world's leading multinational pharmaceutical companies, which supply life-saving medications and health supplements globally. The new medical device park represents a pivotal development not only for Himachal Pradesh and Northern India but also for India's broader goal of manufacturing costly medical, hospital, and healthcare equipment domestically. This initiative aims to reduce reliance on imports and is a crucial step toward achieving self-sufficiency in India's medical device sector in the future.

#### Identified Segments for the Medical Device Park in Himachal Pradesh

**Medical Electronics**

1. Medium-Sized Devices: Ultrasound machines, C-Arm systems, X-ray machines, automated laboratory analyzers, and more.
2. Compact Home Healthcare Devices: Glucometers, blood pressure instruments, thermometers, oximeters, and similar items.
3. Wearable Devices: Examples include wearable patch monitors for electrocardiograms (ECG), electromyograms (EMG), electrooculography (EOG), fitness wearables, drug delivery wearables, and wearable heart rate monitors. Additionally, this segment covers embedded software and mobile phone-based applications, data informatics, artificial intelligence (AI), and IoT (Internet of Things)-based technologies.

**Medical Equipment**

1. Operating theatre (OT) and intensive care unit (ICU) equipment: This category encompasses equipment used in operating rooms and ICUs
2. Diagnostic equipment: Instruments used for medical diagnosis
3. Anesthesia and medical oxygen supply systems: Devices related to anesthesia administration and oxygen supply in medical settings

**Implants**

Intraocular lens (IOL) and implants: Including stainless-steel alloy-based orthopedic implants or plastic and ceramic-based implants.

**Instruments**

Analytical instruments: These can be electrical or electronic devices used for testing and analysis.

Endoscopy and laparoscopy instruments: Surgical instruments, often made from stainless steel, used for procedures like endoscopy and laparoscopy.

#### 17.10.1.2 Andhra Pradesh Med-Tech Zone (AMTZ)

Inaugurated in 2016, the Andhra Pradesh Med-Tech Zone (AMTZ), located near Visakhapatnam, India, is a major state-led initiative focused on enhancing the medical device industry. This zone is committed to promoting innovation by facilitating research and development, providing critical testing services, and supporting emerging enterprises. During the COVID-19 crisis, AMTZ swiftly adapted by commencing the production of rapid diagnostic kits in April 2020, followed by the creation of other essential medical apparatus, including ventilators. Additionally, AMTZ is home to the Bio Valley Incubation Council, which benefits from the backing of the Department of Biotechnology and the Kalam Institute of Health Technology.

**Salient Features**

1. Manufacturers interested in establishing operations can lease prefabricated production facilities on plots ranging from 0.25 to 2.0 acres.
2. Office space for interested government/private organizations to help the zone function.
3. Exclusive world-class scientific facilities required for medical device manufacturing, which are very capital intensive and operate in a Public-Private Partnership (PPP) mode.
4. Designated partners for technology exchange, workforce management, compliance with quality and regulations, project coordination, and financial assistance.
5. Close collaboration with industry and government to develop and pursue policy and procedural interventions required for industry growth.

## Hubs Under AMTZ

(a) *BIOVALLEY*: India's largest incubator for life sciences, the Bio-Valley Incubation Council, provides a distinct environment designed to nurture start-ups. This ecosystem grants emerging companies access to cutting-edge technologies without limitations and offers guidance to help them successfully navigate market entry.
(b) *MEDIVALLEY*: Supported by NITI Aayog through the Atal Innovation Mission, the Medi Valley Atal Incubation Council functions as the innovative branch of the Andhra Pradesh MedTech Zone (AMTZ), a leading hub for medical device manufacturing.
(c) *KIHT*: Backed by the Department of Biotechnology, the Kalam Institute of Health Technology (KIHT) is an initiative launched by the Government of India to drive innovation in the medical technology sector. KIHT's mission is centered on the advancing research and development, promoting industry expansion, shaping policies, and managing vital knowledge.
(d) *IBSC*: Acknowledged by the National Skill Development Agency (NSDA), the Indian Biomedical Skill Consortium (IBSC) functions in accordance with the National Skill Qualification Framework (NSQF) established by the Ministry of Skill Development and Entrepreneurship (MSDE). The consortium is committed to the growth of the biomedical skills sector across India, aiming to foster innovation and expansion within the field. Its efforts are directed toward creating and refining job roles, improving industry standards, and enhancing workforce competencies to meet evolving demands in the biomedical sector.
(e) *Artificial Limb Center*: AMTZ partnered with Sri Gurudev charity trust to setup their Artificial Limb Centre at the campus of AMTZ. In this center, the manufacturing and production of various types of assistive devices such as artificial limbs (below knee, above knee, below elbow, above elbow), wheelchairs, tricycles, motorized wheelchair, standing frame, corner table, commode chair, and ankle foot orthosis, is being carried out under the supervision of AMTZ, Visakhapatnam. The process is extremely transparent, and the beneficiaries are often offered same day service.
(f) *COE Additive Manufacturing*: Transforming the creation of durable and precise components, additive manufacturing (AM), or 3D printing, markedly reduces both the time and expenses involved from initial design to final production. The Centre of Excellence–Additive Manufacturing (CoE-AM) at Andhra Pradesh Med-Tech zone is a leader in this field, encompassing a range of specialized facilities. These include the Material Analysis Centre for metal 3D printing, the Advanced Assembly Technology Centre, the Polymer Additives Production Centre, the Polyethylene Extrusion Centre, and the Radiation Protection AM Centre. Each of these units plays a vital role in advancing the development and application of additive manufacturing technologies.
(g) *COE Medical Electronics and Biophysics*: The Center of Excellence (CoE) for Medical Electronics and Biophysics is a key player in the development and prototyping of electronic components, ensuring their effective integration into

critical medical device assemblies. Beyond its technical achievements, the center is heavily focused on pushing the boundaries of research and innovation in medical electronics. It is also actively engaged in bio-physics research, exploring complex areas like bio-organs and electro-organs, while prioritizing the creation and evaluation of essential electro-potential based components.

#### 17.10.1.3 Medical Device Park: Hyderabad

Since its establishment in 2017, the medical devices park in Sultanpur, Telangana, has successfully attracted over 50 companies, resulting in a total investment of Rs. 1424 crore and generating more than 7000 direct jobs. Recently, seven companies, including Promea Therapeutics, Huwel Life Sciences, Akriti Oculoplasty, Arka Engineers, SVP Techno Engineers, Kelvion, and Rees Medilife, have invested Rs. 265 crore, significantly boosting the state's capabilities in medical device manufacturing and research. Together, these companies aim to create approximately 1300 additional jobs in the region.

#### 17.10.1.4 Med-Spark, Kerala

Situated in Thonnakkal's Life Science Park in Thiruvananthapuram, Med-Spark is a specialized medical devices park focusing on the critical medical device sector. This is a collaboration between the Kerala State Industrial Development Corporation Ltd (KSIDC), the industrial and investment promotion unit of the Government of Kerala, and Sree Chitra Tirunal Institute for Medical Sciences & Technology (SCTIMST), an independent body under the Government of India's Department of Science and Technology (DST). Med-Spark offers a comprehensive range of industry services, including support for research and development, trials, and assessments.

Med-Spark aims to harness Kerala's prominent position in high-risk medical device manufacturing, aspiring to make the state the leading hub for the medical device industry in India. By focusing on essential areas such as surgical implants and external medical devices—fields where SCTIMST has extensive expertise—the park offers vital resources and support to emerging and mid-sized companies throughout the country. The state already boasts a number of medical device enterprises with yearly revenues above Rs. 750 crores, many of which utilize technologies pioneered by SCTIMST.

#### 17.10.1.5 Medical Device Park, Oragadam, Tamil Nadu

The Medical Devices Park to be built in Oragadam will attract investments worth 3500 crores and will employ about 10,000 people directly and indirectly. The cost for building the park is expected to be 450 crores. After accepting the state government's plea, the Union government granted in-principal approval and said it will grant up to 100 crores for the park in Kancheepuram district. The park, which would span 350 acres in the SIPCOT (State Industries Promotion Corporation of Tamil Nadu) Industrial Complex in Oragadam, would produce ventilators, blood pressure monitors, pacemakers, surgical equipment, and other medical necessities. These parks will have modern infrastructure facilities such as common effluent treatment plant (CETP), steam systems, warehouses and cold storage, R&D centers, testing facilities, and so on.

## 17.11 ICMR Center for Innovation and Bio-Design (CIBioD), PGIMER, Chandigarh: As a Med-Tech Hub

Located at the Post-Graduate Institute of Medical Education and Research (PGIMER) in Chandigarh, the ICMR-Centre for Innovation and Bio-Design (CIBioD) is committed to advancing healthcare technologies and diagnostic tools. This initiative aims to create a collaborative environment by partnering with top tech organizations and companies. It has several specific objectives, all designed to support the overarching goal of enhancing healthcare accessibility and cost-effectiveness for all:

1. Developing local innovations and solutions to enhance the accessibility of healthcare.
2. Creating and implementing locally developed healthcare technologies and tools.
3. Crafting strategies and methods to address prevalent health challenges.
4. Providing training and skill development for researchers, healthcare practitioners, and educators in the medical field.

CIBioD has set a Brain Trust by signing 26 different MoU (memorandum of understanding) between CIBioD and various institutes/industries like IIT (Indian Institute of Technology), Ropar, NIT (National Institute of Technology), Jalandhar, Council of Scientific and Industrial Research–Central Scientific Instrumental Organization (CSIR-CSIO), IIM (Indian Institute of Management), Calcutta, NCKUH (National Cheng Kung University Hospital), Taiwan, and Tata Communications. They have started "CIBioD-Innovation Cell" to involve their students, scientists/professionals, and faculty. A steering committee, working group, and innovation panel, composed of prominent medical experts, researchers, business leaders, and financial backers, have been formed to oversee and manage the initiatives. CIBioD started prototyping, IPR (intellectual property rights) protection, and incubation of 36 project ideas. Some of these projects are low-cost MRI (magnetic resonance imaging), tele-cardiology coroquick, quantitative sensory testing, electronic medical record system, virtual super specialty clinics, JEE-1, e-stethoscope, and Arogya Sahayak. CIBioD has started incubating start-up Sri Venkteshwara Healthcare for promotion of telemedicine and artificial intelligence (AI-based solutions for integrated care in tier II and III cities and rural areas. It took initiative to provide healthcare services by accelerating telemedicine during COVID-19 pandemic by setting-up six telemedicine units at various places in Himachal Pradesh and Punjab. It is also mentoring a start-up AVISHKAR for successful commercialization of products developed at CIBioD. CIBioD is also mentoring Arogaya-CIBioD, a section-8 company, for promotion of med-tech industry in India.

ICMR-CIBioD's major focus thrust areas and planned activities are shown in Figs. 17.14 and 17.15, respectively.

*ICMR-CIBioD is also providing mentorship to Medical Device Park, Nalagarh, Himachal Pradesh.*

**Fig. 17.14** ICMR-CIBioD's major thrust areas

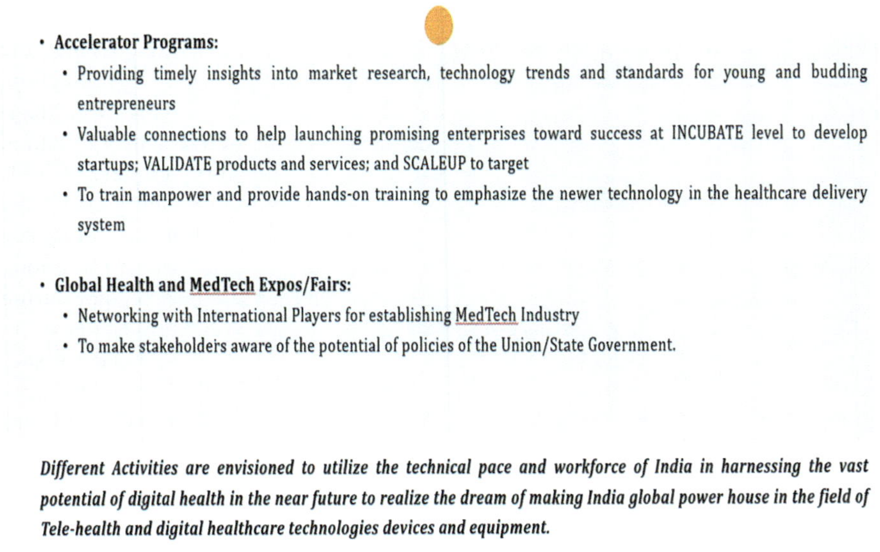


**Fig. 17.15** Planned activities

The Government of Himachal Pradesh signed MoU with CIBioD, PGIMER, Chandigarh, as technical partners to provide mentorship to medical device park, Nalagarh.

## Reference

1. Medical Devices Market Size, Growth Report, Trends, 2023–2032. n.d.. https://www.precedenceresearch.com/medical-devices-market.

GPSR Compliance

*The European Union's (EU) General Product Safety Regulation (GPSR) is a set of rules that requires consumer products to be safe and our obligations to ensure this.*

*If you have any concerns about our products, you can contact us on ProductSafety@springernature.com*

In case Publisher is established outside the EU, the EU authorized representative is:

Springer Nature Customer Service Center GmbH
Europaplatz 3
69115 Heidelberg, Germany

**Batch number: 10732090**

Printed by Printforce, the Netherlands